The Yanks Are Coming
Over There

The Yanks Are Coming Over There

Anglo-Saxonism and American Involvement in the First World War

Dino E. Buenviaje

McFarland & Company, Inc., Publishers
Jefferson, North Carolina

All illustrations are courtesy of the Cartooning the First World War
project at Cardiff University

LIBRARY OF CONGRESS CATALOGUING-IN-PUBLICATION DATA

Names: Buenviaje, Dino E., 1975– author.
Title: The Yanks are coming over there : Anglo-Saxonism and American involvement in the First World War / Dino E. Buenviaje.
Description: Jefferson, North Carolina : McFarland & Company, Inc., Publishers, 2017. | Includes bibliographical references and index.
Identifiers: LCCN 2017042777 | ISBN 9781476668932 (softcover : acid free paper) ∞
Subjects: LCSH: World War, 1914–1918—United States. | United States—Foreign relations—1865–1921. | Nationalism—United States—History. | Anglo-Saxon race.
Classification: LCC D619 .B753 2017 | DDC 940.3/73—dc23
LC record available at https://lccn.loc.gov/2017042777

BRITISH LIBRARY CATALOGUING DATA ARE AVAILABLE

ISBN (print) 978-1-4766-6893-2
ISBN (ebook) 978-1-4766-3019-9

© 2017 Dino E. Buenviaje. All rights reserved

No part of this book may be reproduced or transmitted in any form or by any means, electronic or mechanical, including photocopying or recording, or by any information storage and retrieval system, without permission in writing from the publisher.

Front cover: World War I poster art promoting United States liberty bonds, 1918 (Library of Congress)

Printed in the United States of America

McFarland & Company, Inc., Publishers
 Box 611, Jefferson, North Carolina 28640
 www.mcfarlandpub.com

In Memoriam
Howard G. Bryden
Who embodied the best qualities
of an educator and a human being

Table of Contents

Acknowledgments   ix

Introduction   1
    The Roots of Anglo-Saxonism 7 • Anglo-Saxon Myths 8 • Bede, *The Anglo-Saxon Chronicle* and the Making of England 9 • Geoffrey of Monmouth's History of British Kings and the Arthurian Legend 11 • Post-Norman England 13

Chapter I. Anglo-Saxonism and American Culture, 1895–1914   15
    The Roots of American Anglo-Saxonism 15 • Late-Nineteenth- and Early Twentieth-Century Anglo-Saxonism 17 • The Anglo-American Community 28 • The White Anglo-Saxon Protestant 30

Chapter II. The German-American Connection, 1850–1914   38
    Early German Migrations 39 • The Revolution of 1848 41 • German-Americans and Politics 44 • German-Americans and German Unification 46 • Germans and Anglo-Saxonism: Common Origins and Anxieties 53

Chapter III. Anglo-Saxonism in the Foreign Policy Establishment   75
    The Rise of the United States 77 • William H. Seward: The Architect of Empire 78 • Changes in American Society 80 • Alfred Thayer Mahan and the New Navy 82 • Mahan's Influence on U.S. Foreign Policy 87 • Theodore Roosevelt 90 • The Anglo-American Rapprochement of the 1890s and its Impact on U.S. Foreign Policy 95 • The Experience of the Philippines and Anglo-Saxonism 101 • The Philippine Commissions 105 • The Boer War: A Crisis in Anglo-Saxonism and the Anglo-American Rapprochement 109

Chapter IV. Anglo-Saxonism in the First World War   118
American Neutrality 120 • William Jennings Bryan vs. Robert Lansing 129 • The Role of the American Clergy in the First World War 135 • The British and American Propaganda Machines 137 • The Anglo-American Connection 144 • Anglo-Saxonism and the First World War 148

Conclusion   171
Chapter Notes   179
Bibliography   194
Index   201

Acknowledgments

It is truly a humbling experience when I consider the people and institutions that have contributed to this work. First of all, I would like to thank my dissertation committee chair, Dr. Brian Lloyd, for his patience and mentorship in helping me to analyze the role of Anglo-Saxonism throughout American history and for making me keep sight of my purpose. I am also grateful to Dr. Roger Ransom for his support early in my graduate program, and Dr. Thomas Cogswell for his support at a crucial point in my doctorate program. I also would like to thank Dr. Kenneth Barkin for his suggestion that I add a German-American chapter in order to make my study of American society during the First World War more well-rounded. I also would like to thank the staff of the history department at the University of California, Riverside, for helping me navigate the various stages of my doctorate program. I am especially grateful to the University of California, Riverside, for all the material and financial support it has provided me throughout my graduate education, such as the use of the Tomás Rivera Library, the Dean's Fellowship, the Dissertation Year Fellowship, as well as valuable teaching experience through teaching assistantships.

My gratitude extends beyond UC Riverside. I would like to thank California State University for its support in my graduate program through the Chancellor's Doctoral Incentive Program and the late Dr. Gordon Bakken, who served as my mentor in the application process. I owe my gratitude to the libraries of the Claremont Colleges, the University of North Carolina–Chapel Hill, Duke University, the Newberry Library, DePaul University, and the Missouri Historical Museum, as well as the archives of the National World War I Museum in Kansas City, Missouri, in helping me conduct my research, as well as Cardiff University in Wales. The information I gathered at these institutions helped guide the direction of my work.

The road toward the completion of my work on Anglo-Saxonism goes back even further, and I owe many others my thanks toward this end. The two anonymous readers who reviewed early drafts of the manuscript provided valuable feedback. I also owe my thanks to Dr. Arthur Hansen, Dr. Roshanna Sylvester, and the late Dr. Warren Clark Davis at the California State University, Fullerton, for teaching me what was expected of me at the graduate level during my master's program. I remain grateful to Dr. David Burton, whose article, "Theodore Roosevelt and his English Correspondents," became the kernel of my master's thesis, which became the launching point for my dissertation. I owe my thanks to Dr. Jon Jacobson of the University of California, Irvine, whose dedication to the discipline of history inspired me to pursue a graduate education. I also wish to thank my high school history teacher, Mr. Calwell, for helping me realize that history is more about connections, rather than dates, and to ask "so what?" in understanding the past, which led me to pursue history as a major. I especially wish to thank my fifth grade teacher, Mrs. Hales, and my principal at Mariposa Elementary School, the late Howard G. Bryden, for believing in me so early in my education.

Finally, I am grateful to my friends, both inside and outside of the history department at UC Riverside, such as Adam Messinger, Stephen V. Cole, and Patrick O'Neill, for their camaraderie and support. I would also like to express my heartfelt gratitude to Dr. Michael Shanahan for his friendship throughout my graduate programs and my wife, Sandra Xochipiltecatl, for her patience. I would also be remiss if I did not include another special friend, my cat, Riley, who sat with me quietly throughout the entire writing process. Above all, I owe my sincerest thanks to my family, my stepfather, Roger Knipp, who has been a father in all the ways that matter, and especially my mother, Soledad Knipp, whose strength and perseverance has always served as an example to me in all my endeavors.

Introduction

The entry of the United States on the side of the Allied powers in 1917 was a turning point in the First World War. For three years, there had been a stalemate on both sides, particularly along the Western Front. Britain, France, and Germany (the latter having counted on a swift victory in 1914), witnessed a carnage on the Western Front that drained all three nations in blood and treasure. The unprecedented nature of the war, which saw the introduction of new technology, prevented either side from gaining an advantage; at home, the pressures of the war significantly altered social relationships in terms of politics, class, and gender, sweeping away pre-war assumptions. Once the United States had cast its lot with Britain and France, the balance tipped in the favor of the Allies through the injection of fresh recruits, American industrial power, and American credit. The addition of the United States into the ranks of the Allies did not only pave the way for victory. Its involvement in the First World War introduced the "crusading" theme of American foreign policy when President Woodrow Wilson declared that the world be "made safe for democracy," which continues to have relevance in the early years of the twenty-first century.

The First World War was a significant moment in the history of American foreign policy as well as a cataclysmic baptism by fire for much of humanity. While at first glance it may appear that investigating "The War to End All Wars" would have little else to yield, there are still some unanswered questions. Before writing this book, there were some questions about the role of the United States in the First World War that had been nagging me. What induced the United States to join the side of the Allies during the First World War? How could the United States have entered on the side of Great Britain in 1917 when Irish-Americans and German-Americans, who formed significant portions of the population, were hostile to the British? By what means did the United States government convince the American public that joining the side of the Allies was a just and noble cause?

The answer I found to these questions was, then, summed up in one word: Anglo-Saxonism. Briefly, Anglo-Saxonism is the belief that those of Anglo-Saxon origin, particularly the peoples of the British Isles and their descendants in the United States and the "White Dominions" of the British Empire (Canada, Australia, New Zealand and South Africa), contained virtues and qualities that made them naturally "superior" to other ethnic groups. Among the virtues highly prized by Anglo-Saxonists include courage, thrift, independence, and self-control, culminating into "self-government," unique to these peoples. These qualities, therefore, were thought to explain the economic success of the United States and the British Empire and to justify imperial expansion during the late nineteenth century.

Anglo-Saxonism has undergone an evolution throughout its long history; over the centuries, people in both Great Britain and the United States used Anglo-Saxonism to suit the needs of the time. In its original sense, Anglo-Saxonism refers to the founding myths, which would be written down in documents by chroniclers such as Geoffrey of Monmouth and Bede the Venerable, that defined the English people during the early Middle Ages, as migrations of Germanic peoples settled in what would become England after the collapse of Roman rule. Such myths included the founding of the ancient Britons by survivors of the Trojan War and the stories of King Arthur and the Knights of the Round Table. These early myths created a sense of national identity for an island populated by Angles, Saxons, and Jutes, during the period often referred to as the "Dark Ages," when the light of Roman civilization had been snuffed out from Britain after the fifth century.

After about a thousand years or so, Anglo-Saxonism underwent a transformation. By the time of the Reformation in the sixteenth century, the early myths no longer sufficed, and Anglo-Saxonism was recast as assuming the banner of Protestantism against the Roman Catholic Church, a struggle most notably illustrated by the defeat of the Spanish Armada by the English navy and its subsequent destruction by the "Protestant Wind," a claim to divine favor. Puritans and other groups reinterpreted the Anglo-Saxon stories to denounce Rome's deviation from the original scriptures, as well as the corrupt Stuart monarchy and Anglican hierarchy that was still heavily influenced by the Catholic Church. Because of the influence of the Calvinism espoused by English Puritans, the idea of the English-speaking peoples as the "Chosen People" became part of the narrative of Anglo-Saxonism, especially as they began to settle North America to create a "city on a hill" amidst the "heathen" Native Americans.

Anglo-Saxonism would be reinterpreted by the leaders of the United States, both to provide a sense of continuity from the English tradition as well as to emphasize the ideals of liberty that the ancient Anglo-Saxons represented to the Founders, which would later on evolve into "American exceptionalism." The leaders of the American Revolution looked to the Anglo-Saxon myths as containing the kernels of American democracy, particularly that of limited government and popular sovereignty, ideals espoused before the Norman Conquest in 1066, which introduced the bondage of feudalism. The American Revolution also coincided with the Enlightenment principles of natural rights, and served to contrast the fledgling United States from the corrupt British monarchy.

Starting in the middle of the nineteenth century, Anglo-Saxonism shifted from its emphasis on liberty to racial ideology. The application of Charles Darwin's theory of natural selection added a pseudoscientific component to Anglo-Saxonism, which had originally been a combination of literary and religious myths. Darwin's theory of natural selection lent an aura of scientific credence to Anglo-Saxonism, as his ideas were appropriated and adapted to classifying ethnic groups into a hierarchy. The Anglo-Saxon peoples were placed at the top of the human evolutionary chain because, under this paradigm, the world had become a battleground of limited resources with each of the races competing for survival; the Anglo-Saxons were deemed the most successful in utilizing those resources. Anglo-Saxonism also served to promote Manifest Destiny, which decreed that the American descendants of the Anglo-Saxons were ordained to expand from the Atlantic to the Pacific, and that the Native Americans and Mexicans who stood in their way would either be subjugated or exterminated. Additionally, Anglo-Saxonism became a tool to justify southern slavery by reinterpreting the story of Noah's children to sanction the bondage of African-Americans, both before and after the Civil War. As the United States engaged in large-scale industrialization, Anglo-Saxonism also reflected the fears of "old-stock" Americans, such as the patrician Boston elite, who feared of being overrun by the "new immigrants" from southern and eastern Europe, as well as east Asia. These fears, coupled with the geopolitical realities of the 1880s and 1890s, would prompt a further redefinition of Anglo-Saxonism that would fit with the new international role of the United States in the aftermath of the Spanish-American War.

During the late nineteenth and early twentieth centuries, the *rapprochement* that developed between the United States and Great Britain allowed both countries to set aside old disputes and embark upon a new century with the possibility of future cooperation. That *rapprochement* was possible through the belief in Anglo-Saxonism shared between the ruling classes of both countries. Anglo-Saxonism provided a pseudoscientific justification for late nineteenth century imperialism that neatly explained how one quarter of the globe fell under the dominion of the British Empire, as well as explaining the rise of the United States. It is this shared affinity held by the White Anglo-Saxon Protestant (WASP) establishment that gradually pushed the United States and Great Britain closer together by resolving their final outstanding disputes in the Western Hemisphere and that allowed the Britain to relinquish dominance over Latin America to the United States. The goodwill provided by the British government toward the United States in the Spanish-American War was an example of Anglo-Saxon solidarity against the "Latins" represented by Spain and presented the possibility of a geopolitical partnership.

During the late nineteenth century, Anglo-Saxonism included not only the peoples of Great Britain and the United States but also Germany due to linguistic similarities and a seemingly shared culture. The Teutonic theory held that the seeds of Anglo-Saxon culture and its qualities, particularly that of self-government, lay in the distant past in the forests of Germany and northern Europe that, over the ages, would later spread to the British Isles and eventually the United States, making the German people "close relatives" of the Anglo-Saxon family. Since the colonial period, most notably in the mid-nineteenth century, there had been a stream of German immigration as the result of revolution and nationalist struggles in Europe. German culture was held in high esteem, and many German-Americans contributed greatly in the political, economic, and intellectual spheres of American life. By the turn of the twentieth century, American progressives looked to the Wilhelmine period in Germany as the model for social legislation and as an alternative to British *laissez-faire* capitalism. It would appear to Anglo-Saxonists that it would be a matter of time for the peoples of Great Britain, Germany, and the United States to forge their solidarity as a larger Anglo-Saxon family.

However, in the decade or so before the First World War, there were tensions within the Anglo-Saxon community that would later prompt another redefinition of Anglo-Saxonism. The twentieth century began with the Boer War between the British and the descendants of Dutch settlers in what is now South Africa. Proponents of Anglo-Saxonism in Great

Britain and the United States were at a loss to explain how the British army could be fighting the Boers, who were fellow Anglo-Saxons, and who exhibited the qualities of independence of self-government in the Veldt of Africa. Additionally, in the years before the outbreak of the First World War, Germany became a source of ambivalence to American visitors. While many Americans were impressed with the progress achieved in areas like medical insurance and housing for workers, they were uneasy with the increasing militarism, hypernationalism, and preponderance of the state in Kaiser Wilhelm II's Germany, which was competing against the British for global dominance, one of the long-term causes of the First World War.

The outbreak of the First World War caused a break in the Anglo-Saxon family, creating a narrower definition of Anglo-Saxonism based not on race, but on culture. Even though the German people had been originally included due to racial and linguistic affinities, by World War I it was culture that disqualified the Germans from membership in the Anglo-Saxon family. Political culture also became important as a characteristic of Anglo-Saxonism. Proponents of Anglo-Saxonism claimed that it was the ancient Anglo-Saxons who sowed the seeds that would grow into the traditions of self-government and individual liberty that were clearly evident in Great Britain, its dominions, and the United States by the turn of the twentieth century. Thus, Germany could not be included because it had developed into a conservative monarchy dominated by the descendants of Germanic warlords. It then fell to the WASP foreign policy establishment to use Anglo-Saxonism to sway American public opinion to support the Allied cause despite the significant influence of German culture in the United States. Propaganda was crucial in the redefinition of Anglo-Saxonism. The atrocity stories regarding the German occupation in Belgium and France, as well as the sinking of the *Lusitania,* circulated by the British and later American propaganda machines, excluded the German people from the family of Anglo-Saxons by highlighting the barbarity of German soldiers against civilians. Anglo-Saxonism, then, was defined by the war as representing "civilization" and democracy in the form of the Allies, versus the militarism and "savagery" represented by Germany. By couching the war in these terms, the foreign policy establishment of the United States gained the support of a diverse public whose backgrounds would not otherwise have had a natural affinity with the aims of the WASP elite and the Entente. The most tangible result, therefore, would be the entrance of the United States in the war as one of the Allied powers.

Anglo-Saxonism is crucial to understanding the foreign policy of the United States during the early twentieth century. Anglo-Saxonism fulfilled various functions. First, Anglo-Saxonism gave a sense of origin. As the United States became a haven for the "new immigrants" from Southern and Eastern Europe during the closing years of the nineteenth century, both the mythic and pseudoscientific components of Anglo-Saxonism gave solace to the "old stock Americans" who wished to preserve their predominance in an increasingly urbanized and industrialized society. Secondly, Anglo-Saxonism provided a new purpose. The old admonitions of the founders for the United States to stay aloof from international affairs became inadequate in an age of industrialization, global markets, and colonial expansion. By declaring a crusade for "civilization," Anglo-Saxonism served to cloak the new foreign policy establishment's rush to imperial adventures in the Philippines and Latin America, which resembled the *Realpolitik* and old diplomacy of the European powers. Anglo-Saxonism allowed the United States and Great Britain to extinguish ancient grievances. The resulting *rapprochement* that occurred during the late nineteenth and early twentieth centuries between these two great English-speaking powers served as a foundation for a new relationship that made it possible for the United States to enter as an ally of Britain by 1917.

Anglo-Saxonism continues to be relevant in American society in the twenty-first century. It continues to shape the worldview of Americans, consciously or sub-consciously. During the 1920s, Anglo-Saxonists lobbied to restrict immigration to the United States to northern Europeans to prevent American society from becoming diluted by immigrants from southern and eastern Europe, coinciding with the brief revival of the Ku Klux Klan. This immigration policy had disastrous results because it subjected millions of Jews and Slavs to the gas chambers of the Nazis during the Holocaust. A notable byproduct of Anglo-Saxonism is the idea of "American exceptionalism," the idea that the United States is unique among all nations because of its place as a beacon of liberty. Thus, the United States government is thought to know what is best for the rest of the world. This belief has been used to justify interventions for less-than-noble reasons in Latin America and other parts of the world throughout the twentieth century, engendering a legacy of resentment and suspicion that continues today, preventing much constructive global action. Even today, we can still see the legacy of Anglo-Saxonism in the discussions over "white privilege," and its role in the inexorable persistence of inequality in American society. The unlikely victory of Donald Trump in the 2016 presidential election could also be tied to Anglo-Saxonism because Trump courted disaffected working-class whites by promising them a way of life that they and their ancestors once knew by "making America great again." By understanding the role of racial ideology in the First World War, we can perhaps discover a common humanity, which binds all of us, regardless of our nationalities.

The Roots of Anglo-Saxonism

Anglo-Saxonism began as the mythic and literary origins of the English people who settled in the British Isles following the end of Roman rule in the fifth century. After the withdrawal of Rome's legions, waves of Germanic migrations, such as Angles, Saxons, and Scandinavians from northern Europe, began extinguishing five hundred years of Roman civilization. In order to integrate a diverse island, the narrative of the Anglo-Saxon people began to be written down, explaining their mythic origins.[1] The main message from these myths was that the English-speaking peoples inherited from their ancestors the legacy of a free people, which made them better than anyone else because they inherited qualities conducive to self-government, such as courage, independence, thrift, and self-control. These qualities would guide the English-speaking peoples throughout England's history, culminating in the rise of the British Empire.[2]

The beginnings of "England" can be traced to the end of Roman rule. When Emperor Honorius withdrew the Roman legions in AD 410, four hundred years of Roman civilization came to an end. In *The Ruin of Britain*, written about 540, Gildas blamed the iniquities of the Britons for the collapse of civil order in Britain, precipitating the Anglo-Saxon invasions. He cited the letter of Honorius admonishing the Roman citizens of Britain to look after their own defenses, for they would expect no more help from Rome's legions.[3] The collapse of Roman authority in Britain in the fifth century AD brought about the end of Roman culture. The language of the Britons gradually replaced Latin. Bureaucratic institutions, such as the civil service, withered away. As a result, the withdrawal of the legions meant that Roman money no longer held any value. The roads, villas, and other monuments to Roman rule decayed. The industries that had supported a Roman infrastructure fell idle. The urbanized market economy that had flourished in Roman Britain for almost four centuries reverted to the conditions that Julius Caesar found in 55 BC, i.e., a warrior agrarian society.[4]

The years following the collapse of Roman rule become more a matter of speculation than that of historical record. Gildas's work remains one of the few accounts of Britain at the advent of the Anglo-Saxon invasions. This passage by Gildas gives a vivid description of the collapse of Roman civilization:

> ...Our citizens abandoned the towns and the high wall. Once again they had to flee; once again they were scattered, more irretrievably than usual; once again there were enemy assaults and massacres more cruel. The pitiable citizens were torn apart by their foe like lambs by the butcher; their life became like that of beasts of the field. For they resorted to looting each other, there being only a tiny amount of food to give brief sustenance to the wretched people; and the disasters from abroad were increased by internal disorders, for as a result of constant devastations of this kind the whole region came to lack the staff of any food, apart from such comfort as the art of the huntsman could procure them.[5]

Without Roman protection, Britain was subject to Germanic invasions. Various tribes such as the Alemanni, Angles, Frisians, Saxons, and Swabians settled throughout the southern portion of the island of Britain.[6] The Anglo-Saxon tribes overran Britain and established strongholds, thus filling the void left by the Romans. Rather than an elaborate bureaucracy and infrastructure, a warrior aristocracy predominated in which authority was based on military prowess. In place of the Latin language and literature, the Germanic languages of the Anglo-Saxons dotted the island, whose influence can still be placed in modern England. Norse and Germanic gods replaced the Christianity brought by the Romans, who still reign over the days of the week throughout the English-speaking world.[7] It was during this period, however, when myths could flourish that would gradually unite this island and create "England."

Anglo-Saxon Myths

The collapse of Roman rule in Britain meant a lack of reliable sources describing the years since 410, when the last Roman legions withdrew from the island. In place of official record keeping, myths served to fill the void left by the Romans. These myths were stories brought over by various Germanic peoples who encroached upon the Western Roman Empire and the island of Britain. A few examples of the myths that have been preserved have Germanic origins, from the tales of *Sigmund* and *Weland and Beaduhild*, which originated from Norse mythology, to the incorporation of *Aetla* (Attila) the Hun, whose exploits caused the Germanic incursions into the Roman Empire.[8]

The Anglo-Saxon myths that prevailed during the Early Middle Ages fall into two categories. The first category of myth is the myth of migration. In a myth of migration, the story is structured around the need for more space for a people to thrive, which is often patterned after the Jewish narratives of the Old Testament.[9] The second category is known as "conquest mythology." These myths revolve around the establishment of the Anglo-Saxon kingdoms in Britain. Their stories are similarly structured, revolving around an exodus from an ancestral birthplace, a series of trials to be overcome in the new homeland, a sign of divine sanction, the conversion from paganism to Christianity, and the defeat of a traditional enemy.[10]

The latter category of mythology gives insight into the formation of Anglo-Saxon identity. In one example, the tale of Hengest exemplifies military prowess as one of the chief qualities of the Anglo-Saxons. In another example, Beowulf epitomizes the ideal relationship between lord and warrior, as shown in the expectations of generosity by a lord to his retainer upon a successful campaign.[11] In the narrative translated by Kevin Crossley-Holland, Hengest is the hero who leads the Danes after the death of their leader Hnaef to victory over their enemies.[12] Also central to the Anglo-Saxon myths is the idea of the Anglo-Saxons as a "chosen people." Gildas took a disparaging view of what he saw as Britons' the lack of moral fortitude, which explained their conquest by the Romans and their subsequent degradation upon the collapse of Roman rule.[13] The narratives of the Anglo-Saxon myths, such as that of Hengest, describe the ancient Britons as unworthy, which would justify their conquest. The story of Hengest would suggest that because of his victory, the Anglo-Saxons had a right to establish their dominion in what would become the kingdom of Kent, from whom its royal line was derived, serving as the nucleus for the English state.[14]

Bede, The Anglo-Saxon Chronicle *and the Making of England*

Bede's *Ecclesiastical History of the English People* is one of the earliest attempts write down the common history of what would become "England." Rather than simply describe the history of the "Saxons" or "Jutes," Bede's original title, *Historia Ecclesiastica Gentis Anglorum* implies a common people that transcends the various Anglo-Saxon kingdoms that existed in by the seventh century.[15] Bede writes his *Ecclesiastical History* from a particular standpoint. As a member of the Church, his work reflects the unity of the Roman Catholic Church, rather than the political loyalties of each particular kingdom.[16] Bede does this by beginning his work with a description of the island of Britain. He describes the geographical features, some of the local flora and fauna of the island, and the climate of the island, rather than dwelling on the particularities of any of the Anglo-Saxon kingdoms.[17] Secondly, Bede takes note of the languages that were in use in England. However, he emphasizes the fact that what unites the speakers of English, British (or Welsh), Irish, and Pictish, is the Latin language of the Roman Catholic Church, suggesting that it is spiritual unity that makes up the English people.[18]

Bede's description of Britain under Roman rule differs vastly from Gildas's *Ruin of Britain*. Though not intended to be a history of Britain, Gildas's work is often treated thusly because of its eyewitness account of Britain immediately following the end of Roman rule. Gildas prefaced his history by declaring his intention to "deplore with mournful complaint … a general loss of good, a heaping up of bad." That is, his goal was to serve as a warning against spiritual laxity, not unlike the epistles of St. Paul in the New Testament.[19] Bede's *Ecclesiastical History*, however, was intended as a history, written using the documents of his day as corroborating evidence. Bede consulted historians such as Pliny, Solinus, Eutropius, Sain Germanus, and Gildas, as well as the archives in Canterbury, Kent, and gained access to papers from Rome.[20]

Bede's *Ecclesiastical History* delves into more detail on the political and social developments of England during and after Roman rule without providing as much admonishment as Gildas's work. For example, for the years surrounding Rome's fateful decision to withdraw its legions from Britain, Bede describes the historical context that led to Rome's withdrawal from Britain by citing the invasions of the Germanic tribes that swept into Gaul, the rampant political instability in Rome, and the sacking of Rome by the Goths.[21] In contrast, Gildas describes the same period with more commentary on the shortcomings of the Britons without the same attention to detail and historical analysis as illustrated in *Ecclesiastical History*.[22]

Perhaps where Bede and Gildas coincide is their treatment of the Anglo-Saxon invasions. Both scholars heap condemnation on the Britons' sins as the reasons for the Anglo-Saxon invasions. Gildas refers to the invasions as God's way "to purge his family and to cleanse it from such an infection of evil…."[23] Bede also gives a Biblical analogy to the Anglo-Saxon invasions by likening them to the destruction of Jerusalem by the Babylonians as a means of divine punishment.[24] Where Bede differs from Gildas is in his treatment of the myth of Hengest. Gildas only refers to the raiding party of Hengest as "three keels," referring to their ships. Bede, however, describes the arrival of the Saxons, Angles, and Jutes. He traces the royal lines of the Anglo-Saxon kingdoms to Hengest and Horsa, describing them as "sons of Woden" from Norse mythology.[25] Like, Gildas, Bede considered the Anglo-Saxons justifiable. He believed that because of their sinfulness, the Britons deserved their punishment and were not fit to rule Britain. Thus, Bede traces the beginnings of the English people to the Anglo-Saxon invasions, rather than with the ancient Britons, themselves.[26]

Likewise, *The Anglo-Saxon Chronicle* takes its cue from Bede's *Ecclesiastical History*. *The Anglo-Saxon Chronicle* begins with a description of the island. It also emphasizes that among the languages spoken on Britain, Latin is a uniting factor for the island.[27] Perhaps even more explicitly than Bede's *Ecclesiastical History*, *The Anglo-Saxon Chronicle* makes more of an effort to include Britain in the larger Christian community by including the events in the New Testament as part of the history of Britain before any mention of the Anglo-Saxon rulers.[28]

Unlike Gildas's *On the Ruin of Britain* and Bede's *Ecclesiastical History*, *The Anglo-Saxon Chronicle* was written specifically to praise the Anglo-Saxon kings. While both Gildas and Bede condemn the moral torpor of the ancient Britons, *The Anglo-Saxon Chronicle* makes no mention of them and credits the Anglo-Saxons with the establishment of the English nation.[29] Of the three works, *The Anglo-Saxon Chronicle* gives the most historical credence to the myth of Hengest. *The Anglo-Saxon Chronicle* lists the exploits of Hengest in detail, from his arrival at the request of Vortigern to the establishing of the kingdom of Kent.[30] As its title suggests, *The Anglo-Saxon Chronicle* traces the beginnings of the English nation to the creation of the Anglo-Saxon kingdoms, rather than the ancient Britons. The *Anglo-Saxon Chronicle* creates what Benedict Anderson calls an "imagined community," by using language to construct a larger Anglo-Saxon, hence "English," community out of an island of various kingdoms that were often in conflict with one another.[31] By its nature, *The Anglo-Saxon Chronicle* establishes the primacy of the Anglo-Saxons through its celebration of the military conquests of the Anglo-Saxon kingdoms, and it gives a sense of purpose above mere conquest and booty to the Anglo-Saxons who settled into Britain.[32]

Geoffrey of Monmouth's History of British Kings and the Arthurian Legend

Geoffrey of Monmouth's work *Historia Regnum Brittaniae* was written in 1136, far beyond the era of the Anglo-Saxon invasions. Geoffrey's purpose was to include the Normans, who were the last wave of invaders to overtake England, into the English community. Rather than to condemn the Britons as Gildas and Bede had done, Geoffrey sought to include the early Britons by connecting the Normans to the Arthurian legend. By connecting the Normans to the ancient Britons, particularly King Arthur, Geoffrey's work would establish a line of continuity, thus providing the Normans with a sense of legitimacy.[33]

Geoffrey's history of England delves more into myth than does Gildas, Bede, or *The Anglo-Saxon Chronicles*. Like Bede and *The Anglo-Saxon Chronicle*, Geoffrey gives a geographical preface as an introduction, perhaps consciously imitating the previous works' style, so as to lend legitimacy to his history of Britain.[34] While Gildas and Bede write from an ecclesiastical perspective, Geoffrey writes from a lay secular point of view. Geoffrey delves into Roman mythology to explain the origin of the Britons. According to Geoffrey, Britain was founded by Brutus, a grandson of Aeneas, who escaped the fall of Troy. Like the origin myths of other peoples, Brutus was given a divine commission by the goddess Diana to establish a kingdom in "an empty land" beyond Gaul and be the father of a line of kings.[35] After years of wandering, Brutus came upon the island of Albion, which he renamed "Britain," and established his capital at Troia Nova, where he established a people from which the Britons were derived by the time of the Roman conquest.[36]

Geoffrey's approach to the ancient Britons differ markedly from that of Gildas, Bede, or *The Anglo-Saxon Chronicle*. Rather than condemning them or ignoring them altogether, Geoffrey puts the Britons in a more positive light. Instead of blaming the sins of the Britons for the Anglo-Saxon invasions, Geoffrey blames the political instability of the Roman Empire for the demise of Roman rule in Britain and its indefensibility against the invaders.[37] Like Bede and *The Anglo-Saxon Chronicle*, Geoffrey weaves the myth of Hengist into the narrative of the founding of the English nation through their defeat of Vortigern.[38]

Geoffrey wrote his *History* during the civil war between Stephen and Matilda in 1138. He goes beyond the earlier works mentioned in this paper and provides the narrative of Arthur, a Welsh chieftain. The Arthurian legend served various purposes. One of them was to cast Arthur as the ideal model for the feudalism that was established since the Norman Conquest. The Arthurian legends, aside from regaling its audiences with deeds of knightly valor, served to teach the morals of chivalry and the importance of maintaining the bond between lord and vassal.[39] While Gildas, Bede, and *The Anglo-Saxon Chronicle* ignore the Arthurian narrative altogether, Geoffrey takes great pains to connect Arthur to the recently established Norman rulers. Geoffrey was one of the first medieval scholars to cast Arthur in a heroic light. He does this not only for the sake of literary flair but also for the purpose of establishing legitimacy for his patrons, the Normans, who came over with William the Conqueror in 1066. Firstly, Geoffrey's narrative of the Arthurian legend establishes a sense of continuity by linking the Normans to the ancient Britons. Secondly, Geoffrey bypasses the Anglo-Saxon kingdoms, the last of which the Normans overthrew because of their fractured nature. By tracing royal genealogy back to the British, the Normans would be able to justify the centralization of England with the creation of a strong bureaucracy.[40]

Post-Norman England

In the centuries following the Norman Conquest, Anglo-Saxonism would continue to play a role in the shaping of the British people. The theme of the English people as a "chosen people" gained new meaning during the English Reformation of the sixteenth century, when Henry VIII broke England away from the Roman Catholic Church. John Bale, a former Carmelite priest who joined the Church of England, re-cast the Anglo-Saxon story *The Actes of the English Votaryes* as an allegory of the struggle between the English church and a corrupt Roman Catholic hierarchy by emphasizing the sexual appetites of Roman Catholic priests, who did not spare even young English boys. In doing so, Bale gave credibility to the idea that Henry VIII's decision to declare himself the supreme head of the Church of England was a holy cause rather than a political expedience. Therefore, since the Roman Catholic Church had been divided between the Bishop of Rome and the Patriarch of Constantinople, the Anglican church was the "true church." This decision would be further vindicated under the leadership of Elizabeth I, when England escaped the clutches of the Catholics by a failed invasion attempt from the Spanish Armada.[41]

Just as Anglo-Saxonism was used to justify the English Reformation, the British people drew upon their Anglo-Saxon narrative in the struggle between absolute and constitutional monarchy throughout the seventeenth century, with the emphasis on liberty, as interpreted by the Whig faction that overthrew James II. In their triumph over the Stuart dynasty's pretense of divine right, the Whigs drew upon England's Anglo-Saxon past as an example of the ideal society. Sir William Temple, who wrote *An*

Introduction to the History of England, idealized the Goths as "civil, orderly, and virtuous," in contrast to the absolutist tendencies of the Romans whom they vanquished. Therefore, it was in the spirit of the Goths that, during the Glorious Revolution of 1689, the Whigs overthrew James II for imposing Catholic absolutism upon the English people.[42] The succession of the German Hanoverians to the British throne in the early eighteenth century, a result of the 1701 Act of Settlement, was celebrated by Whig leaders as a reunion of the English people to their Saxon relatives, drawing upon their common ancestry and the Protestant cause.[43] As the Whig version of history emerged in the seventeenth and eighteenth centuries, historians supporting the Whig cause, such as John Oldmixon, connected their revolution against absolutism and the constitutional monarchy to Anglo-Saxon institutions like the *witenagemot* from which Parliament was derived. The goal of these fledgling institutions was to prevent monarchical tyranny, a cause that would be carried on to Britain's North American colonies.[44]

CHAPTER I

Anglo-Saxonism and American Culture, 1895–1914

The Roots of American Anglo-Saxonism

Like England, the United States was created in the eighteenth century out of a melting pot of peoples from all over Europe, bringing diverse creeds and traditions. As the early Republic was established, its founders appropriated Anglo-Saxonism to establish a national identity that Americans would use to further differentiate themselves among the various European ethnic groups settling in the country, distinguishing the "civilized" from the "savage." During the first decades of the Republic, a narrative arose to define who was an "American" and to outline the ultimate destiny of the American people. First, the Americans were descended from ancient Anglo-Saxons with a tradition of liberty before the Norman Conquest. This included a Protestant identity, which drew heavily on Calvinism, that declared the Americans to be an "elect" who shared a covenant with God to spread Christianity. Founding Fathers such as John Winthrop, George Washington, and Thomas Jefferson were part of this Anglo-Saxon pantheon, from which the American nation would spring. The American people were therefore the heirs to the ancient Anglo-Saxons and would continue the legacy of liberty and Protestant Christianity upon the North American continent.[1] Anglo-Saxonism would provide a common narrative for the fledgling republic during the nineteenth century, as the United States endured the growing pains of nationhood and its expansion westward in the decades before the Civil War.[2]

American imperial expansion can be more clearly illuminated by using the template of Anglo-Saxonism. The peoples of Great Britain and their descendants in the white dominions—such as Canada, Australia,

New Zealand, and South Africa—and in the United States shared a common sense of origin and destiny by the end of the nineteenth century. Referring to themselves as the "English-speaking race," Anglo-Saxonists believed that inherent in their shared character were the qualities of self-government, liberty, and rule of law. In addition, Anglo-Saxonists claimed for their own the virtues of intelligence, temperance, efficiency, and moral consciousness.

Anglo-Saxonists drew upon the cultural and literary heritage connecting Britain and America. They claimed for their own the ancient myths of the founding of the British people and the heroic epic of King Arthur.[3] Anglo-Saxonism added a religious component during the Protestant Reformation and the Commonwealth with the belief that they were "God's Chosen People," which was likewise transplanted in Massachusetts by the Puritans.[4] During the founding of the United States, the Anglo-Saxonists of the early nineteenth century took liberty as an inherent characteristic, and at the time brooked no *rapprochement* with the British, whom they saw as hopelessly corrupted by monarchy. It was this interpretation of Anglo-Saxonism that fueled the idea of "Manifest Destiny" and justified the expansion of the United States across the North American continent at the expense of Mexico and Native Americans.[5] During the 1840s, when famine in Ireland drove unprecedented numbers of Catholic Irish immigrants to American shores, nativists feared for the future of the United States, particularly whether Catholicism would undermine American democratic institutions. Anglo-Saxonism thus provided a shared American identity by stressing Protestantism.[6]

The leaders of the American Revolution drew upon Anglo-Saxon themes as part of their cause for liberty against despotic monarchical rule, based upon the belief that ancient England under the Anglo-Saxons was free until the Norman invasion of 1066. During the early years of the republic, the leaders of the new nation equated Anglo-Saxonism with freedom.[7] Likewise, Jefferson, who saw the independent yeoman farmer as the backbone for the new American society, also believed that the entire North American continent belonged to the United States.[8] By the 1830s and 1840s, Manifest Destiny had become synonymous with Anglo-Saxonism and served as the justification for American expansionism. Many Americans believed that it was the destiny of the young republic to expand from the Atlantic to the Pacific because of the supposed divine sanction of the Anglo-Saxon heritage. Americans began to see non–Anglo-Saxons, i.e., African-Americans, Mexicans, and Native Americans, as incapable of governing themselves responsibly. By 1850, Manifest Destiny provided the justification for the acquisition of Texas, the Oregon Country, and California because, under the wise tutelage of American Anglo-Saxons, those areas would supposedly progress much farther than if they had been left to their own devices. Once the United States had reached the Pacific, Asia and the Caribbean lay next within the sights of Anglo-Saxonists with the same goals.[9]

Late Nineteenth- and Early Twentieth-Century Anglo-Saxonism

During the late nineteenth century, proponents of Anglo-Saxonism defined what it meant to be an American by adding scientific racism and social Darwinism to the existing literary and religious narratives, giving different kinds of Anglo-Saxonists something to offer. For example, American historians and ethnologists of the 1890s, such as Herbert Baxter Adams, John Fiske, John W. Bergess, and James K. Hosmer, continued to draw from the forests of northern Europe as the origins of American "self-government" and bolster the identity of an Anglo-Protestant America.[10]

Frederick Jackson Turner, known for his prominent Frontier Thesis, would at first glance appear to refute Anglo-Saxonism's role in shaping American culture by stressing westward expansion's role in creating an egalitarian and democratic society. In actuality, Turner's intellectual pedigree included the Anglo-Saxonist Herbert Baxter Adams as his mentor. Turner assumed that Americans of Anglo-Saxon descent comprised the "native stock" of the United States, and it was this Anglo-Saxon stock's sense of liberty and agrarian impulse that conquered the western half of North America.[11]

By the end of the nineteenth century, the concepts of liberty and self-government as unique to Anglo-Saxonism continued to be part of the intellectual discourse, going back, at least, to medieval England. In the 1891 edition of the *Harvard Law Review*, the legal tradition of the Magna Carta was a major influence upon the federal and state constitutions, which inculcated the sense of "liberty" as part of the American identity. The author, Charles Shattuck, argues that the concepts of private property, religious liberty, freedom of speech, and trial by jury, etc., as protected by the Declaration of Independence, the Constitution, and the Bill of Rights, are a continuation of the Anglo-Saxon traditions enshrined in the Magna Carta, the Petition of Right, the Habeas Corpus Act, and the English Bill of Rights.[12] Shattuck traces the protection of the rights to "life, liberty, and property" to Teutonic origins that were gradually transmitted to England by the time of the Norman Conquest in 1066.[13] Shattuck refers particularly the thirty-ninth article of the Magna Carta which declares that "No freeman shall be taken, or imprisoned, or disseized, or outlawed, or banished, or any ways destroyed; nor will we pass upon him, nor send upon him, unless by the legal judgment of his peers, or by the law of the land."[14] This has been interpreted as the origins of due process, the foundation of American jurisprudence that protects a citizen's right against imprisonment or having his property seized by an arbitrary and tyrannical government. Shattuck considers this article of the Magna Carta especially important because it would serve as a foundation upon which traditional English liberties would be built, which he ascribes as one of the chief qualities of the Anglo-Saxon peoples. He best articulates this with the following:

> Personal liberty was a common-law right in England in 1215, and long before; it was one of the great rights declared in the thirty-ninth article of the Great Charter; it was insisted upon in all the confirmations of that article, and is there always found in connection with the rights of life and property; its infringement was the chief complaint in the Petition of Right of 1627, and the Habeas Corpus Act of 1679 was passed solely to secure it against usurpation. Altogether, it may be said that the history of the growth and development of the right of personal liberty is the main element in the history of early English constitutional law, that the idea of personal liberty pervades the history of the Anglo-Saxon race, and that it is, therefore, not surprising to find it classified with the rights of life and property as one of the three greatest civil "liberties."[15]

The rights to life, liberty, and property guaranteed in the Magna Carta, according to Shattuck, became enshrined in the federal and state constitutions, culminating in the Bill of Rights, particularly the Fourteenth Amendment, which protects against the seizure of life, liberty, and property without the due process of law. The Fourteenth Amendment would be tested in the "Slaughterhouse Cases," which decided whether butchers in New Orleans were being deprived of their livelihood when the state government of Louisiana created a monopoly and, in the name of public health, restricted the area in which butchers could ply their trade.[16] Shattuck noted that the dissenting justices cited the Anglo-Saxon legal heritage enshrined in the Magna Carta that depriving one's ability to earn a livelihood was the same as depriving one's property, which was an infringement of liberty as stated in the Fourteenth Amendment.[17] Shattuck further uses the development of liberty to differentiate English-speaking countries from non–English-speaking countries.[18]

Because of the inherent love for liberty held in the hearts of the English-speaking peoples, the case for Anglo-Saxonism, as inherent in the political blueprint of the United States, continued to be a topic of intellectual debate in the late nineteenth century. Anglo-Saxonists tied American political institutions to the primeval forests of the Germanic peoples, who held the kernels of representative government.[19] The September 1895 issue of *The Annals of the American Academy of Political Science* states that the American federal system that emerged in the late eighteenth century was not a new system but rather had its roots in the ancient Germanic tribes. While the author, William Morey, notes that similar movements had occurred in the ancient Greek and Roman city-states, he suggests the Germans were successful because they did not fall to anarchy, and eventually, autocracy, as had occurred with the ancient Greeks and Romans.[20]

Morey examines further the development of Anglo-Saxon institutions transplanted from Germany, which held the seeds of the future American government that would blossom centuries later. Like many Anglo-Saxonists, Morey considered the village structure to be the basis for the New England village, which he believed was a miniature model of American representative government. At the lowest level was the town meeting or *tun-gemote,* which elected its own chief magistrate, known as the *tun-reeve.* At the next level was the hundred, made up of a collection of towns, that elected the *hundred-reeve,* which had an assembly, known as the *hundred-gemote.* A group of "hundreds" composed the shire, which had an assembly called the *shire-mote,* made up of the freeholders of the shire, who elected their "earldorman," the chief executive, and the *shire-reeve,* from which the title of "sheriff" is derived. In his publication, Morey argues that the organization of the "town meetings," "hundreds," and the shire would serve as the template for the American federal system because it would provide the conditions necessary for self-government, which would later distinguish the English-speaking peoples from all others.[21] Consistent with other Anglo-Saxonists, Morey argues that the free institutions established by the early Anglo-Saxon tribes were brought to an end after the Norman Conquest of 1066, which introduced feudalism and centralized government. The shire, for example, became reduced to an administrative unit rather than a self-ruling entity. The sheriff was no longer an elected position, and the earldorman was appointed by the Crown. According to Morey, in the centuries after 1066, England, culminating in the Tudor and Stuart dynasties, would copy its continental neighbors' centralization of government.[22]

By the 1890s, Americans took a great interest in the Anglo-Saxon language, which was available at more than three dozen schools, making the United States the country with the most abundant Anglo-Saxon courses in the world, compared to the 1840s, when there were only four schools that taught Anglo-Saxon. Proponents of Anglo-Saxonism believed that the American people were the heirs to the Anglo-Saxons by linking American political institutions with their own decentralized tribal systems.[23]

In his article, Morey argues that the Pilgrim fathers and the Puritans who settled in Massachusetts were part of an "Anglo-Saxon revival" because they escaped the centralized "tyranny" they had known in England and re-established the institutions that existed before the Norman Conquest. Morey considered the New England townships in Massachusetts, Rhode Island, and Connecticut as models of Anglo-Saxon "self-government" that had no parallels in the world of the seventeenth century. From the New England town, therefore, sprang forth the seeds of American federalism, which could be seen in the Albany Plan of Union proposed in 1754, culminating into the federal Constitution that was ratified in 1787.[24]

Likewise, in an address to Syracuse University in 1875, attorney Dexter Hawkins attributed love of liberty to be unique in the Anglo-Saxon people, particularly its influence behind the creation of American institutions. As the descendants of the ancient Anglo-Saxons settled into North America, they transplanted Anglo-Saxon institutions. In the aftermath of the American Revolution, the leaders of the new American polity could further fulfill the ancient liberties of their Anglo-Saxon forebears because they would be free of the trapping of hereditary monarchy, landed aristocracy, and an established church, which had so corrupted England, the ancient homeland. Hawkins considered the American Civil War to be the last battle for Anglo-Saxon freedom, which eliminated slavery, something he termed a remnant of "barbarity."[25]

After the Civil War, white southerners would turn to Anglo-Saxonism to establish a new narrative to replace the world they had known, which was built on slavery. This was a change in attitude from the antebellum period: then, white southerners identified more with the Normans, as the planter class desired to link themselves to the English aristocracy who traced their ancestry to the Norman Conquest in 1066. When the Civil War broke out, white southerners identified with the "Cavaliers" of the English Civil War of the seventeenth century, compared to the "Puritan" northerners.[26] Throughout the antebellum period, southerners held to a code of honor that was reinforced by slavery. When the American Civil War broke out, white southerners counted on that sense of chivalry in order to prevail against the commercial barbarians of the North.[27]

With the defeat of the Confederacy in 1865 and the Reconstruction that followed, white southerners had to establish a new identity for themselves and reinterpret the Anglo-Saxon stories. During the 1890s, Anglo-Saxon studies became part of the southern curriculum because of increasing demand for university courses by white southerners, who used Anglo-Saxon linguistics and ideals to define themselves, in light of the disruptions caused by the Civil War and Reconstruction.[28] White southerners saw themselves in the stories of the Anglo-Saxon people who fought against oppression, whether it be from the Romans or the Normans. Therefore, white southerners saw the Civil War, fought between 1861 and 1865, as not so much over the subjugation of African-Americans as it was a struggle against the oppression of the federal government, which was their contemporary version of the Norman invaders.[29] An article by W. P. Trent in the *Sewanee Review* in 1901 justified the South's secession on the grounds that the states had the right to govern themselves as they saw fit, including on the issue of slavery. States' rights then became the mid-nineteenth century equivalent of the Anglo-Saxon virtue of self-government, which southern intellectuals appropriated as they began to give their accounts of the Civil War after 1865.[30]

The aftermath of General Robert E. Lee's surrender at Appomattox Courthouse would, for many southerners, usher in an era of humiliation and degradation, as they would have to endure the abolition of slavery as the source of their wealth, military occupation, disfranchisement, and the onslaught of Northern carpetbaggers. White southerners felt this was akin to the defeat of the Anglo-Saxons after the Battle of Hastings in 1066, as well as similar to the military dictatorship established by Oliver Cromwell in the aftermath of the English Civil War in the seventeenth century.[31] In his article, Trent argued that Reconstruction was even more excessive than the military government imposed by Cromwell after the establishment of the Commonwealth of England after 1649. Trent blamed the Radical Republican faction led by Thaddeus Stevens for suppressing the South's inclination to Anglo-Saxon self-government by imposing military occupation upon the former Confederacy and using African-American suffrage as a cudgel to keep southern whites in a "vanquished" state.[32] He also thought it was a "delusion" to give freed African-Americans the same rights of citizenship and the vote because of their "inherently" inferior nature; he further thought that universal suffrage would require countless generations of Anglo-Saxons' tutelage, which to him was among the chief reasons that Reconstruction failed.[33]

With the abolition of slavery, white southerners used Anglo-

Saxonism to refashion a new identity for themselves. They likened themselves to the Anglo-Saxon tribes, themselves occupied by the Norman invaders, and sought to create similar institutions that would recreate the liberty lost by the Norman Conquest. White southerners identified with the qualities of temperance, duty, and endurance, which facilitated self-government.[34] As a result, white southerners believed that even though they were unsuccessful in the military struggle during the Civil War, they could preserve their heritage by using the Anglo-Saxon language and its institutions against northern carpetbaggers. The southern appropriation of Anglo-Saxonism, therefore, would save American culture, as a whole, from the forces unleashed by the Civil War, most notably the emancipation of African-Americans.[35] Southern white proponents of Anglo-Saxonism used the literary and linguistic traditions of the ancient Anglo-Saxons as tools in the disfranchisement of African-Americans by condemning African-Americans' use of language to the periphery, declaring that it was inferior compared to the language of Beowulf. Therefore, southern Anglo-Saxonists argued against what they called the "linguistic miscegenation" between African-American English and the "pure" English, which descended from Anglo-Saxon languages, and used it as another justification for racial segregation.[36]

It is therefore no surprise that southern whites used Anglo-Saxonism as part of their arsenal in the subjugation of African-Americans in the late nineteenth century. Southerners used Anglo-Saxonism to further differentiate themselves from African-Americans, and, despite the abolition of slavery, they believed that African-Americans could therefore never rise to the levels of southern whites. An article in the June 1900 issue of the *North American Review* addressed the question of whether African-Americans could ever be integrated into the wider American society. The author, Professor John Roach Straton of Mercer University in Macon, Georgia, argued that the education of African-Americans in the decades after the Civil War had done little good: to the contrary, education had only encouraged "their tendency to immorality and crime," compared to the antebellum period when he stated that African-Americans were a more docile people in their ignorance.[37] Straton cited a direct relationship between the rise of spending on education of African-Americans with the increase in the crime rate. For example, he listed that between 1870 and 1880 the crime rate among African-Americans increased 25 percent, and that between 1880 and 1890 it had increased to 33 percent, while between 1865 and 1890, spending on the education of African-Americans totaled to $100 million. Like many southerners of his time, Straton linked African-

Americans with the crime of rape, particularly against white women, which he believed to be intrinsic to their nature.³⁸

While one does not have to be an Anglo-Saxonist to espouse racist ideology, Straton saw civilization as inherent in the Anglo-Saxon peoples. Stratton emphasized the fact that though one might wish to share the fruits of civilization with "savages," they would not be able to digest them, rather such fruits would be harmful to them by their sudden introduction. Straton expressed this position best with the following:

> The true civilizing process is not a sudden and artificial development from without, but a gradual and harmonious growth from within. Plato's dwellers in the cave could not be suddenly transferred from their accustomed darkness to the dazzling light on the out side. The African cannot be lifted to the plane of the Anglo-Saxon by the use of either logarithms and Greek roots or formulae for cultivating a field or constructing a pair of shoes. The Anglo-Saxon has reached his present high civilization after a long and laborious struggle upward. Through a series of well defined steps, he has risen from barbarism to his present plane. The system in which he now dwells is the logical outcome of all that has gone before, and consequently the white man of to-day is thoroughly suited to his environment. Now, it is reasonable to think that, since Anglo-Saxon civilization is thus the culmination of a series of steps, all the steps must be taken before it can safely be reached.³⁹

Furthermore, Straton argued that exposure of non–Anglo-Saxon peoples to the Anglo-Saxons had generally led to their extinction. He cited historical examples of contact—such as between the British and the indigenous peoples of Tasmania, between the British and the Maoris in New Zealand, between Europeans and the native Hawaiians, and between Europeans and native Americans—all of which led to drastic declines in indigenous numbers because of the attempts of well-meaning Europeans to "civilize" these populations.⁴⁰ In the case of African-Americans, Straton concluded that while there might be remarkable individuals like Booker T. Washington, whose emphasis on "industrial education" he supported wholeheartedly, Straton believed that as a whole, "lifting them up" by education would have disastrous consequences. Because the Anglo-Saxon peoples took millennia to develop into a "civilized" race, Straton believed that the sudden introduction of education and technology wrought by emancipation would lead to the ultimate destruction of the African-American people, releasing their propensities toward "degeneracy."⁴¹

The transformation of Anglo-Saxonism from the optimism of liberty to a message of racial struggle occurred in the mid-nineteenth century with Charles Darwin's *Origin of the Species: The Preservation of Favoured Races in the Struggle for Life*, published in 1859. Anglo-Saxonists freed Darwin's theory of natural selection from its biological application, utilizing it for the human world. For example, even though the term "races" in the subtitle of the work referred to animal species, Anglo-Saxonists of the period extended the definition to include humans. Darwin's subsequent work, *The Descent of Man* (1871), argued that the laws of evolution and natural selection also applied to human beings, particularly those of the Anglo-Saxon race. As a result, Darwin's works provided a scientific explanation for the "superiority" of some races and the "inferiority" of others. Adding science to the Anglo-Saxonists' arguments provided an intellectual foundation from which to draw and a means from which to gain credibility.[42] These ideas would then be applied to American foreign policy at the beginning of the twentieth century, as the United States embarked upon an expansionist agenda by projecting its power beyond its shores. Anglo-Saxonism and whiteness complemented each other perfectly by declaring that the white race had an obligation to "civilize" and "Christianize" the "savages" of the world.[43]

Darwin's theories of evolution and natural selection became sources from which Anglo-Saxonists from both sides of the Atlantic could expand their theories of racial superiority. Increasingly, intellectuals from the United States and Great Britain looked to Anglo-Saxonism as a reason for the incredible success of their respective countries; it was assumed that the United States and Great Britain working together in concert would be a force for greater good. In the years following the publication of *Origin of the Species*, various writers also used the themes of racial struggle to justify the dominance of the Anglo-Saxon peoples. Benjamin Kidd, a British civil servant, published *Social Evolution* in 1894. Therein, he contended that human societies were subject to the same biological laws that governed other organisms.[44] A similar Anglo-Saxonist, Karl Pearson, wrote in 1900 *National Life from the Standpoint of Science*, which suggested that nations were engaged in perpetual struggle, particularly in economic and technological competition. As a result of this struggle between nations, the "suffering" of individual members of society, i.e., workers, was a price for progress, whose ultimate goal was civilization.[45]

By the late nineteenth century, Anglo-Saxonists used history to justify the superiority of the Anglo-Saxon civilization of Britain and the United States. Anglo-Saxonist historians argued that the ancient Anglo-Saxon race developed the free institutions of Britain and America. James Hosmeer, a contemporary historian of the 1890s, remarked the following:

> Representation, the principle that pervades the whole apparatus for law-making and administration in the higher ranges of politics, is distinctly an Anglo-Saxon idea, proceeding probably from the earliest times. If America resembles the ancient

mother, in no less degree does England resemble her.... The blood and fibre of the whole great English-speaking race, in fact, is derived from those Elbe and Weser plains; government of the people, by the people, for the people, which is as the breath of its life wherever that race may be scattered, is the ancient Anglo-Saxon freedom.[46]

Similarly, in the August 1898 issue of *Living Age*, the director of the American Archaeological School in Athens, Dr. Charles Waldstein, opined that the peoples of the United States and Great Britain shared a common history. He claimed that before 1776, the year of the American Revolution, the history of America lay *not* with the Native Americans, but with England. He also made the claim that the history of Great Britain, therefore, would not be complete *without* including the histories of the United States and its settler colonies of Australia, Canada, and New Zealand.[47] In regards to the American Revolution, Waldstein did not interpret it as a schism between the two English-speaking peoples. Rather, the revolution and the founding of the United States complemented England's enterprise of self-government in America. Thus, the peoples of Great Britain and the United States, deduced Waldstein, were far more united because they shared the same institutions of self-government.[48]

Another method of manipulating history to justify the superiority of the Anglo-Saxon peoples was the "Teutonic" theory, which held that the ancestors of the British and American people hailed from Germany, and over the centuries established themselves in England and America, bringing their ideas of self-rule with them. Among the scholars who supported the "Teutonic" theory was John Mitchell Kemble, who in his work *The Saxons in England* traced the development of the English institutions of representation and self-government to ancient Anglo-Saxon assemblies. Edward Freeman, Regius Professor of history at Oxford University, promoted the idea of race in English history. In his lectures between 1881 and 1882, titled *The English People in its Three Homes*, Freeman wrote that there were three points of origin of the English-speaking peoples: "Old England" was in northern Germany, whose people migrated to "Middle England," which was Britain, and whose people then migrated to "New England" in the United States. Freeman toured the United States, giving lectures on the origins of the English-speaking peoples, and was enormously popular. Freeman contributed to the field of Anglo-Saxonism by emphasizing the unity of the peoples of Britain and America based on race and language.[49]

Sir Walter Besant best expressed the "Teutonic" school of Anglo-Saxonism in the August 1896 issue of the *North American Review* when he summarized the history of the Anglo-Saxon peoples as coming from

> ...a cold, sterile and ungenial tract of country in the midst of which now stands the very noble city of Hamburg. They came over in hordes; they settled down on the English coasts; whole districts of their native land were deserted; they came in tribes and in families; wherever they sat down, they brought with them, as part of themselves, not to be changed, their laws and their customs and their language. These survived, and remain to this day in essentials the language, the laws, and the customs of their countries.[50]

Besant further argued that, throughout the centuries, the Anglo-Saxons who settled in England rooted out the indigenous peoples of Britain. Instead, the Anglo-Saxons absorbed other peoples who crossed their path in succeeding migration waves. He viewed Americans as having the same trait as their Anglo-Saxon forebears as they settled the frontier, absorbing not only indigenous populations but also previous colonizers:

> The United States of America in the same way covers ground which has been Spanish, French, Dutch, and Swedish. What trace do you find [of] Spanish occupation?—an ancient town. What trace do you find of the Dutch?—a few houses here and there which remind one of Amsterdam. Anglo-Saxon America is constantly engaged in absorbing.[51]

Besant concluded that the Anglo-Saxon people were a "stiff-necked race ... which cannot change its mind—as regards laws and manners—for the mind of any other race ... a people, which if it settles down anywhere, means to go on living as before and to make other people live in the same way."[52] Besant further suggested that this restless spirit and the ability to absorb foreign elements had allowed the Anglo-Saxon races to expand their dominion throughout the globe:

> This then is the present position of our race; we possess the finest and most desirable parts of the earth; we are more wealthy than the rest of the world put together; we are connected by a common ancestry; by a common history up to a certain point; by the same laws which we have inherited from our common ancestors, by the same speech; by the same religion; by the same literature.... It would be difficult to find stronger bonds: they are such as nothing in the world can cut asunder.[53]

Culture also provided another dimension of Anglo-Saxonism. An editorial in the April 30, 1898, issue of *The Spectator* argued for the inclusion of the United States, despite its immigrant population, among the Anglo-Saxon peoples. According to the editorial, the American people were predominantly Anglo-Saxon based upon its leaders in government, religion, the legal system, and literature.[54] With the exception of Martin Van Buren, all of America's presidents had been of English descent. Additionally, then-current President McKinley's cabinet consisted of men of British descent. English common law also served as one of the hallmarks of Anglo-

Saxonism, according to the editorial, which cited the Supreme Court's ruling that the common law of England was also part of the United States. As for literature, because Anglo-Saxons claimed English as a mother tongue, all English-speakers from both sides of the Atlantic shared the same appreciation for the great literary works of, such as Shakespeare or Coleridge. Having common cultural affinities, then, regardless of ethnicity, illustrated the potential for inclusion as Anglo-Saxon.[55]

Anglo-Saxonists used contemporary statistics to justify their belief in the superiority of the English-speaking peoples. In the March 14, 1896, issue of *Outlook,* editorialist Reverend George Payson echoed the social Darwinist belief in race as the basis for future conflict. He dismissed the French and Germans as viable contenders to Britain and the United States because of their lower birth rates and their "lack of pluck and grit."[56] He stated that, as of 1895, Great Britain and the United States combined controlled thirty percent of the earth's surface; twenty-five percent of the world's population; raised more than sixty-six percent of the world's wheat; and accounted for sixty-six percent of the world's tonnage. To Payson, these facts gave uncontestable proof that "the history of this race, its genius for government, its enterprise, and its devotion to civil and religious liberty, fit it for the noblest destiny."[57] As early as 1850, an editorial in the *Christian Observer* predicted that the Anglo-Saxon race would expand to as much as eight hundred million in the distant future because of its inherent superiority in fertility, language, and literature.[58]

Anglo-Saxonism became a lens through which to interpret the historical development of the United States. By the nineteenth century, Anglo-Saxonists saw demographics as crucial to the cultural and economic development of the United States. In an article for *The New York Times,* Edward E. Cornwall, MD, took pains to refute an argument that Americans had no close connection to Britain or Germany. He concluded that, out of a population of about fifty-five million white Americans in the 1890 census, thirty-three million, or sixty percent, were considered to be of Anglo-Saxon heritage, meaning they were descended from settlers from the British Isles. All other groups, such as Native Americans or African-Americans, according to Cornwall "have no part in the destiny of the American people."[59] It is not surprising, then, that the racial component of Anglo-Saxonism flourished as American society faced an influx of "new immigrants" from southern and eastern Europe, which terrified old-stock Americans.[60] Rather than celebrate the cultural diversity of the United States through immigration, Anglo-Saxonists argued for what they saw as the racial "purity" of the Anglo-Saxon heritage of the American people.

The Anglo-American Community

Despite the acrimony that resulted from the political separation between the United States and Great Britain, both English-speaking countries continued to be enmeshed economically, intellectually, and culturally. The cities of Boston, New York, Liverpool, and London were integrated into the Atlantic economy, which had its roots in colonial period. British capital helped finance American industrialization during the early nineteenth century until the Civil War.[61] British political radicals and intellectuals looked to the United States as a model for liberty, while American abolitionists worked with their British counterparts.[62] As a result of these intertwined networks, an Anglo-American community emerged that would provide the foundation for the *rapprochement* between both countries at the turn of the twentieth century, which would later become the "Special Relationship."

Britain's economic ties with the United States can be traced to the seventeenth century with the creation of the Virginia Company in 1606. Envious of the wealth pouring into Spain from its Latin American colonies, the English government hoped to repeat Spain's success by founding its own colonies on the North American continent. However, even after those colonies had achieved political independence, the United States remained economically dependent on European manufactured goods, European markets, and European capital, particularly British capital.[63] Between 1820 and 1860, half of American products went to British markets, and by 1860, Great Britain accounted for eighty percent of foreign tonnage arriving in American ports.[64] Cotton, however, proved to be the most valuable economic link between Great Britain and the United States. American cotton fed the British mills of Lancashire between 1820 and 1860, which in turn provided American consumers with cheap clothing and other manufactured goods.

In addition to economic ties, the United States and Britain maintained an intellectual community. During the early decades of the nineteenth century, the United States was a model for liberty, particularly to British intellectuals. The Jacksonian Democracy of the 1820s and the 1830s fired the imaginations of British liberals and religious non-conformists, who chafed under a political system dominated by the landed nobility and a society groaning under the overwhelming influence of the Church of England.[65] American society was a favorite topic for British authors such as Frances Trollope, Charles Dickens, and Harriet Martineau who wrote about their travels to a hungry British audience—these works would continue to inspire generations of British immigration.[66]

I. Anglo-Saxonism and American Culture, 1895–1914

British immigration to the United States was crucial to the formation of the Anglo-American community. It is important to note that for the purposes of this chapter, "British immigration" refers to the countries of Great Britain, i.e., England, Scotland, and Wales. Emigration from Great Britain to the North American colonies had been a fact of life since the seventeenth century. By the mid-eighteenth century, an average of 125,000 people left Britain for North America, mostly to escape its caste-ridden society.[67] An emigrant from Scotland, Alexander Thomson, best expressed such sentiment, writing that, unlike in Scotland, "...we have no tithes of general taxes, or.... We have the privilege of choosing our ministers, schoolmasters, constables, and other parish officers for laying and collecting the necessary assessments..."[68]

During the first United States Census in 1790, approximately sixty percent of the white population of the United States was of English and Welsh descent. British immigration to the United States continued in the decades after independence. After a long lull because of the Napoleonic Wars and the War of 1812, immigration to the United States totaled 15,837 between 1820 and 1830.[69] Between 1851 and 1860, immigration to the United States from England alone totaled 247,125, a significant jump from just 32,092 a decade before. Immigration to the United States from England peaked between 1881 and 1890 at 644,680.[70]

The impetus for these demographic shifts was the Industrial Revolution, which dislocated traditional trades in Britain through mechanization.[71] As mechanized looms priced out traditional weavers by the late eighteenth century, the United States became a beacon of economic opportunity. Between 1826 and 1827, Parliament started an inquiry into the economic effects of industrialization and its relationship to British emigration, concluding that there were destructive effects of mechanization on the textile industry.[72]

In addition to economic necessity, it was personal ambition that induced many Britons to come to America. The prospect of owning land lured many emigrants to cross the Atlantic, without even the scantest information of where they were settling or the costs involved. Many British immigrants were inspired by the Jeffersonian ideal of the independent yeoman farmer. What coincided with mid-nineteenth century British immigration to the United States was the availability of land. With the land readily available, all that was needed was capital, prompting relatively well-off Britons to contemplate emigration across the Atlantic.[73]

For the great majority of British immigrants, their experiences in settling in the United States were atypical to what was experienced by their Irish brethren and counterparts from southern and eastern Europe. With English as their primary language, immigrants of British descent had none of the usual impediments facing other immigrants, which allowed them to bypass the typical adjustment period of entry-level work and provided upward mobility through the next generation.[74] As a sign of true acceptance, British workers eventually adopted the same racial prejudices as their American counterparts. They equally shared the same disdain for southern and eastern European immigrants and adopted the same anti-immigrant attitudes that the "new immigrants" were taking away good jobs and debasing the American way of life, thus perpetuating Anglo-Saxonism.[75]

The White Anglo-Saxon Protestant

By the late nineteenth century, the migration of British settlers, along with their Anglo-Saxon narratives, to the thirteen colonies culminated into the creation of the White Anglo-Saxon Protestant, or WASP, which emerged as the ruling class of the United States, dominating its political, economic, and social institutions until the mid-twentieth century. In a 1991 essay by Richard Brookhiser, being a WASP required subscribing to a set of ideals: conscience, anti-sensuality, usefulness, civic-mindedness, industry, and success. These ideals regulated the actions, beliefs, and motivations of the WASP elite, which in some ways filtered down to the white working classes throughout the history of the United States. According to Brookhiser, these qualities not only explained the rise of the WASPs but also informed the Puritan work ethic espoused by the WASP elite, which contributed to the rise of the United States as an economic superpower.[76]

The proponents of Anglo-Saxonism in the United States were the Anglo-American community, whose members could trace their lineage to British colonists who settled in the original thirteen colonies. The colonial experience of these early English settlers influenced the formulation of what would become WASP culture. Of the original one hundred and five settlers in Jamestown, thirty six were listed as "gentlemen" and expected to live the life to which they had been accustomed. Thus, even in a new world, class assumptions began to be planted, as manual labor was not fitting for the "gentlemen" ancestors of the WASP elite.[77] In contrast to Jamestown, for the Puritans who settled New England in the 1630s, religion, rather than commerce, was their motivation to leave Europe.

John Winthrop wrote that one of the justifications for settling in New England was to spread the gospel into hitherto unknown regions of the world and to check the influence of the Catholic Church in the New World.[78]

As the thirteen colonies grew from isolated outposts of England's seventeenth-century colonial empire to part of an emerging Atlantic eighteenth-century economy, the concept of "whiteness" further evolved out of the growing tensions between an increasingly powerful planter class and their dispossessed indentured servants and, relatedly, between the colonies and their home country.[79] Indentured servitude was gradually phased out with the introduction of Africans as a new source of labor to be exploited. As African slavery became a more common part of colonial life, especially in the southern colonies, English settlers defined their whiteness even further by distinguishing themselves from "Negro labor." By the eighteenth century, there arose a gradation of occupations that were deemed suitable for white workers and those that were reserved for African slaves. Slavery provided a means for working class whites to share the same dignity as the planter class because they could both use their white skin color for solidarity.[80]

While the institution of slavery created social cohesion within the colonies, a widening gulf existed between the colonies and the British motherland. Despite the commonalities between the settlers and their British brethren in culture and language, the tensions simmering between the colonies and Great Britain during the 1760s and early 1770s exploded into the American Revolution. At the heart of the matter was the colonists' resentment of not having the same rights as British subjects. The rhetoric of "slavery vs. liberty" was commonly used in the political tracts of the day, particularly regarding the arbitrary rule of Parliament over the colonies on matters such as taxation and settlement on Indian lands west of the Appalachians, tensions that culminated into Thomas Jefferson's Declaration of Independence.[81]

Like his contemporary Jefferson, James Iredell, future Associate Justice of the Supreme Court, made his own personal declaration of independence. A patriot from a distinguished family in North Carolina and a descendant of Oliver Cromwell, Iredell renounced his allegiance to George III on March 1777 after considerable deliberation:

> Severe and painful, indeed was this Duty. I loved my Country; I once loved my Prince. Would have been the greatest blessing in life to me had it been in my power to continue my attachment to both. This would have been the Case, Sir, if your Majesty had not adopted measures of the most fatal tendency; measures insup-

portable to freemen, and which perhaps in the end may prove personally ruinous to yourself. I cannot yet, Sir, without emotion, think of the complicated miseries yourself, as much as your Subjects may endure, from your haughty and precipitate conduct.[82]

Iredell accused George III of ruling arbitrarily and depending upon ministers who give false information about the thirteen colonies—ministers who were mostly dependent on the good graces of the Crown rather than on the citizens of the colonies. As a result, Iredell concluded that the king of Great Britain had endangered the liberty of the colonies, which he was expected to protect as part of his royal duties.[83] This infringement upon their liberties was, to Iredell, what impelled the political separation from Great Britain.[84]

"Whiteness" as an identity came further into focus during the first years of the Republic in the political and economic spheres, which further evolved into the conventions of the WASP elite. In 1790, Congress decreed that "all white persons" would be given the full rights of citizenship.[85] The motivation behind this piece of legislation was to associate the rights, privileges, and responsibilities with a free white citizenry. Thus in 1790 it would be inconceivable to ascribe American citizenship to African-Americans or Native Americans.[86]

The ideal of republicanism was not purely a political ideology. Rather republicanism was also applied to the workshop, as it filtered down to the working classes, eager to establish their identities as distinct from the degradation of slavery. For example, Thomas Jefferson believed that the cornerstone of the early Republic lay in the yeoman farmer.[87] To be white was to be accorded all the privileges of citizenship, which would establish who would have political participation, as well as clarify people's positions in the socioeconomic ladder.[88] Whether they were yeoman farmers, or shop apprentices, labor republicans sought to eliminate inequality among white workers. On the shop floor, there was to be no distinction of who was the "master" or who was the "servant."[89]

With the Jacksonian democracy of the 1830s, the ruling class widened to include white males, Anglo-Saxon Protestants who had a perceived stake in the socioeconomic structure.[90] To be a "freeman" was the highest honor coveted by the white working class because it rejected the dichotomy of *master* and *slave*. The connotation of the term "freeman" was that of independence and control over one's destiny.[91] However, as white males were granted access to political participation, there was an equally strong movement to ensure the political and economic marginalization of African-Americans. During the 1830s, state constitutions across the North sharply restricted the rights of free blacks, so that by 1860 only one African-American in fourteen would have had the right to vote.⁹² The result was what sociologist Pierre L. van der Berghe called "*herrenvolk* democracy" because in his studies of South African society during *apartheid* and the United States under segregation, wherein the dominant racial group enjoyed democracy and the benefits of citizenship, while minorities lived under oppression.⁹³

In addition to liberty and citizenship, religion was another pillar in American white identity, namely Protestantism, which played an important role in the founding of the thirteen colonies. It is important to note that, contrary to what is generally believed, people settled in the colonies not for the sake of their religious liberty, but rather to practice their faiths to the exclusion of all else.⁹⁴ Even though the United States Constitution enshrined the separation of church and state in the Bill of Rights, Protestantism remained the default religion for the overwhelming majority of Americans in the early decades of the republic. Yet there remained a tension over the identity of the United States, whether it was a "Christian" nation, meaning Protestant, or a secular "republic," which had gained a negative connotation during the French Revolution.⁹⁵ The consensus followed, then, that while the Founders of the early republic shed the new nation of all trappings of monarchy and state-sanctioned religion, they still believed in the idea that the United States was analogous to the Biblical covenant between God and the children of Israel.⁹⁶

Out of this milieu of political, economic, and social assumptions came the dominance of the WASP elite that lasted until the latter half of the twentieth century. The term "White Anglo-Saxon Protestant" was introduced in the 1960s by the sociologist E. Digby Baltzell in *The Protestant Establishment: Aristocracy and Caste in America.* Baltzell defined the WASP elite as being traced to the East Coast establishment, bearing a resemblance to the British aristocracy in the mannerisms and upbringing that had emerged by the mid-nineteenth century.⁹⁷ The origins of the WASP elite could be traced to the founding of the thirteen colonies, which occurred in different circumstances, from the backwoods of Virginia to the rocky soil of New England.

Throughout the seventeenth century, a clique of wealthy planters often dubbed the "First Families," emerged in Virginia society. Land was the foundation of wealth in Virginia, and a prerequisite for any kind of social pretension. Tobacco, then, became the engine for economic stability in Virginia. As long as there was a demand in Europe and the prices were high, tobacco proved to be a source of the fortunes of the First Families.⁹⁸

Because the terrain and the climate of the southern colonies provided for the rise of a planter elite, New England was different in terms of its settlement and the eventual rise of its elite class. While Virginia was settled by adventurers from the Virginia Company, Massachusetts was founded on religion.[99] Over time, Massachusetts and the rest of New England evolved from a spiritual community to an economic center in the Atlantic trade.[100] Starting with the Navigation Acts of 1660 and 1673 and the Staple Act of 1673, Parliament regulated colonial trade by restricting the transport of colonial goods through British merchants and shippers. All goods going to the colonies had to go through the British Isles. From this wealth, a handful of families clustered in Boston emerged, such as the Adamses, Cabots, Lodges, Tyngs, and Ushers. Though they may have had different origins, these families shared the same economic interests. By the eighteenth century, the "First Families" of Boston used marriage to protect their assets, even marriage among first cousins, a practice that had originally been forbidden by the Puritans.[101]

After the Civil War, a new industrialist class emerged. To add legitimacy to their new-found wealth, these Gilded Age millionaires formed genealogical societies such as the Sons of the American Revolution and the Society of Mayflower Descendants. In doing so, not only did they appear respectable, but they also provided a sense of continuity in a society undergoing large-scale industrialization, urbanization, and immigration.[102] Among this WASP elite were men of letters such as Henry Adams who reflected the apprehensions of the late nineteenth century. With the "new immigrants" from Eastern Europe streaming into Ellis Island year by year, Anglo-Saxonists like Adams felt increasingly out of touch with the accelerating changes overcoming American society.[103]

It was primarily this WASP elite who was most in favor of American imperial expansion. Using Darwin as a guide, they saw a world of limited resources with nations, like organisms, fighting for survival. As they saw it, the world of the turn of the century was divided among the "Latin race" (represented by France), the "Teutonic" race (represented by Germany), the "Slavic race" (represented by Russia), and the "Anglo-Saxon race," which was represented by the British Empire and the United States. To them, it was a natural conclusion, therefore, that Britain and the United States would join forces against such antagonistic rivals and spread the benefits of civilization.[104]

Anglo-Saxonists translated their numbers as justification for the expansion of the United States, Great Britain, and Germany at the beginning of the twentieth century. An article in *The Maine Farmer* connected the American victory in the Spanish-American War, Britain's victory in the Boer War, and the eventual domination of Russia by Germany as proof of Anglo-Saxon superiority.[105] He argued that since the Anglo-Saxon races had contributed to the technological progress of the nineteenth century, as well as dominating global trade, culture, and literature, it stood to reason that Anglo-Saxons were best suited to manage humanity.[106] To support this argument, the article compared the low birthrate of France with the high fertility of Britain and the United States, as well as the slow economic development of Latin America and colonies administered by Latin countries in Africa. Anglo-Saxonism, then, was clearly the preferred model for colonization, a practice which would then be undertaken by the United States.[107]

Anglo-Saxonism was an integral component of American colonial rule in the Philippines. The victory of the United States in the Spanish-American War and the acquisition of the last remnants of Spain's colonial empire marked the debut of the United States as a major world power. Having at last realized the responsibilities of colonial rule, American foreign policy makers could embark upon the United States's *rapprochement* with its old adversary Great Britain.[108] American control of the Philippines was Anglo-Saxonism in action. While it was one thing to extol the past glories of the Anglo-Saxon race, it was another thing to apply the credos of Anglo-Saxonism in the Philippines. Politicians could no longer talk about the *potential* benefits of American rule, but instead of how to bring "civilization" to the Philippines.[109]

For some American Anglo-Saxonists, colonial rule over the Philippines was more than a strategic or economic necessity. Rather it was part of a missionary impulse of spreading Christianity and civilization to a "benighted" part of the world. In an article in *The Arena*, George F. Pentecost best summarized the American Anglo-Saxon as a lover of liberty, an individual, and a Protestant.[110] To Pentecost, the rise of the United States as an industrial power, culminating in the annexation of the Philippines, was part of a divine will, and the American people had a destiny to fulfill.[111] Pentecost believed that the purpose of American colonization was to bring "universal education, political freedom ... the modern mechanical arts and sciences ... and Christian civilization at the front door of Asia."[112]

The realities of colonial rule gave a rude awakening to Anglo-Saxonists. The "bully little war" in which Theodore Roosevelt charged to battle gave way to a protracted guerrilla war in the Philippines, led by Emilio Aguinaldo, who believed that the Philippines would be given independence after the war with Spain. This forced Americans to confront which the direction the United States was headed, whether it was to serve as a beacon for liberty, or whether it was to be just another colonial empire. In an address on October 7, 1899, Secretary of War Elihu Root justified America's role in the insurrection and the actions of the military. Root argued that the United States was the only civilizing force in the Philippines, which would fall into the anarchy of tribal warfare should the Filipino people be left to their own devices. He described Aguinaldo's forces as "men who prefer a life of brigandage to a life of industry" and Aguinaldo as a "military dictator ... who has attained supreme power by the assassination of his rival, and who maintains it by the arrest and punishment of every one who favors the United States, and the murder of every one whom he can reach who aids her."[113] In the same breath, Root extolled the Anglo-Saxon virtues of the American soldiers in the Philippines, even though he did not mention Anglo-Saxonism by name. To him, the American soldier

> ...carries with him not the traditions of a military empire, but the traditions of a self-governing people. He comes from a land where public discussion has educated every citizen in the art of self-ggovernment ... where the affairs of city and county and town and village, have made the art of government the alphabet of life for every citizen, where every citizen has learned that obedience to law, and respect for the results of popular elections is a part of the order of nature.[114]

The guerrilla war ended with the capture of Aguinaldo, thus allowing the United States to begin its "civilizing mission" in the Philippines. Despite the goals of bringing self-government to the Filipino people, American policy makers enabled the landowning elite to dominate the political and economic systems. The United States ensured the primacy of the elite through the creation of the Philippine Civil Service. The members of the Taft Commission had hoped that the creation of a civil service in 1901 would eliminate corruption and establish an efficient colonial structure.[115] Through the *pensionado* system starting in 1903, the goal for children from elite families would be to spend some time in the United States, studying and becoming acculturated to American values, then returning to the Philippines to honorably take up posts in the Philippine Civil Service.[116] However, the opposite proved to be true:. corruption became rampant in all areas of government as networks of patrons and clients emerged, whereby political bosses handed out offices to their supporters. The vicissitudes of American politics also accelerated the pace at which corruption developed as autonomy was gradually handed over to Manila. In a twist of irony in its colonial experience, the United States failed in its all-important mission, which was to teach the values of self-government and democracy.[117]

Anglo-Saxonism in American culture evolved over a long period of time, with its roots stretching back to the founding myths of the English people. As English settlers established the thirteen colonies, they adapted their myths to their new surroundings and created a new narrative that established a shared identity of "whiteness," which distinguished whites from the indigenous peoples of North America and the African slaves who were first imported into the thirteen colonies in the seventeenth century. By the eighteenth century, as the thirteen colonies became integrated into the Atlantic economy, Anglo-Saxonism took another turn when attempts at centralization by the British government clashed with the ideals of liberty and self-rule resulted in the American Revolution, establishing the United States. Yet despite the political separation between Great Britain and the United States, the economic, social, and cultural connections between both English-speaking peoples continued throughout the nineteenth century. As the United States by the 1890s emerged to become an industrial giant, Anglo-Saxonism became an expression of this new self-confidence and the willingness of the American people to take a more forceful role in world affairs with the British Empire as their partner.

CHAPTER II

The German-American Connection, 1850–1914

Though not always recognized today, German-Americans played a major role in the settling of the United States and were part of the American social fabric generations before the First World War. German culture influenced many areas in American cultural and intellectual life, which ran just as deep as English culture. In the late nineteenth century, the German people were closely affiliated with, if not part of, the Anglo-Saxon family through the "Teutonic Theory" of Anglo-Saxonism, by theories establishing the forests of Germany as the primordial homeland of the Anglo-Saxon peoples, who eventually migrated to the British Isles and, later, the United States. Thus, by 1914 and the outbreak of the First World War, alignment with Britain was not a foregone conclusion, with a large German-American population that, at best, was indifferent to the British cause or, at worst, was utterly hostile.

Nevertheless, Anglo-Saxonists still felt ambivalence about adding contemporary Germany, a rival to the rising power of the United States, to the Anglo-Saxon family. This ambivalence was because of the Prussian military and political apparatus put in place by Otto von Bismarck after 1871, which contradicted with the ideals of self-government and liberty that were cherished by British and American Anglo-Saxonism. Tensions between the United States and Great Britain on the one hand, and Germany on the other, were exacerbated after Bismarck's fall from power in 1890, when Kaiser Wilhelm II advocated a more aggressive foreign policy. By the turn of the twentieth century, American foreign policy makers regarded Germany a threat as both countries competed for influence in Asia and the Pacific and also when Germany began its encroachment in Latin America, which the United States regarded to be part of its informal empire. Thus the rivalry between both countries would become a source of tension leading to the beginning of the First World War.

Early German Migrations

The contributions of the German people to the United States stretch far back beyond the creation of the United States. In 1507, Martin Waldseemüller, a German cartographer, was the first to refer to the New World as "America." In 1626, Peter Minuit, another German, negotiated the purchase of the island of Manhattan from its indigenous inhabitants.[1] German immigration to what would become the United States began during the seventeenth century with the establishment of Jamestown, when some German settlers formed part of John Smith's party. The first German permanent settlement in the colonies consisted of thirteen Mennonite families from Krefeld in western Germany, who in 1683 settled in the future community of Germantown, outside of Philadelphia. William Penn encouraged German immigration to the newly established colony of Pennsylvania. The Mennonites shared many similarities with Penn's church, the Society of Friends, more commonly known as the Quakers, particularly their inward spirituality, as opposed to the ritualism of other denominations. After some meetings with Penn's associates, a group of German Mennonite leaders formed the Frankfurt Company and purchased twenty-five thousand acres in the wilderness of Pennsylvania. On August 20, 1683, the first German immigrants arrived in Philadelphia who would form the community at Germantown.[2]

The first German settlers generally resided in the mid–Atlantic colonies of Maryland, New York, Pennsylvania, and Virginia. In addition to seeking religious freedom, another reason for immigration to the colonies was to escape war. During the first half of the seventeenth century, the German people in the Rhineland Palatinate suffered tremendously during the Thirty Years' War.[3] In 1688, Louis XIV of France again invaded the Rhineland Palatinate in order to expand French influence, resulting in the expulsion of nearly half a million Germans.[4] By the mid-eighteenth century, colonists of German descent comprised two hundred fifty thousand, or eight to nine percent of the population. Many Germans contributed to colonial society, including John Peter Zenger, who established the foundations of freedom of the press. Germans fought on both sides of the American Revolution: examples are Hessian mercenaries who supported the British; the American heroine Molly Pitcher, born Maria Ludwig; and Baron Frederick von Steuben, who transformed the Continental Army from a mob of farmers into a professional fighting force, contributing to eventual victory over the British.[5]

After independence, the United States established its initial diplomatic contacts with the German states, notably Prussia. On September

10, 1785, the United States and Prussia entered into a commerce treaty that called for "trade reciprocity and freedom of the seas for neutral vessels, even in time of war." The treaty was renewed thirty years later and reinforced with the Treaty of 1828. Despite such friendly beginnings, trade between the United States and Prussia did not blossom to any significant extent for much of the nineteenth century: Prussia had neither overseas possessions and did not invest in international trade, and the United States did not wish to become involved in European affairs. Neither country even considered it necessary to maintain diplomatic representation in each other's capitals until the first quarter of the nineteenth century. Thus, because there were few common political interests between the United States and Prussia, relations were cordial.[6]

While prospects for diplomatic cooperation between the United States and German states were miniscule, there was room for cultural exchange. For the Germans who immigrated in the nineteenth century, America represented a utopia, the perception of which originated from the American Revolution. German immigrants perceived America as a *"tabula rasa,"* an empty space upon which they could build a new life, one that held little to none of the cultural baggage of the old world: established religion, class structures, princes, and an overwhelming state. Germans immigrating to America believed that America was an abundant land that would reward hard work.[7]

The events of the American Revolution influenced German perceptions of the United States. The writings of Benjamin Franklin and the accounts of the Marquis de Lafayette reinforced the picture of America as a land of religious freedom. In fact, to many of the Pietist clergy, America represented a "city on a hill" where Protestant religion flourished, unmolested by the religious skepticism unleashed in Europe by the Enlightenment. Fueled by positive reports of American life, immigration by Germans into the United States held at a steady rate between 1783 and 1800 of five hundred and ten per year, totaling to eight thousand seven hundred immigrants.[8] During the first half of the nineteenth century, Germans established "colonies" all over the United States, not in the traditional imperialistic sense, but in the sense of establishing a community whereupon one may lay down roots. Because of their belief in America as a new and as an "empty" land, in exchange for the riches they were extracting, German settlers believed they were contributing by infusing their own culture. The Germans who settled in the United States resisted the temptation to assimilate into the larger Anglo-American society, believing in the superiority of their own culture.[9]

Americans formed differing perceptions of Germans when traveling abroad, both complimentary and uncomplimentary. These perceptions were often based on the purpose of their journeys. During the nineteenth century, there emerged three groups of American travelers to Germany. The first group of Americans traveled to Germany chiefly to study in German universities. The second group traveled to Germany as part of a larger comprehensive education in European and classical culture. The third group was comprised of American tourists and those seeking novelty.[10] Between 1800 and 1839, fifty-one American citizens traveled to Germany, of which the majority came from New England. Of those fifty-one, two-thirds came from the educated classes, such as clergymen, students, and scholars.[11]

Among the most common comments traveling Americans had was that the Germans they encountered were cordial and hospitable. However, many of the travel journals of the period reflected cultural differences between Germans and Americans. Among such observations were that Germans enjoyed eating and drinking too much, wasted time in celebrations, were in less of a hurry than Americans, and subjected their women to hard labor.[12] It is not surprising that these comments were from New Englanders who grew up with Puritan backgrounds, as the United States was in the midst of the religious revival of the Second Great Awakening and the reform movements of the 1830s.[13] However, Americans were not the only ones who were disenchanted. Some German visitors to the United States found themselves repulsed by American democracy in the form of universal manhood suffrage. Others complained about the lack of culture and the American obsession with commerce, conflicting with traditional German connections to agriculture. However, such sentiments did not abate the emigration of Germans to the United States.[14]

The Revolution of 1848

The Revolution of 1848 was a turning point in the history of the German people, and it would also have repercussions in the United States. The influence of the French Revolution hung over Europe during the first half of the nineteenth century, as liberals clashed with conservatives, and nationalists clashed with ancient dynasties of central Europe. Dissatisfaction with the settlement of the Congress of Vienna in 1815, which ended the Napoleonic Wars, caused Germans to rebel against the old order. German liberals and nationalists aspired to break free from the domination of the Austrian Empire and the petty princes of the German Confederation to forge a united Germany based on democratic principles. The economic effects of the Industrial Revolution made their way to Germany, as cheap mass-produced British goods ruined the livelihoods of traditional artisans. These conditions made Germany ripe for revolution.[15] Following the same pattern as the French Revolution, the Frankfurt Assembly drafted a Declaration of the Rights of the German People, which was based on liberal principles such as civil liberties and constitutional government that were taken from the Declaration of Independence and the Declaration of the Rights of Man. In 1849, the Frankfurt Assembly drafted its constitution, which was much along the same lines as the French and American models.[16]

American public opinion was sympathetic to the cause of revolution in Europe. To many Americans who paid attention to foreign affairs, Europe—with the exception of Great Britain—stood for tyranny, especially in the form of the Holy Alliance, whose goal was to stamp out democracy. American publications such as the *American Quarterly Register, Brownson's Quarterly Review,* and the *New York Tribune* speculated on the course of events in Germany and predicted that a unified German state would emerge with a federal system based on that of the United States.[17] It is important to note, however, that American interest in European affairs depended largely upon the region. While the Northeast paid rapt attention to the events of 1848, the newspapers in the South and the West were mute on the subject matter and focused primarily on domestic issues—this was due to a range of reasons. The western states were absorbed with internal development; the South's main focus was on slavery and its extension to the West, as well as small numbers of immigration, which remained concentrated on the Northeast.[18]

The United States government expressed its support of the goals of the Frankfurt Assembly and extended the good wishes of the American people to the German people. President James K. Polk quickly promoted Andrew J. Donelson, the minister to Prussia, to "Envoy Extraordinary and Minister Plenipotentiary to the Federal Government of Germany," based upon the optimistic assumption of success upon the part of the revolutionaries.[19] Donelson was instructed to go to Frankfurt and observe the proceedings there. Meanwhile, the Frankfurt Assembly prevailed upon the United States to give material support by lending experienced men, particularly requesting that an American officer serve as an admiral in the fledgling German navy. Polk, however, was reluctant to go to that extent, since it would mark an unprecedented break from traditional

American foreign policy. Commodore Foxhall Parker was also instructed to go to Frankfurt and discern what aid the United States could give. When he arrived, Parker learned that the Frankfurt Assembly was interested in purchasing a frigate from the United States Navy in anticipation of a war with Denmark over the disputed province of Schleswig-Holstein. Parker concluded in a report that civil war in Germany was imminent and advised against any American officers serving in Germany. The election of Zachary Taylor rendered moot any future assistance to the Frankfurt Assembly because Taylor saw that German unification was not realistic.[20]

Despite its lofty goals, the Frankfurt Assembly failed for a number of reasons. The main contributing factor to this failure was the body's inability to enforce the plans set forth. The Frankfurt Assembly had no army, and therefore it had no credibility among the German states. Secondly, the princes of the German states were jealous of their individual sovereignty, and they were loath to lose themselves in a greater German state. The Declaration of the Rights of German People offended non–Germans within the German states, such as the Poles, because it specifically applied to just the German people, unlike the universal premises of the French and American models. The role of Austria in the new Germany was especially troublesome for the Frankfurt Assembly because of the traditional leadership of the Habsburgs. By excluding Austria, more than a millennium of tradition would be terminated. However, including the Austrian Empire with its non–German peoples would have been problematic for the Frankfurt Assembly. These setbacks caused the prominent German-American politician Carl Schurz to doubt the success of the Assembly. In a letter, he declared, "If the German nation makes itself ridiculous now, it will be ridiculous for a long, long time."[21] Thus the Frankfurt Assembly disbanded in late 1849, having lost the opportunity to bring democracy to the German people. Many of the German liberals who supported or sympathized with the Frankfurt Assembly left for the United States and became known as the "Forty-Eighters."[22]

In the aftermath of the failure of the Revolution of 1848, and particularly the Frankfurt Assembly, there followed an exodus of German immigrants to the United States. Between 1850 and 1870, the number of German immigrants in the United States had swollen from six hundred thousand to 1.7 million. Between 1852 and 1854, there were as much as five hundred thousand immigrants entering the country alone.[23] As with other waves of immigration, nativist sentiment existed against German immigrants, due to the way they kept to themselves and their fondness for beer. Nevertheless, on the whole, the American public largely welcomed German immigrants, which eased their assimilation into the larger culture. American newspapers praised German immigrants for their education, their thrift, their work ethic, and, particularly, the money that they brought with them. Thus, to the eyes of many Americans, Germans were prime candidates for citizenship.[24]

German-Americans and Politics

No sooner had they left their homelands than many of the forty-eighters began to adopt American culture and participate in antebellum politics. While previous German immigrants praised American culture for its adherence to Protestantism, the forty-eighters saw American democracy as political model to emulate. As a whole, the generation of the forty-eighters abandoned their former allegiances and took up the banner of republicanism.[25] Carl Berthold, a middle class immigrant from Waldeck in western Germany, gave an account of the 1852 elections with great interest:

> The [Whigs], or "aristocrats" ... wanted to treat the Germans unfairly, they were supposed to have to wait to become citizens until they'd been in the country for 21 years, that's almost like it is in Germany with the princes, they want to rule over the Germans like that, but they got their necks broken. Democracy won out by a great majority, and in a few weeks a true Democrat [Franklin Pierce] will ascend the presidential chair. The [Whigs] are now trying all sorts of tricks to get back in, like the big wheels tried to do with the people in [the Revolution of 1848] but flattery doesn't get you anywhere here.[26]

Until the early 1850s, the majority of forty-eighters sided with the Democratic Party because of their belief in the Jeffersonian and Jacksonian principles of popular sovereignty. However, as sectionalist tensions flared, the forty-eighters eventually switched to the newly-formed Republican Party after 1854 because of their abhorrence for slavery.[27]

Within the emerging German-American community being forged by the forty-eighters, slavery was as much a controversial topic as it was for the larger community. Many German-American publications took the position of "free soil" and "free labor." Periodicals such as the *New Yorker Demokrat* and the *Anzeiger des Westens* frequently questioned the position of the Democratic Party on the issue of slavery.[28] The election of 1854 was a turning point in the political allegiance of German-Americans over the issue of Stephen Douglas's Kansas-Nebraska Act. Because of Douglas's pro-slavery position, German-Americans defected from the Democratic Party and sought out a party that was more in tune with their interests.[29]

Carl Schurz, among the more prominent German-Americans of his generation, escaped Germany in the aftermath of the failed Revolution of 1848; because of his activities, he sought refuge in the United States. There he joined the Republican Party because it shared his opposition to slavery. In 1855 Schurz denounced the Kansas-Nebraska Act because it did not really resolve the controversy of slavery and was nothing more than a cover for Douglas's political ambitions.[30] By the mid–1850s, Schurz had not only settled successfully in Wisconsin, he even began to venture into American politics with great relish. He ran for the Wisconsin legislature as a Republican in 1856. Even though he was defeated, Schurz made his mark as a rising star in the Republican Party. Of his first experience in American politics, Schurz wrote the following to his friend Henry Meyer:

> You over there in your decrepit Europe can hardly understand any more how a great idea can stir the masses to their depths and how an enthusiastic fight for principles can displace all other interests; even, for a time, materialistic ones. It is the first time in seven years that I have taken part in politics—in a time which arouses even the sleepiest and in a cause which is second to none in the world in reach and greatness.[31]

Of the prospects of the Republican Party, Schurz continued:

> At last a regular, intense struggle against slavery has arisen in the United States; and the party of freedom, while defeated in the first election contest, despite its youth and deficient organization, has shown so much strength and won so much territory that it can look to the future with the confidence of victory.[32]

While German-Americans gradually abandoned the Democratic Party, the Republican Party was not entirely welcoming to them. There was still a nativist force that prevented German-Americans from taking leadership positions in the Republican Party. Secondly, the Republicans ran on issues that were culturally insensitive to German-Americans. In 1855, the temperance movement dominated state elections in New York, Wisconsin, and Illinois, which alienated German-American support and crippled the chances of German-American candidates.[33]

This experience showed the Republican Party leadership, that if it wanted German-American votes, then it would have to change its campaigning strategies. That meant denouncing nativist rhetoric while emphasizing its support for free-soil in its platform. However, state republican platforms maintained their support for temperance, which left German-Americans dissatisfied.[34] During the presidential election of 1856, these lessons were learned as the Republican Party nominated John C. Fremont as its first presidential candidate. The Republican platform endorsed a more inclusive position, which pushed for equality for all citizens. By denouncing nativism, more forty-eighters fled from the Democratic Party and swelled the numbers of the Republican Party, which stood for "free soil, free labor, free men and Fremont."[35] Though many German-Americans remained within the Democratic Party, they no longer voted as a single bloc. By the eve of the Civil War, most of the forty-eighters who had joined the Republican Party supported Lincoln's policy of preserving the Union.[36]

Throughout the wars that the United States had fought during the nineteenth century, from the War of 1812 to the Spanish-American War, German-Americans had served their country with distinction, from the rank and file to the officers' corps. The Civil War was another conflict that had a large proportion of German-Americans soldiers. In the Union army alone, German-born soldiers numbered over 176,000 out of two million total mobilized troops.[37] Most German-Americans volunteered for service either for ideological reasons or out of financial necessity. About one out of six German-Americans was conscripted. German-Americans accounted for five to fifteen percent of most regiments in the Union army and were often placed into "German companies" in order to accommodate the language barrier. More than thirty thousand German-Americans served in around thirty "German Regiments," which consisted of German soldiers and officers at the beginning of the war; in the latter phases of the conflict, German soldiers were placed randomly throughout the ranks.[38]

German-Americans and German Unification

During the 1850s and 1860s, much of the American public was preoccupied with sectionalist rivalries and, ultimately, the Civil War. Thus, the events unfolding in Germany, particularly the process of unification undertaken by Prussian Chancellor Otto von Bismarck, had less priority in American newspapers. However, of what was reported on Germany, American public opinion weighed in on the side of the Prussians because of their Protestant affiliations, albeit with some reservations because of the martial mentality within Prussian society.[39] Diplomatic relations between the United States and Prussia had generally been amiable. However, between 1848 and 1871, one thorny issue for both countries revolved around Prussia's compulsive military system during the 1850s: whether a Prussian soldier who came to the United States without completing his military service could be considered a United States citizen. Ultimately, the case was deemed not worth fighting over and was resolved by the Bancroft Treaties of 1868. Bismarck had greater matters to attend to.[40]

As Bismarck executed his machinations during the 1860s, American public opinion rallied around the cause of German unification. The experiences of the Civil War caused many Americans to sympathize with the issues of "national unity" vs. "states' rights," which were thrown around in Germany, albeit under different contexts.[41] American public opinion was divided over the rivalry between Prussia and Austria for leadership among the German states. *The New York Times*, a pro–Austrian newspaper, saw Bismarck as an unprincipled and calculating politician who used German unification as a pretext for Prussia's aggrandizement at the expense of Austria and smaller German states.[42] However, the *New York Herald* favored Prussia as an agent for change and progress against Austria's feudalism.[43] Nowhere was this division of opinion more evident than in the German-American community. The victories of the Prussian army over the Austrians aroused celebrations in many German-American communities in New York and Chicago. German-American organizations raised $600,000 for German charities. The forty-eighters who had left German despotism praised Bismarck. In a letter to his wife, Schurz gave his appraisal of Bismarck and the possibility of unification:

> The development of affairs in Europe is surprising.... And since the attainment of these results depends wholly upon the energy and the success of Prussia, my sympathies are naturally with the Prussian side. At present, it is all off with the revolution; and the attempts at revolutionary organization which are still underway here and there are supremely absurd. Bismarck can now be more useful to Germany than any other man if he can only be forced into the right track.[44]

Schurz's high opinion of Bismarck originated from a meeting between the two on January 28, 1868, during a visit to Berlin. Schurz had some misgivings that German unification might simply be a mask for Prussian expansionism. In their conversation, Bismarck became pleased when Schurz relayed the support of the German-American community for his policies.[45] In a letter to his friend, Adolf Meyer, Schurz described Bismarck as a man of strong will and character, qualities that he believed to be necessary for the monumental task of uniting the German people.[46] A few German-Americans, however, such as forty-eighter and radical journalist Karl Heinzen, could not celebrate the reactionary Prussian government, still steeped in absolutism and militarism, that was poised to bring all of Germany under its control.[47]

The issue of German unification culminated with the Franco-Prussian War in 1870. Bismarck used a succession crisis in Spain as a pretext of eliminating France as the last obstacle to a Prussian-dominated Germany.[48] Despite the historic ties between France and the United States, by 1870 American public opinion had turned against the French government, particularly Napoleon III, who Americans distrusted because they believed he betrayed the Second Republic in 1851. Americans saw the conversion of the Second Republic into the Second Empire as a move toward reactionary despotism, rather than toward democracy.[49] Americans not only had philosophical disagreements with Napoleon III, but they could point to instances of French meddling in American affairs, particularly during the 1860s, when the events of the Civil War had shown France to be sympathetic toward the Confederacy. Particularly unforgivable to many Americans was Napoleon III's ambition to restore a French colonial empire in the Western Hemisphere by installing the puppet government of Archduke Maximilian in Mexico between 1862 and 1867, which was a direct attack on the Monroe Doctrine. These memories were still fresh in the minds of the American public as the Franco-Prussian War broke out in 1870.[50]

Although it declared its neutrality, the United States was clearly sympathetic to Prussia. Elihu Root, the minister to Paris, intervened on the behalf of Prussians trapped in France on the outbreak of war. The United States rebuffed offers by the European powers to mediate an end to the conflict, which was in line with the policy of the Prussian government. The United States closed its ports to belligerent vessels of both sides. In the aftermath of France's defeat, the United States was wary of the Paris Commune that emerged after the abdication of Napoleon III. During negotiations, the United States did not press Bismarck to abandon his demand for Alsace-Lorraine, much to the dismay of the French minister in Washington. Bismarck never forgot the goodwill expressed by the United States in his hour of need, and would therefore make it a policy to accommodate the United States.[51]

German unification in 1871 was greeted with enthusiasm in the United States. American historian and diplomat George Bancroft expressed high hopes for the Second Reich. In his reports, Bancroft stated that the new German Empire closely mirrored the United States in many ways, particularly its federal structure, and universal manhood suffrage for the Reichstag. Bancroft thus declared that this "United States of Germany" would be the most liberal government in all of Europe, and it would be in the best interests of the United States to cultivate the friendship of the most rapidly growing power in Europe.[52] Schurz, despite his liberal credentials, greeted Germany's victory over France in 1870 with great joy. In a speech he gave in St. Louis, Missouri, commemorating the end of the Franco-Prussian War, Schurz referred to German unification as "a portentous event which shifts the political center of gravity on the continent of Europe, and annihilates the empty and hollow phrase of the European balance of power which had aimed at defrauding Germany of her achievements, independence, and power...."[53] Schurz credited the victory over France to the "physical courage, impetuous attack, skillful handling of arms, and intellectual education of the German soldier."[54] He gloried in the rise of Germany, so much so that he raised the flag of the new German Empire from the building of the *Westliche Post*, where he worked in St. Louis. He shared in the jingoistic rhetoric of his fellow German-Americans, declaring that Germany was the greatest nation in Europe and had fulfilled the goals of the Frankfurt Assembly in 1848.[55]

During the 1870s, diplomatic relations between the United States and Germany were especially amiable. Even though the United States did not factor greatly in international events, Bismarck was careful to prevent antagonizing American public opinion, especially in Latin America, where he would most likely run afoul of the Monroe Doctrine. Bismarck's government consulted the State Department over how best to resolve differences between German citizens and Latin American governments. In turn, the United States government requested Kaiser Wilhelm I to arbitrate in the long-running border disputes with Great Britain over Canada.[56] As chancellor, Bismarck made security a priority for the newly-unified Germany by establishing alliances to isolate a vengeful France, eschewing colonial expansion, and not constructing a large deep-water navy, which would antagonize Great Britain. These policies assured Germany's neighbors, as well as the United States, of a peaceful and contented Germany.[57]

Bismarck's domestic policies met with high American approval. In the late 1870s, suspicious of the loyalties of the German Catholics, Bismarck embarked upon his *Kulturkampf* policy. Under this policy, the Jesuits were expelled from Germany; bishops lost power; German education fell under secular, rather than religious, control; and civil marriage was instituted. Bancroft reported the *Kulturkampf* as a sign that Germany was freeing itself from feudalism and was emulating the separation of church and state.[58] When Bismarck turned his attention to the socialists, he again garnered high praise in the esteem of many Americans. Bismarck's outlawing of the Social Democratic Party assured the United States that Germany was committed to *laissez-faire* capitalism.[59] As the United States celebrated its centennial anniversary, both Bismarck and Kaiser Wilhelm I expressed their congratulations to the American people and voiced their hope that the peaceful relationship, which had existed since the days of Frederick the Great, would continue.[60]

In the last quarter of the nineteenth century, cultural exchanges between the United States and Germany accelerated. The most significant impact German culture made on American intellectual life had its roots in the late eighteenth and early nineteenth century with Wilhelm von Humboldt's essay "The Limits of State Action," written in 1792, which supported academic freedom. In 1810, Humboldt founded the University of Berlin.[61] Humboldt's counterpart in the United States was Thomas Jefferson, who devoted forty years of his life to establishing a public university in Virginia, where he believed that it would be possible to pursue truth based on reason. Due to the influences of the Enlightenment, the American and French Revolutions, and the Romanticism prominent on both sides of the Atlantic, many Americans developed an affinity for the German people, who appeared to be on the same road toward liberty and progress.[62]

Nowhere was this affinity more evident than in the realm of education. The Revolution of 1848 had caused a massive exodus of German liberals to the United States; these immigrants wanted to reform education from an exclusive place for the elite into an arena where democratic principles could be taught to new generations. This was the beginning of the *kindergarten* movement, which was first begun by Friedrich Froebel in Germany in 1837, and in 1856 was transplanted to Watertown, Wisconsin, by Margarethe Schurz, wife of prominent German-American politician Carl Schurz. The establishment of the first kindergartens coincided with the public education movement in the United States. The kindergarten was based on the assumption that the child was inherently good and should be taught the principles of democracy at an early age, and thus the child would later make a positive contribution to society.[63] Thereafter, kindergartens would open throughout New England in 1867 due to the influence of Henry Barnard and Elizabeth Peabody, who were connected with the Schurzes. In 1873, the future of the kindergarten as the foundation for the modern American public education system was secured when William Harris, the superintendent of schools in St. Louis, Missouri, established the first kindergarten in a major metropolitan area. The kindergarten was especially useful in helping immigrants assimilate into American society by fostering a sense of citizenship.[64]

American adoption of German pedagogy did not stop with the kindergarten. During the nineteenth century, American educational figures established the elementary and secondary educational system based on the Prussian system of education. Because of the perception of Prussian society as hierarchical and militaristic, Calvin Stowe, an education reformer, believed that the Prussian system could not simply be transplanted, but rather it should be modified to fit the democratic aims of the American public school system. Based on his observations in Prussia, Stowe wrote a report to the Ohio legislature outlining what would become the foundations of the American educational system: the need for trained teachers, the credentialing of teachers, compulsory education for all children, a school system based on discipline and the authority of the teacher, (whom parents must respect), and the advancement of students through the educational system based on comprehension of the learning material. The revolution in American primary and secondary education that resulted from Germany's influence neatly coincided with the intense industrialization and the rise of the United States as an economic power in the years following the Civil War.[65]

The crowning touch to this educational revolution in the United States was in the creation of the research university, established as a result of German-American cultural exchange. Studying at German universities was a profound experience for many Americans. Oxford or Cambridge might appear to have been choice for study because of the shared linguistic and cultural heritage of the United States and Great Britain; however, Americans were eager to establish their own identities during the first decades of independence. Additionally, the British erected obstacles to American students by establishing quotas.[66]

The German universities at Berlin and Göttingen offered different models for learning. While many American and European universities of the early nineteenth century were still based on classical studies and liberal arts since the Middle Ages, German universities, under the vision of Humboldt, focused on expanding knowledge and directly applying that knowledge to society, again coinciding with the visions of Benjamin Franklin, Alexander Hamilton, Thomas Jefferson, and James Madison. Unlike their British counterparts, who would have snubbed their American cousins, German universities went to great lengths to welcome American scholars. During the first half of the nineteenth century, around two hundred American students matriculated at German universities. However, by 1900, that number had mushroomed to nine thousand due to advances in travel and the growing popularity of German education. Many prominent Americans such as George Bancroft and John Lothrop Motley had German educations, and a new generation of Americans who grew up in the Midwest used their experiences in Germany to reform American universities.[67] What arose from those reforms was the modern research university that stressed teaching and research, the ideal of academic freedom, and an emphasis on the sciences. Crucial to this vision was the concept of the graduate education, which culminated in the doctoral degree and fostered specialization and the addition of new knowledge to a discipline, paving the way for American leadership in research in the twentieth and early twenty-first centuries.[68]

The application of these American Progressives' educational experiences in Germany was first expressed in economics and social legislation. By the second half of the nineteenth century, the ideal of *laissez-faire* and free trade as espoused by Britain began to be challenged for its inattentiveness to the resulting inequities of wealth in society.[69] After unification, Germany's rapid industrialization was from the result of government protection. Also, it was Germany that pioneered the first pieces of social welfare legislation, such as unemployment insurance, disability insurance, and old-age pensions.[70] These were important lessons to be learned by a new generation of German-trained American economists. American universities forged connections with German economic departments. For instance, the University of Pennsylvania's Wharton School of Finance and Economy sent ten to fifteen graduate students to Halle by the 1890s.[71]

The exposure to German economic theories showed American scholars a wider world of possibilities and alternatives to the British economic model. Bismarck's social welfare legislation of the 1880s, originally a compromise between conservative and socialist factions in the Reichstag, caught the interests of American labor leaders, who were dismayed at the lack of progress in the United States.[72] In 1905, the American Association for Labor Legislation (AALL), an offshoot of the International Association for Labor Legislation, was founded to advance the interests of American workers. The AALL was founded by Henry Farnam from Yale University and Adna F. Weber from the New York Bureau of Labor Statistics, both of whom were students of German economist Gustav Schmoller. Originally an "educational" association that published an English-language version of its European counterpart, *The Bulletin,* which advanced progressive legislation, the AALL eventually transitioned into a lobby for more stringent regulations in the match industry.[73]

By the Progressive era, factory legislation, minimum wage laws, and pensions had been integrated into state laws. The next obstacle was social insurance. Carroll D. Wright, the U.S. Commissioner of Labor, commissioned John Graham Brooks in 1891 to compile a report on German compulsory insurance. Brooks, in his investigations into the effects of social legislation, was less than enthusiastic and made no recommendations. The Socialists then took up the mantle for social insurance. When it first organized in 1900, the Socialist Party included social insurance in its plank. Eugene Debs had recommended the German model to the chair of the Minnesota Employees' Compensation Commission as a source of information during a fact-finding mission in 1908. Because of the Socialist Party's strong advocacy for social welfare legislation, social insurance became associated with radicalism in the perceptions of American voters, despite its conservative roots under Bismarck.[74]

In tandem with social insurance, workers' compensation was a German innovation that caught the interest of American reformers. Industrialization exacted a heavy toll from American families, who could be financially ruined when the sole breadwinner became unable to work due to a workplace injury. In the first decade of the twentieth century, only a small portion of injured workers or their families received any kind of compensation. In Pittsburgh steel mills alone, between 1906 and 1907, a quarter of families went uncompensated. Less than a third received $100 for burial expenses. Even if a case was brought to litigation, the courts often ruled in favor of the employer.[75]

The German accident insurance law, enacted in 1884, was considered a model for American progressive reformers. Under Bismarck's plan, employers were organized into networks of compulsory quasi-public employers' mutual associations, called the *Kassen*. Employees would be compensated according to a fixed scale. By 1903, funding for accident insurance came from a variety of sources: seven percent from the government, forty-seven percent through employer taxes, and forty-six percent from employees.[76] Americans of all stripes supported compensation for workplace injuries. Theodore Roosevelt championed workmen's compensation as part of his overall policy of establishing the government as the protector of the people against exploitation by powerful companies. Even employers supported to escape litigation and as an opportunity to steal the thunder from labor unions. By the eve of the First World War, twenty-one states enacted legislation establishing workmen's compensation, and Germany was seen as being at the vanguard of social legislation and a beacon for American progressives. It would appear to many Americans that Germany and the United States would grow closer together.[77]

Germans and Anglo-Saxonism: Common Origins and Anxieties

By the late nineteenth century, proponents of Anglo-Saxonism extended the Anglo-Saxon family beyond the British Isles and into Germany with the "Teutonic origins theory." The idea sprouted from early nineteenth century Romanticism and nationalism, when scholars began to construct narratives based on common linguistic and national origins. The Teutonic origins theory held that Germany was the home of the Anglo-Saxon tribes; from there they scattered to the British Isles and, ultimately, the United States. Thus, the kernels of Anglo-Saxon virtues, such as self-control, independence, and self-government, were also held within the German people, making them part of the larger Anglo-Saxon family.[78] As a result, compared to other European immigrants—most notably the Irish and Italians—German immigrants were greeted far more warmly and were integrated relatively seamlessly into American society due in no small part to the racial affinities between Anglo-Saxon and Teutonic stocks.[79] Quite similarly, in the early twentieth century, German scholar Albert Bernhardt Faust, who devoted his career to the fostering of friendship between Germany and the United States, attributed characteristics such as duty, honesty, loyalty, industry, and respect for law to German-Americans, which were consistent with the larger Anglo-Saxon family. To Faust, these characteristics helped form American society, which suggested that German-Americans were part of the Anglo-Saxon family.[80] An article in *The New York Times* by Medill McCormick, publisher of *The Chicago Tribune*, acknowledged that far more substantive ties existed between the German and American peoples; the article suggested that the *rapprochement* between Great Britain and the United States was not as solid as it appeared, claiming that any sentiment regarding Shakespeare, the Bible, and the Magna Carta was "perfunctory" and could not make up for the years of "condescension" on the part of the British government. This was clearly articulated:

> We not only exchange professors with German universities ... we import historians, psychologists, and chemists for our best chairs. Whereas a generation ago we looked to Oxford and Cambridge for inspiration, now we turn to Heidelberg and Leipzig. We have Germans on the bench, in business, in the law, in office, and seeking it. English with a German accent is more familiar to our ears than English with an English accent.[81]

Perhaps the closest articulation of attaining these hopes occured in a speech in commemorating Kaiser Wilhelm II's visit to Britain, when British foreign minister Joseph Chamberlain, himself a fervent Anglo-Saxonist, in his tireless efforts to secure an alliance between Great Britain and Germany, suggested an alliance among the "Germanic empires," meaning Germany, Great Britain, and the United States.[82]

In his 1872 *Outlines of History*, British historian Edward A. Freeman traced the Anglo-Saxon peoples to the Teutonic peoples of Germany, who in turn were descended from the Aryan migrations into Europe in the distant past, from whom all Germanic peoples were descended.[83] The Angles, Saxons, and Jutes settled the British Isles during the fifth century A.D. and displaced the Celts. Freeman attributed to the Angles, Saxons, and Jutes characteristics of independence, describing them as unwilling to assimilate Roman culture by keeping their language and stubbornly clinging to their religion. These peoples, according to Freeman, established the ethnic and cultural foundations of the English people.[84]

Likewise, an article by J. W. Jackson in *The Journal of the Anthropological Institute of Great Britain and Ireland* argued that the Teutonic peoples, who became the modern Germans, had been a force for racial and cultural invigoration in Europe for millennia; Jackson suggested this occurred from the Middle Ages, when the Franks mixed with the Celtic population of Gaul after the collapse of the Roman Empire, through the end of the Franco-Prussian War in 1871.[85] Jackson described the Teutons as follows:

> Tall of stature and large of limb, fair-haired, and blue-eyed, they present us, more especially in the Scandinavian variety with the beau ideal of robust, vigorous, and large-hearted humanity, dwelling in a temperate clime. They are framed on a large scale, and are obviously intended as providential instruments for the effectuation of vast deeds and the utterance of profound thoughts.... They are the reserve force of the West, which always comes into play when the more nervous races have been exhausted by the morbid excitement of their corrupt civilization. They are the osseous and muscular pole of European humanity.... Modern Europe is their making. It is impossible to over-estimate our obligations to such a race. They made medieval Italy differ from Greece, and it is their larger presence in Britain which differentiates her from ethnically exhausted France.[86]

Jackson listed the accomplishments of the Germanic peoples throughout the centuries. For example, in the field of music he listed Handel, Haydn, Mozart and Beethoven; in philosophy and literature, Immanuel Kant, Georg Hegel, Johann von Goethe, and Johann von Schiller; Martin Luther for the Reformation; Alexander Humboldt and Carolus Linnaeus in science; and Helmut von Moltke in military strategy.[87] He argued that the Franco-Prussian War of 1870 was the latest chapter of the continuing struggle between the Celts and the Teutons. However, even though the Germans had achieved the goal of unification, Jackson said they were not yet poised for European leadership because they had not shaken off feudalism.[88] However, Jackson had more confidence in another branch of the Teutonic family: the Anglo-Saxons in Great Britain, a branch that had grown into a worldwide empire and the center of civilization and commerce, and, by extension, the United States. The main difference, according to Jackson, between the Germans and the Anglo-Saxons, was that the latter had developed constitutional government, placing emphasis on liberty.[89]

James K. Hosmer further elaborated on the Teutonic theory of Anglo-Saxonism. In his work *A Short History of Anglo-Saxon Freedom*, Hosmer traced the ancestors of the Anglo-Saxon peoples to the region between the Weser and Elbe rivers in Germany. He argued that, in these villages across the North Sea, the kernels of Anglo-Saxon institutions were already present.[90] Hosmer credited these peoples' warrior culture as the basis of Anglo-Saxon freedom that had been ingrained in the English-speaking peoples of the late nineteenth century, particularly in its organization. For example, the origin of the New England township, according to Hosmer, was based on freemen who could bear arms, upon which the *tun-scipe* was formed, which was organized into the hundred, and the shire. The *aethling, ceorl, lathe,* and *slave* formed the social hierarchy of the Germanic tribes that settled England.[91] The *Cyningas,* or king, was a military leader who was chosen by the local communities, made up of landowning freemen, and as such did not hold absolute power. The *tun-moots* became the foundation of representative governments that checked the power of the king. Thus, when the first English settlers arrived in Jamestown, it was from these humble Germanic beginnings, Hosmer concluded, that the American constitutional government of checks and balances was established.[92]

In the realm of religion, prominent American Anglo-Saxonist Josiah Strong credited the rise of the "true faith" of Protestantism with the German reformers of the sixteenth century, who freed Western Christianity from papal absolutism, which he attributed to the Celts and "Latins." Strong considered Protestantism to be another sign of what it meant to be Anglo-Saxon and consistent with the Anglo-Saxon ideals of liberty and self-government. Strong believed that Anglo-Saxonism was divinely ordained to spread the ideals of liberty and self-government, considered unique to the Anglo-Saxon peoples, to the rest of the world.[93]

While Hosmer and other Anglo-Saxonists established the Teutonic theory as part of the origins of the Anglo-Saxon people, they were nonetheless careful to distance contemporary Germany from the United States and Great Britain, the contemporary Anglo-Saxon nations. This distance was necessary because the unified German state established by Bismarck did not adhere to Anglo-Saxon principles of self-government and liberty, which the British and American peoples espoused in the late nineteenth century. Instead, Hosmer described Wilhelmine Germany as based on the Prussian military state, dominated by its Kaiser and court and covered over with a veneer of parliamentary government.[94] Hosmer reflected:

> Under able leaders she has shown herself marvelously powerful. As regards the people, however, what the world has had occasion to notice particularly is the docility with which they have suffered themselves to be led. The initiative has been from the ruling [Hohenzollern] dynasty and its great servants. The Court has supplied the plan of action, the brains, and the energy for carrying it out, using the resources and mighty strength of an unresisting people to secure objects undoubtedly adapted to promote the well-being of the people.... It has been said that the Germans of to-day are cheated by a mere counterfeit of representative institutions, while real freedom is far away from them. To some extent, the remark is true. Though the German Parliament debates and votes, the power of the [Hohenzollern] dynasty is very great and not diminishing.[95]

This tendency toward absolutism was literally written into the person of Germany's first emperor, Kaiser Wilhelm I, who in his earlier capacity as King of Prussia ruled, as well as reigned, without regard for the consent of his subjects and who was fiercely opposed to the notion of democracy. After his death in 1888, the *North American Review* gave a retrospective of his tenure as king and Kaiser in these words:

> In both his functions, as King and as Emperor, William repeatedly found himself in a sea of trouble. He persistently refused any interpretation of either constitution, royal or imperial, which conferred on the ministry, as in England, the power to govern with its related responsibility to the Legislature. He often protested that he had not given up, and would never abandon the hereditary right to rule, as well as to reign. The legislative bodies had their functions, but they did not include in any form the executive power. They would censure his ministry and could refuse proposed laws, and budgets; but they could not overthrow his ministers. His Cabinet was responsible to himself, and not to the law-making power.[96]

Similarly, Strong noted that while self-government and the love of liberty were part of the early Teutonic ancestors of the Anglo-Saxons, that flame had burnt out in the Germans, to be replaced by militaristic regimentation. Spiritually, Strong condemned German Protestantism for falling into the same regimentation, and thus lapsing into "formalism," meaning that German Protestants were more concerned with ritualism than with having a full spiritual experience. Strong supported his argument by the fact that German missionary societies received only a fraction of the donations that were normally given to British and American missionary societies, implying that German Protestants lacked the spiritual zeal held by their British and American counterparts.[97]

In addition to misgivings on issues of religion, Anglo-Saxonists also shared reservations about Germans in the realm of foreign policy during the late nineteenth century. Theodore Roosevelt best expressed the ambivalence toward Germany's inclusion into the Anglo-Saxon family. Roosevelt's capacities both as a private citizen and as president lend a unique insight into the attitudes of late nineteenth century WASP elites and their worldviews. Like the Anglo-Saxonists of the late nineteenth century, Roosevelt was a follower of the Teutonic theory, which included Germany as the primordial cradle of the Anglo-Saxon people and praised the warrior spirit of Norse mythology.[98] Roosevelt also acknowledged, in a speech given to a German-American association, the "increasing importance" of the German identity that had been felt throughout the history of the United States from early colonization; he credited German-Americans' defense of the Union during the Civil War and particularly praised their involvement in preventing Missouri from joining the Confederacy.[99] In a similar speech given in Baltimore, Roosevelt evoked the Teutonic spirit of adventure and perseverance as he described the hardships of the German colonists who settled in the Thirteen Colonies, whose blood he said flowed into the American people.[100]

Roosevelt, on several occasions, expressed his admiration for the accomplishments of the German people, particularly their unification into one nation-state, and he hoped for a closer relationship between Germany and the Anglo-Saxon powers. During his presidency, Roosevelt and Kaiser Wilhelm II made overtures toward cementing the friendship between their respective countries. In some ways, both men shared similarities in their childhoods. Both Roosevelt and Wilhelm II overcame physical challenges in their childhood through a strict physical regimen; they both came to power at a relatively young age; they both saw the potential greatness of their respective countries; and they both saw naval power as crucial to their countries' national interests. Wilhelm II hoped that he could court Roosevelt and persuade him into forming a German-American alliance.[101]

Toward that end, in 1902 Wilhelm II sent his brother, Prince Henry, to promote German-American friendship, which included presenting a statue of Frederick the Great in Washington, D.C., as well as donating models of German sculpture and architecture to Harvard University. In 1905, the tradition of exchanging German and American professors was initiated to promote their respective countries' cultures.[102] Schurz gave his perspective on the royal visit and did not ascribe any ulterior motive beyond the promotion of friendship between both countries.[103] He remained skeptical to concerns of German ambitions that threatened the strategic and economic interests of the United States, declaring that it would not be in the interests of Germany to violate the Monroe Doctrine. Schurz refused to consider the prospect of a conflict between the United States and Germany beyond a tariff war, and he concluded that the visit of Prince Henry was a reflection of the naturally warm friendship that existed between the German and American peoples.[104]

In a letter to German diplomat Hermann Speck von Sternberg, Roosevelt described Wilhelm II as "a fit successor to the [Holy Roman Emperors] Ottos, Henrys and Fredericks of the past."[105] Later, in a letter to American newspaper editor and politician Whitelaw Reid, Roosevelt expressed his gratitude for Kaiser Wilhelm II's support in his mediation ending the Russo-Japanese War, for which he won the Nobel Peace Prize.[106] Roosevelt noted in a letter to Senator Henry Cabot Lodge that Kaiser Wilhelm's efforts in persuading Czar Nicholas II to make concessions to Japan showed that Germany had the potential to become a strategic ally in American foreign policy.[107]

However, like other nativist Americans, Roosevelt had misgivings over the influence of German-Americans in American society at the beginning of the twentieth century. The large waves of German immigrants arriving on American shores at the close of the twentieth century made Roosevelt and others concerned that, rather than assimilating into the larger Anglo-American society, German immigrants would instead transform the United States into what they had left behind in Europe. Roosevelt and other nativists pointed to German-American associations, such as the National German-American Alliance, as examples of the "Germanization" of America, when instead these associations' main goal was simply to promote German culture.[108]

Nativists like Roosevelt at the turn of the twentieth century expressed a distaste for what they called the "hyphenated American," meaning an immigrant who retained elements of his or her cultural heritage rather than assimilating wholly into the larger American and Anglo-Saxon culture. Roosevelt considered the maintenance of one's German heritage by living in German-American neighborhoods, continuing to speak German, and going to German schools to be almost akin to treason and, therefore, anathema to the American ideal of the "melting pot."[109] These views are best articulated in an essay called "The True American," where Roosevelt expressed what it meant to be an American, which is simply to obliterate any signs of the country he or she had left behind. Of European, particularly German, immigrants, Roosevelt exhorted:

> We must Americanize them in every way, in speech, in political ideas, and principles, and in their way of looking at the relations between Church and State. We welcome the German or the Irishman who becomes an American. We have no use for the German or Irishman who remains such. We do not wish German-Americans and Irish-Americans who figure as such in our social and political life; we want only Americans, and provided they are such, we do not care whether they are of native or of Irish or of German ancestry.[110]

For Roosevelt, anyone who wished to be an American could not maintain any cultural connection to the land he or she left behind. Though he originally intended that immigrants should leave behind ancient quarrels—such as that between the Irish and the English or between the French and Germans—to become a true American meant that "He must learn to celebrate Washington's birthday rather than that of the Queen [Victoria of England] or Kaiser [Wilhelm II], and the Fourth of July instead of St. Patrick's Day."[111]

In the realm of foreign policy, despite his personal admiration for the German people, Roosevelt saw Germany as a rival for interests in Latin America and the Pacific, which was a source of tensions for both countries. By the late nineteenth century, the United States and Germany were emerging powers in international affairs. The decades after the Civil War witnessed the rise of American industrial power, led by an Anglo-Saxonist elite that was willing to extend American influence beyond its shores, most notably by the extensive modernization of the U.S. Navy starting in the 1880s. By 1898, the United States made its entrance as a world power with the defeat of Spain and the acquisition of Guam, Puerto Rico, and the Philippines.[112] At the same time, after he had unified the German people, Bismark would in 1890 berewarded with a forced dismissal by Wilhelm II, who wanted a more aggressive Germany through a policy of *Weltpolitik*, or "geopolitics." By the late 1890s, a clique of politicians, aristocrats, and industrialists had formed a lobby that supported Wilhelm II's desire for a powerful navy and a colonial empire in order to aggrandize the newly-formed Reich.[113]

As early as 1889, diplomatic relations between Germany and the United States began to worsen. The Samoa Crisis in 1889 became a nexus that brought Germany, Great Britain, and the United States together, but it also had the potential to unleash a war involving those three countries. A few decades earlier, the South Pacific had been given little attention by the great powers, who were more focused on the Atlantic trade. By the late nineteenth century, however, the islands of the South Pacific were a source of colonial rivalries among the European powers and, later, the

United States. Starting in the 1850s with the discoveries of gold in California, Australia, and New Zealand, more investment was placed in infrastructure and communication to the Pacific, such as telegraph lines and the Transcontinental Railroad. Over the decades, commerce in the Pacific grew, which made the Pacific Ocean and the countries bordering it potential centers of trade.[114]

An article written in 1895 by Lorrin Thurston, the Hawaiian minister in Washington, D.C., declared that the Pacific region should be given as much attention as the Atlantic, if not more so because of the growing trade. Thurston painted stark contrasts between the lack of telephones, telegraphs, and railroads in the countries bordering the Pacific in the 1850s and in the islands of the South Pacific; he described them as being "inhabited by savages and cannibals whose absolute sway was interrupted by an enterprising trader or self-sacrificing missionary."[115] He stated that, since the 1850s, the exports of countries bordering the Pacific Ocean had grown exponentially, particularly those under "dominated by the Anglo-Saxons," and predicted that one day commerce in the Pacific region would rival or even surpass that of the Atlantic.[116] Thurston described the South Pacific as an area of competition among the major powers of Spain, Great Britain, France, the Netherlands, and Germany, each claiming various territories from Australia to Fiji for political and economic interests, emphasizing the social Darwinism of the late nineteenth century as each nation battled each other for limited resources. Nevertheless, Thurston pointed out that the bulk of economic development in the Pacific was under the initiative of the Anglo-Saxon powers, by either Great Britain or its self-governing dominions of Australia or Canada, which emphasized Thurston's support for Anglo-Saxonism as a source for good, at least for the global economy of the late nineteenth century.[117]

In a similar vein, Commodore George Melville, the chief engineer of the U.S. Navy, stressed the importance of the Pacific for the economic growth of the United States. He underscored the fact that the Pacific Ocean covers eight hundred thousand square miles: it would be an excellent outlet for trade and its potential would grow with the completion of the Transcontinental Railroad and a future canal across Central America. According to Melville, the Pacific region would absorb much of the domestic exports from manufacturing, valued at $79.5 million in 1896.[118] He also noted the untapped potential of the markets in Asia and Pacific region. For example, while China imported a total of goods valued at $130 million per year and Japan at 138 million yen, the United States only sent about $25 million dollars' worth of goods to Asia in 1896, and about only 5.69

percent of the United States' total foreign trade passed through its Pacific ports.[119] Additionally, Melville also pointed out that the Pacific coast was a weak spot in the nation's defenses, which had only fourteen vessels, or less than a total 50,000 tons of displacement, compared to Japan's forty-eight vessels at 173,000 tons and Great Britain's forty-one vessels at 91,000 tons. Additionally, it would take about ninety days to send reinforcements from New York to California or longer because the United States did not have many coaling stations in between.[120] Melville thus chided American foreign policy makers for staying aloof while Germany had annexed the Marshall Islands and Great Britain and France had annexed other islands in the South Pacific in the latter part of the nineteenth century.[121]

During the late nineteenth century, however, there was instability in the Samoan political system in the form of rivalry among chiefs competing for the Samoan crown.[122] The continuing conflict among these chiefs coincided with the increasing influence of Great Britain, Germany, and the United States in the region. During the 1870s, the British government made attempts to establish a protectorate over Samoa but was unsuccessful.[123] During the 1880s, Germany began in earnest its acquisition of colonial territory in Africa and the Pacific. Between 1884 and 1885, Germany gained control of part of New Guinea and the Bismarck Archipelago in the Pacific. Samoa, however, was the real prize sought by Chancellor Bismarck.[124]

When civil war broke out in Samoa in 1887, the three powers each supported a candidate for the Samoan throne, which escalated into an international crisis. In 1889, Great Britain, Germany, and the United States sent warships to Samoa, with the German and American warships confronting each other at the Samoan harbor at Apia. On the prospect of a war with Germany, Roosevelt wrote to his close friend, the British diplomat Cecil Spring Rice:

> Frankly, I [don't] know that I should be sorry to see a bit of a spar with Germany, the burning of New York and a few seacoast cities would be a good object lesson on the need of an adequate system of coast defences; and I think it would have a good effect on our large German population to force them to an ostentatiously patriotic display of anger against Germany; besides, while we would have to take some awful blows at first, I think in the end, we would worry the Kaiser [Wilhelm II] a little.[125]

Despite this bellicose rhetoric from Roosevelt, however, the prospects of a war between Germany and the United States over Samoa disappeared when a massive hurricane destroyed the warships on March 15, 1889. The three powers agreed to joint control over Samoa.[126]

II. The German-American Connection, 1850–1914

By 1898, however, conflict once again embroiled the island. British and American newspapers claimed that the German government was behind the outbreak of the Samoan Civil War and was plotting to establish a puppet government, since Germany had the largest economic stake in Samoa.[127] The Samoa Crisis was resolved in 1899, when the British withdrew their claims in Samoa due to the outbreak of the Boer War in South Africa and Germany and the United States split the Samoa islands between them; in addition, Germany purchased the Caroline and Mariana islands from Spain. However, as a result of the Samoa Crisis, the diplomatic tensions between Germany, Great Britain, and the United States were heightened, rather than abated.[128]

The United States had interests at stake in Samoa. According to Henry Ide, who served as Chief Justice in Samoa, the United States since 1872 had established a naval coaling station, a grant of the High Chief of Pago Pago, which was finalized in a treaty between the governments of the United States and Samoa in 1878.[129] According to Ide, Samoa was part of a larger geopolitical game in the South Pacific. As various European powers, most notably Germany and Great Britain, were claiming islands in the South Pacific, the United States was becoming increasingly isolated and could be left out of the potential strategic and economic opportunities in the region. He stated:

> In the South Pacific, European nations have been swift to seize upon the vantage points. With the French in Tahiti and New Caledonia, the Spanish in the Carolines and Philippines, the Germans in the Marshall Islands, New Guinea, New Britain, and other groups, and the British in Australia, New Zealand, Fiji, the Solomons, and many other groups, and exercising a practical protectorate over Tonga, there is no independent group left except Samoa. But these islands, lying south 10 degrees and west 173 degrees, are in the very path of commerce.... If it is appropriated by any foreign power, we have no foothold left south of the equator, no place to which we can go as a matter of right. When we once relax our grasp, we do so forever. Immediate annexation by England or Germany would follow, and those hands never open to release what they have closed upon.[130]

Taking a leaf from Alfred Thayer Mahan, whose works influenced practitioners of late-nineteenth-century geopolitics, Ide stressed the importance of Pago Pago as a naval station because of its harbor. Other nations were also in search of coaling stations to supply their navies, in order to establish a presence in the Pacific. Ide noted that in 1872 German representatives attempted to secure the harbor at Pago Pago but were beaten out by the United States.[131] Ide stated that in 1888, Germany had attempted to take Samoa by force, resulting in a bloody conflict that divided the indigenous population of Samoa into factions supported by German,

British, and American forces; also, German officials imposed martial law, even upon Americans, which raised tensions between the governments of Germany and the United States and could have resulted into war. Ide quoted Secretary of State James G. Blaine's objection:

> To subject the citizens of the United States to the inspection of the German navy; to require reports from each household as to arms kept for its necessary protection; to make permission from the German authorities a needed prerequisite to the natural right of American citizens to guard themselves from danger; to inquire into the character of even their rumored conversations and hold them answerable therefore to the summary proceedings of a German court-martial. All these were trials and indignities to which they ought never to have been subjected.[132]

Ide argued that the presence of the United States in Samoa had benefited the Samoans on the one hand, as well as the Germans and Americans on the other. The establishment of a supreme court in Samoa, under Ide's tenure as Chief Justice, meant that English Common Law was established for Americans or Englishmen, who otherwise would have had to go to a German consulate to redress their grievances. Previous confusion over the validity of land titles were also resolved, as well as the finances of the Samoan government, which hitherto were constantly in debt. Such actions recalled the ideals of the "White Man's Burden," with which Anglo-Saxonism was becoming associated by the late nineteenth century.[133]

The United States and Germany had periods of confrontation in other areas of Asia and the Pacific. A year before the crisis in Samoa had abated, the United States fought its "bully little war" with Spain in 1898. Though it was ostensibly for the liberation of Cuba, the Spanish–American War became a war over the remains of Spain's decaying empire, as well as a European crisis. The Spanish government appealed to Austria-Hungary, France, and Germany for diplomatic intervention on its behalf. However, any intervention, let alone military aid, from the continental powers would have been impossible because of Britain's moral and material support of the United States, despite its official neutrality.[134]

Throughout the war, the British government stoked American suspicions of German designs on American interests in the Philippines and Latin America. Germany, however, also contributed to American suspicions. Since 1897, Wilhelm II had become suspicious of the growing *rapprochement* between the United States and Great Britain; he became convinced that there was an "Anglo-Saxon conspiracy" to dominate Europe economically and called for a continental tariff against the United States.[135] As tensions between Spain and the United States escalated, Wilhelm II called for a pan-European alliance to rally around Spain's cause, which he believed was legitimate. The United States was already designated as a potential opponent in German secret naval documents—had Germany's navy been sufficiently expanded, the Spanish–American War could have become a war between the United States and Germany. With the collapse of Spanish rule imminent, Wilhelm II expressed an interest in acquiring the Philippines.[136] The German government appeared to express an interest in aiding Filipino insurgents in establishing an independent state. Tensions rose particularly through the actions of Vice Admiral Otto von Diderichs in Manila Bay. With the destruction of the Spanish fleet by Commodore George Dewey on May 1, 1898, Manila became an object of interest not just to the United States but to other countries, including Great Britain, France, Germany, and Japan, all of which sent naval observers to protect their respective interests in Manila. The German squadron under the command of von Diderichs was larger than those of the other foreign powers present. Von Diderichs appeared to make aggressive moves, giving rise to a legend that a British squadron intervened to prevent a clash between the German and American warships. The incident in Manila Bay would spark the *rapprochement* between the United States and Great Britain.[137]

Germany's actions in Latin America would continue to fuel American suspicions. For decades, there were large numbers of Germans immigrating to South America for better economic opportunities. According to an article in *The Journal of Race Development* by F.E. Chadwick, Rear Admiral of the United States Navy, there were one hundred and ten thousand total Germans who immigrated to Brazil between 1820 and 1911 at a rate of four thousand a year. Unlike others in the foreign policy establishment, Chadwick did not consider Germany to be a threat to American interests in the Western Hemisphere.[138] On the contrary, he believed that larger numbers of German immigrants in Brazil would be a benefit to the country and argued that if Germans made up the majority of the population, Brazil would be "of a higher type economically and intellectually" to offset the mixed European, African, and indigenous population.[139]

Others, however, were not as optimistic. Attempts to purchase property in Baja California in 1901 for Wilhelm II touched off speculation in the media of a German incursion. In 1902, as Prince Henry was making his goodwill tour, the Danish government rebuffed a proposal for the United States to purchase the Danish West Indies, now known as the Virgin Islands; Senator John Hay and the American press believed that Germany was planning on acquiring them, thus putting pressure on Denmark.[140] In 1897, in his capacity as Assistant Secretary of the Navy,

Roosevelt shared the following with naval strategist Alfred Thayer Mahan on the importance of the Caribbean to the United States and his concerns about Germany:

> We should acquire the Danish [Virgin] Islands, and by turning Spain out should serve notice that no strong European power, and especially not Germany, should be allowed to gain a foothold by supplanting some weak European power. I do not fear England; Canada is a hostage for her good behavior; but I do fear some of the other powers.[141]

Roosevelt expressed similar anxieties in a letter to Spring Rice:

> As an American I should advocate—and as a matter of fact do advocate—keeping our Navy at a pitch that will enable us to interfere promptly if Germany ventures to touch a foot of American soil.... I would simply say that we did not intend to have Germans on this continent, excepting as immigrants whose children would become Americans of one sort or another, and if Germany intended to extend her empire here, she would have to whip us first.[142]

Roosevelt continued in his letter to Spring Rice with an analysis on Germany that became more nuanced. Roosevelt objected to Prussian militarism and the authoritarian government of Wilhelmine Germany, referring to the "imprisoning of private citizens of all ages who do not speak of 'Majesty' with bated breath" as contrary to Anglo-Saxon ideals of liberalism. Of the American public opinion on Germans, Roosevelt found that "Americans don't dislike the Germans, but so far as they think of them at all they look upon them with humorous contempt," and he predicted that in one hundred years the Germans would be of little consequence.[143]

For the time being, however, Germany and the United States would once again confront each other over a crisis in Venezuela. At the beginning of the twentieth century, the Venezuelan government fell behind its debt payments to Germany and other European powers. When Venezuela did not comply with Germany's demands for arbitration, the German government declared its intention of imposing a blockade and seizing some customs houses. Roosevelt and Secretary of State John Hay had no objections, as long as no territory was occupied: such an act would have been in gross violation of the Monroe Doctrine.[144] In a letter to Spring Rice on July 3, 1901, detailing a conversation with German Ambassador Speck von Sternberg, Roosevelt framed the Venezuela Crisis in the context of its significance to the Monroe Doctrine:

> ...the Monroe Doctrine does not touch England in any shape or way, and that the only power that needs to be reminded of its existence is Germany. I explained to the German Ambassador that I did not want to see America get a foot of territory

II. The German-American Connection, 1850–1914

at the expense of any one of the South American states, and that I did not want her to get a single commercial advantage over Germany or any European power save as it was obtained by fair competition by the merchants or by the ordinary form of treaty; but that I most emphatically protested against either Germany or any other power getting new territory in America—just as I am certain England would object to seeing Delagoa Bay [in Mozambique] becoming German or French instead of Portuguese.[145]

However, in December 1902, a combined German, British, and Italian fleet blockaded Venezuela, an act interpreted by the American public as a challenge to the Monroe Doctrine.[146] Congress and American public opinion continued to suspect Germany of harboring territorial ambitions in the Western Hemisphere, while ignoring the British who also took part in the blockade. Roosevelt ordered a fleet to conduct naval maneuvers in the Caribbean as a show of strength. This decision persuaded all the parties to enter into arbitration. The Venezuelan Crisis showed Roosevelt that the United States had to maintain a strong presence in the Caribbean in order to prevent German encroachment.[147]

Roosevelt's ambivalence towards Germany remained prevalent throughout his presidency. Roosevelt's letter to Spring Rice on July 3, 1901, expressed that "it would be most unfortunate if Germany could not continue to get along well with both the United States and England."[148] In his estimation of Kaiser Wilhelm II on May 13, 1905, Roosevelt stated that the German nation was dominated by the Prussian military state, implying a lack of the desired self-government principles associated with Anglo-Saxonism, and, more specifically, was subject to the individual whims of its Kaiser.[149] Again Roosevelt expressed a desire for friendly relations between the United States, Great Britain, and Germany, but at the same time, he considered Germany an unreliable ally due to the policies of Wilhelm II, whom he described as "too jumpy and too erratic."[150]

The Moroccan Crisis of the early twentieth century was an example of Wilhelm II's increasingly aggressive and meddlesome foreign policy. In a letter to William Howard Taft, Roosevelt expressed the balance that he had to maintain in relations between Great Britain and Germany during the Moroccan Crisis in 1905. Roosevelt described Wilhelm II's interference in France's annexation of Morocco as a "pipe dream," which had the potential of starting a war with France's ally, Britain, surmising, "The Kaiser is dead sure that England intends to attack him. The English Government and a large segment of public was sure that Germany intends to attack England."[151] This letter expressed the growing tensions between the British and German governments in the decade before the First World War, as

Britain was trying to maintain its global dominance in light of Germany's rising power. Roosevelt saw the United States as being caught in their competition for global hegemony and had to tread lightly.[152] As the Algeciras Conference was arranged to defuse the crisis in Morocco, in order to placate the German government, Roosevelt had to go so far as to give a speech to German war veterans emphasizing the close ties between the United States and Germany and stressing the magnanimity of Wilhelm II in consenting to negotiate with France.[153]

In the last decade before the outbreak of the First World War, attempts by the German Foreign Office to cement an alliance with the United States began to wind down. Germany was becoming more involved in other areas of the world, such as the Middle East and the Balkans where the United States had not the slightest strategic interest. By 1909, Roosevelt's second term as president had drawn to a close, and his successors, William Howard Taft and Woodrow Wilson, were not as interested in foreign adventures since the United States was in the midst of Progressive Era domestic reform.[154] As he was ending his presidency, Roosevelt wrote Wilhelm II a farewell letter, rich in sentimentality, and when he stopped in Berlin in 1909 as part of his world tour, Wilhelm II publicly declared him his friend. Roosevelt was awarded an honorary degree from the University of Berlin and established a Roosevelt Professorship to promote German-American friendship.[155] However, despite the exchanges of platitudes between Roosevelt and Wilhelm II, any hope for a formal alliance between the United States and Germany would not be forthcoming. Roosevelt never fully trusted Wilhelm II's intentions, nor could he truly believe that Germany lacked territorial ambitions in the Western Hemisphere. German-American relations remained much as they were during the 1890s, as Europe and the world were set on a path toward the Great War.[156]

At the turn of the twentieth century, the doubts expressed by Roosevelt and other policy makers, both in the United States and Great Britain, centered on the anxieties caused by the economic rise of Germany after its unification in 1871: particularly of concern was the uncertainty created in the wake of Bismarck's dismissal in 1890 and the more aggressive and bellicose foreign policy of Wilhelm II that followed.[157] Historian J. Barker Ellis expressed these tensions between Germany and the Anglo-Saxon powers in his article "The Future of Anglo-German Relations," published in *The Eclectic Magazine of Foreign Literature*. Ellis's article was a rebuttal to the British industrialist Lord Avebury, who gave an optimistic view of the global economy. Ellis, instead, pointed out the challenges posed by Germany to Britain's leadership at the turn of the twentieth century. Ellis subscribed to the social Darwinism of the late nineteenth century, which became injected into Anglo-Saxonism, pitting nations and peoples against one another in the never-ending struggle for survival, including the Anglo-Saxons, whom he described as "a little tribe of Northmen," and the Hohenzollerns of Prussia as "a poor Swabian family," who came to power "by right of the stronger."[158] Ellis, in no uncertain terms, considered Germany's foreign policy under Wilhelm II as a challenge to Britain's naval and economic supremacy. He considered the Anglo-Saxon and Teutonic peoples to be two completely different peoples, rather than close cousins under a large family tree. He repudiated the utopian visions held by previous generations of economists that free trade was the catalyst toward world peace and that international arbitration would abolish war. Rather, Ellis fell back on Niccolo Machiavelli's dictum that force was a necessary means for a state or a ruler to survive.[159] He best articulates the Prussian philosophy of using force to achieve political ends by saying:

> The cause of Prussia's marvelous growth can be summed up in one single word, which is worth noting, exists only in the German language. It can be summed up in the word "Machtpolitik," which translated into English, means "the policy of force." "Machtpolitik" is a word which is consequently on the lips of every German who discusses foreign policy, and has no wonder, for Prusso-Germany has put all her trust in the policy of force, which is her traditional policy and which has stood the test of ages. If we read the history of Prusso-Germany we find that by the constant use of force Prussia has become great and powerful, and has welded into a homogeneous mass the numerous nationalities and races which originally inhabited modern Germany.[160]

Ellis's article raised the warning flag that Germany sought to challenge the supremacy of the Royal Navy, and by extension, Britain's colonial empire, which he considered to be the most serious challenge since the Napoleonic Wars. He cited Germany's expanding naval budget, in which the German electorate voted to spend £200 million to be spent over several years, more than the British government spent on the Boer War, alone.[161] Ellis concluded with a warning:

> At present Germany dominates the Continent, but if her frontiers should become further extended she would rule it, and Germany's military, naval, and industrial power might become irresistible. She might then become able to vanquish not only Great Britain, but the United States, as well. Anglo-Saxon civilization might eventually be replaced by German civilization the world over. For these reasons it may be expected that Great Britain would feel impelled to assist the weaker European Powers in opposing any further extension of Germany. Germany seems to be standing at the parting of the ways, and a few years may decide the fate of Europe and perhaps that of the world.[162]

The British writer, Sydney Brooks, gave his assessment of American suspicions of Germany's strategic ambitions. In an essay in *The Living Age,* Brooks outlined the reasons that American foreign policy makers considered Germany to be a rival in the geopolitics of the early twentieth century. Brooks's article foreshadowed the coming confrontation between the Anglo-Saxon and Teutonic peoples, which would also include the United States despite the traditional aloofness held by American public opinion in matters regarding European diplomacy.[163] Brooks surmised that Americans were far more hostile to German institutions than to British institutions, explaining that unlike Great Britain, which had a fundamentally democratic system of government within its constitutional monarchy, Germany was, at heart, an autocracy thinly veiled by a parliamentary system, resting on a "military, aristocratic, and bureaucratic caste." Thus such a political system was incompatible with American democracy and the "free institutions" of other Anglo-Saxon peoples.[164]

It was not simply a matter of political differences between the two countries that Brooks noted the antipathy of the United States toward Germany. He also stated that Germany's policies in Latin America and Asia had been considered threats to the economic and strategic interests of the United States. For example, he noted Secretary of State John Hay's suspicions that German influence might have been involved in the cancellation of the sale of the Danish West Indies, now the Virgin Islands, to the United States in 1899. Brooks concluded that Wilhelm II and his foreign policy makers were plotting to undermine the Monroe Doctrine by expanding German influence in the Western Hemisphere through emigration to relieve social pressures at home, gaining economic influence in Brazil, and culminating in the installation of a naval base in the Caribbean by attempts to lease land from Venezuela.[165] The Spanish–American War was also an example of Germany's meddling and obstruction of American efforts to establish the position of the United States as a newly-emergent power, thus raising warning flags for American foreign policy makers, as Brooks argued:

> The futile rudeness of the German squadron in Manila Bay, the Kaiser's swoop down the *disjecta membra* of the Spanish Empire in the Pacific, the clash over Samoa, and many smaller but not less irritating incidents expanded the distrust of German policy of national prepossession. Within a year of the signing of the Peace of Paris, the Kaiser and the [German foreign office in] Wilhelmstrasse had between them contrived to oust Great Britain from her old position as the supreme object of American suspicion. All the doubts and apprehensions, the willful misunderstandings, and irrational animosities that Americans used to project in their dealings with [Great Britain], they have, since 1908, brought to bear against Germany.[166]

Brooks considered attempts of Wilhelm II at gaining the friendship of the United States—through the visit of Prince Henry of Prussia, educational exchanges, and overly complimentary articles by Ambassador Baron von Sternberg—to be facile, at best, and had done little to remove American doubts about German intentions, but rather merely covered for German ambitions in Latin America, the Pacific, and elsewhere. On the contrary, Brooks argued that American foreign policy makers were far more comfortable with Great Britain's global dominance because Britain, with its naval supremacy, has seen fit to recognize the Monroe Doctrine, and therefore accepted American hegemony over Latin America. Additionally, he expressed the belief that, in a future conflict, the United States would provide more than moral support for Great Britain and the survival of its empire because German supremacy would be an obstacle to the rise of the United States as a world power. Brooks cited Mahan's analysis as an example showing that, if Germany gained command of the sea, the U.S. Navy would be no match in a naval battle and American commerce would be strangled by blockade.[167] Brooks concluded his article expressing his confidence that, though the United States was still new to the uncharted waters of being a world power, that its foreign policy would ultimately mature and accept the fact that alliances are necessary. When that time came, Brooks predicted that the friendship between the United States and Great Britain would be more cemented and less dependent on mere sentimentality.[168]

The rise of Germany as a naval power was also a concern for American foreign policy makers at the beginning of the twentieth century. An article by W. G. Fitzgerald in the *North American Review* declared that Germany, under the direction of Wilhelm II and his ministers, was on its way toward building an offensive navy. The expansion of the navy was part of Wilhelm II's *Weltpolitik*, which aimed at German supremacy in international diplomacy at the expense of the Anglo-Saxon powers, notably, Great Britain. According to the Navy Act of 1900, "Germany must have a fleet of such strength that a war, even against the mightiest naval power, would involve risks threatening the Supremacy of that Power."[169] Toward that end, Fitzgerald detailed the increased military spending by the Reichstag, which totaled approximately $4 billion in the preceding decades. With the unveiling of the British dreadnoughts, which would be far more powerful than any ship of the German navy's existing fleet, the German government, according to Fitzgerald, planned on constructing its own versions of the dreadnought in order to keep pace with the Royal Navy.[170] The implications of Germany's naval expansion were evident to

American foreign policy makers. By threatening Great Britain's naval supremacy, Germany would also be threatening American interests, as well. Fitzgerald noted that Germany's foray into colonization in Africa was a disappointment. At $175,000,000, the costs of maintaining its colony in German Southwest Africa (present-day Namibia) far outweighed any benefits, particularly in light of a brutal colonial war to pacify the colony.[171] Thus Latin America, particularly Brazil, would be a more lucrative target for German ambitions, and the Monroe Doctrine was the only obstacle toward achieving that end. Not surprisingly, Fitzgerald made the observation that the German government refused to entertain any proposal of limiting its armaments at the Hague Peace Conference.[172]

The suspicions of American foreign policy makers regarding Germany's ambitions toward Latin America remained in the first few months of the First World War, foreshadowing the tensions that would emerge in the years leading to American involvement. An article in the periodical *Outlook,* dated November 1914, announced that the German government announced on September 3, 1914, that it would respect the Monroe Doctrine and not establish colonies in Latin America. Ironically meant to assuage American concerns, the statement only heightened concerns that Germany might actually have designs somewhere in the Western Hemisphere. Adding to those concerns was a later statement that a German invasion and occupation of Canada would not be in violation of the Monroe Doctrine, since Canada had given military and economic assistance to Great Britain and was therefore "beyond the pale of American protection."[173] Adding weight to these suspicions, the *Outlook* article argued that based on a school of thought among German professors, the fact that the United States maintained colonies, such as the Philippines, invalidated the Monroe Doctrine, and thus Germany would be justified in expanding its influence in the Western Hemisphere. Since Germany had a population growth of eight hundred thousand a year, Latin America was the perfect place where its surplus population could immigrate. This view was also supported by General Friedrich von Bernhardi, who argued that it was hypocritical for the United States to use the Monroe Doctrine to keep European powers from colonizing Latin America, while it was, at the same time, maintaining colonial possessions in the Pacific. He stated:

> While, on the one side she insists on the Monroe Doctrine, on the other she stretches out her own arms towards Asia and Africa in order to find bases for her fleets. The United States aim at the economic, and where possible, the political command of the American continent, and at naval supremacy in the Pacific. Their

II. The German-American Connection, 1850–1914 73

interests both economic and political, notwithstanding all commercial and other treaties, clash emphatically with those of Japan and England.[174]

The *Outlook* article raised concerns whether American citizens who were born in Germany could be counted upon to support the United States should war break out with Germany since, as of the 1910 Census, there were more than two and a half million people of German descent. The article concluded that the great majority of German-Americans would ultimately side with the United States because Prussian militarism, from which they had emigrated, was incompatible with Anglo-Saxon, and therefore American, views of liberty and self-government. This is contrasted with the fact that even though the United States and the British Empire shared a three-thousand-mile border with Canada, neither side held any fortifications because both peoples shared the same world view. The article explained:

> The reason for this history of peace is to be found in the fact that, whatever the failings of the British Empire and the United States may be, both of these great countries are in principle devoted to a common ideal—that the people should control their own government, and not the government its people.[175]

The article concluded that the war between the Allies and Germany was a war between the ideals of self-government, as exemplified by the Allies, and the autocracy, as embodied by Germany. Even though, at this point, the United States had the luxury of neutrality, the encroachment of Germany, with inherently incompatible with the Anglo-Saxon ideals, upon the Western Hemisphere meant that at some point the American people would have to fight to protect those ideals, and that would mean joining forces with its fellow Anglo-Saxons, the British, in order to defeat the forces of autocracy and militarism.[176]

The cultural connection between Germany and the United States was just as deep and long-running as the connection between Britain and the United States. At various times in their histories, both Germans and Americans looked to each other as models, whether it be the American political model of the late eighteenth century or the German social legislation of the early twentieth century. German immigrants contributed to political and cultural life throughout the history of the United States, from colonial times to the eve of the First World War. Thus it would become a challenge for the foreign policy establishment to ask millions of Americans to set these bonds aside during the First World War.

However, despite the cultural connections between Germany and the United States, framing the German people in the context of Anglo-

Saxonism proved more of a challenge. During the late nineteenth century, it appeared that the Teutonic theory of Anglo-Saxonism might have provided a way to include Germans into the Anglo-Saxon family by tracing the ancient origins of the Anglo-Saxon peoples to the forests of Europe, wherein the kernels of self-government and other qualities, such as adventurousness, resourcefulness, and self-discipline, would be fostered and later spread to the British Isles and, eventually, to the United States. However, the contemporaries of late nineteenth century economics and diplomacy prevented the fusion of Teuton and Anglo-Saxon, as Germany and the United States became rising powers, both with leaders who wanted their respective countries to play a much larger role in international affairs, resulting in tension that escalated into confrontation between both countries. Despite overtures of friendship from both governments, the foreign policy establishments of Wilhelmine Germany and the United States retained their mutual suspicions of one another, suspicions that would continue into the outbreak of the First World War.

CHAPTER III

Anglo-Saxonism in the Foreign Policy Establishment

By the beginning of the twentieth century, the United States had not only grown into an industrial power, but it had also entered the ranks of the major world powers with a colonial empire in the Caribbean and the Pacific. Starting with the "Gilded Age" of the 1870s, the United States had begun its recovery from the carnage of the Civil War, and by the last decade of the nineteenth century, there was a shift in the American worldview. Rather than staying aloof from world affairs as it had done since the founding of the republic, the United States began to take a more active role on the world stage, as much of the globe was increasingly partitioned among the European powers and Japan.

The foreign policy elite in Washington, D.C., of the 1890s had a far different outlook from that of the Founders a century earlier. Behind this fundamental shift in foreign policy was a foreign policy elite that used Anglo-Saxonism as the new rallying cry for a more boisterous and aggressive nation seeking to take its place in the world. Anglo-Saxonism was redefined to suit the new foreign policy of the United States, which was heavily influenced by Social Darwinism and other pseudo-scientific ideas, justifying the "inherent superiority" of the British and American peoples. Anglo-Saxonists of the late nineteenth century emphasized the idea that qualities such as self-government, resourcefulness, and intelligence were qualities that justified global domination by Great Britain and the United States. Anglo-Saxonism served a variety of uses for the foreign policy elite. It gave purpose to the foreign policy establishment that sought to break from the tradition of disengagement dictated by George Washington's Farewell Address of the late eighteenth century. By this time, Anglo-Saxonism had gone beyond parlor room discussions among WASP elites and had become part of foreign policy. Because the United States and Great Britain were deemed by Anglo-Saxonists to be "blessed" with the aforementioned qualities of good government, self-control, resourcefulness, and intelligence attributed to Anglo-Saxonism, they had the responsibility of establishing good government and "civilization" to the benighted parts of the world. Anglo-Saxonism thus justified colonial expansion in the Pacific and Caribbean, by calling it the "White Man's Burden," rather than naked imperialistic aggression, a charge by its critics. Anglo-Saxonism provided an outlet for a society whom the establishment feared was being "softened" by urbanization and industrialization with the closing of the frontier, as well as being "diluted" with the arrival of the "new immigrants" from southern and eastern Europe.

From the colonial period through the nineteenth century, the history of the United States had been that of a nation whose people were in constant movement from the Atlantic to the Pacific in search of free land and economic opportunities. Attempts by the British government to hinder that movement—for example, through the Proclamation of 1763, which excluded the Ohio Valley from settlement—were met with outrage and marked as the first steps toward the American Revolution. The Northwest Ordinance of 1787 provided the mechanisms for integrating new territories into self-governing states, in which such residents would be provided the full protection of the Constitution.[1] Anglo-Saxon ideology had become an ingrained influence when Congress passed the Naturalization Act of 1790, which extended citizenship to all free white men. It is worth remembering that as the United States developed throughout its history, so too did Anglo-Saxonism evolve to suit the exigency of the time. At the founding of the republic, Anglo-Saxon myths and icons were appropriated by its Founders to reinforce the ideals of liberty and self-government.[2]

As the United States continued its expansion, the federal government's relationship with Native Americans became a precursor to colonialism after the Spanish-American War. The proclamation of "Manifest Destiny" was really a call for the propagation of Anglo-Saxon hegemony in the guise of "liberty" across North America, regardless of who stood in the way.[3] Thus, even though Native Americans and Mexicans had inhabited those lands, they supposedly used the land inefficiently and perpetuated "savagery" and "backwardness." The proponents of the Mexican–American War of the 1840s justified the conflict by arguing that only the Anglo-Saxon peoples could truly rule the vast expanses of North America because they would establish the principles of self-government in the untamed lands of the West, from Texas to California, because it was a part of their history and ancient past bloodlines. By spreading the ideals of liberty and self-government inherent to Anglo-Saxonism, the West, and even the world, would thus be formed in the image of Anglo-Saxon America.[4]

The redefinition of Anglo-Saxonism in the late-nineteenth century would have significant ramifications upon American foreign policy. By 1890, however, American expansion was not restricted to the spread of liberty and the addition of self-governing states to the Union. The United States government supported expansionist policies for more mundane reasons, such as conquest and access to new markets. Annexing Canada had been an old dream, a dream that had failed twice after ill-planned invasions during the American Revolution and the War of 1812 and instead led to the creation of the Canadian confederation. By 1850, the acquisition of the Pacific Coast, from Great Britain in the Oregon Country and from Mexico through the Treaty of Guadalupe Hidalgo, completed Manifest Destiny. Policymakers began to look to the Pacific and the Western Hemisphere as a new outlet for exports in a new American "empire," as the United States embarked on the course of becoming a major industrial power.[5]

The Rise of the United States

Like Germany, another power rising in the late nineteenth century, the United States as a new arrival among the ranks of the major European powers. Unlike Germany, which was encircled by potentially hostile neighbors, the United States developed its full economic potential practically unmolested throughout the nineteenth century. The United States had many advantages from which to draw: rich agricultural land; vast raw materials; modern technology (e.g., railways, steam engines, mining equipment, etc.); geographic isolation; the absence of foreign enemies; a steady labor force brought in by immigration; and a steady flow of foreign and domestic investment capital.[6] Between 1865 and 1898, the United States devoted its energies to internal economic development. During the thirty-three years between the end of the Civil War and the outbreak of the Spanish–American War, productivity in agriculture and industry jumped to astronomical levels. Wheat increased 256 percent, while corn and sugar increased 222 percent and 460 percent, respectively. Coal production increased 800 percent, while the production of crude petroleum rose from 3 million barrels to 55 million barrels. What especially aided

American economic growth were the millions of immigrants who joined the labor force.[7] The United States truly had an economy of scale. American firms such as Singer, Du Pont, Bell, and Standard Oil were leaders in technology and enjoyed a gigantic domestic market.[8] American foreign trade proved to be more competitive than either Britain or Germany as exports increased sevenfold between 1860 and 1914.[9] Between 1874 and 1900, American exports grew from around $600 million to $1.4 billion. Exports to Canada and Europe grew from about $500 million to $1.1 billion between 1875 and 1900, while exports to Asia and Latin America in those same years grew from $72 million to $200 million. This was not the whole picture, however.[10]

While the United States was indeed an economic power, it was not a military power. In 1900, the United States had only 96,000 military and naval personnel compared to Germany's 524,000 and Britain's 624,000. In warship tonnage, the United States ranked only fourth behind France and Russia.[11] American foreign policy held to the tradition of isolationism, thus steering away from any formal alliance. Geographic isolation had rendered alliances unnecessary for most of its history. This isolation allowed the United States to achieve dominance within the Western Hemisphere. American economic dynamism was thus coupled with the willingness of its policy makers to pursue a more aggressive foreign policy.[12]

William H. Seward: The Architect of Empire

The architect of American imperialism of the late nineteenth and early twentieth centuries was William H. Seward. As Abraham Lincoln's secretary of state, Seward's diplomacy prevented European intervention during the Civil War. He did so by marginalizing the Confederacy by discouraging Great Britain and other European powers from granting it recognition as a sovereign nation. Secondly, he used Canada's vulnerable geographic location as leverage to ensure British neutrality, and, during the *Trent* affair, he did not allow the heat of the Civil War to result in an international war between the United States and Great Britain. In doing so, he ensured the victory of the Union over the Confederacy, setting the foundation for American expansion in the coming decades.[13]

With the Civil War over, the creation of an American empire would dominate the last third of the nineteenth century. American foreign policy was in transition by the end of the Civil War. On the one hand, American presidents and secretaries of state were bound by the tradition of non-engagement in "entangling alliances" going back to the founding of the republic. The Monroe Doctrine served as a bulwark against European meddling in the Western Hemisphere. The American people saw themselves as a "city on a hill" embarking upon an experiment of creating a nation, one not based on blood or ethnicity, but upon the ideals of liberty that would attract the downtrodden peoples of Europe and elsewhere.[14] Seward was the first major policymaker to break away from the traditional paradigm of American foreign policy. As secretary of state, Seward sought to use the economic potential of the United States as the launching pad of a new American empire, coupled with the magnet of immigration that would contribute to American economic power.[15]

Seward saw the domination of Latin America as crucial for the rise of the United States as an imperialist power. His goal was to acquire for the United States a series of naval bases in the Caribbean, particularly Santo Domingo and the Danish Virgin Islands, and the Pacific. The acquisition of Alaska, though known in 1867 as "Seward's Folly," was part of a grander plan to annex Canada: an old expansionist dream of expelling the British from their last North American colony that went back to the American War of Independence.[16] Seward did not wish for the United States to acquire new territory for its own sake. In fact, aside from Alaska, the only mainland territory Seward desired was the Isthmus of Panama—the rest were island acquisitions.[17] Economics was the impetus for late nineteenth-century American expansion. Seward saw the geopolitical position of the United States as the basis of economic supremacy, given its location between Europe and Asia. Rather than a traditional land-based empire, Seward sought to have the Pacific become part of an American commercial empire.[18]

The acquisition of Alaska was part of a larger strategy of establishing an American presence in Asia. A canal through Panama would open markets on the West Coast to the Atlantic. As early as 1863, Seward raised the profile of the American representative in Hawaii and negotiated a trade reciprocity treaty with the Hawaiian government in order to draw it into an American sphere of influence, culminating in Hawaii's annexation in 1898. In 1867, Seward laid claim to the Midway Islands as part of a chain of coaling stations leading through the Pacific to Asia.[19] Once in Asia, Seward vigorously advocated for free American access to its markets. In 1868, he negotiated the Burlingame Treaty, which provided cheap Chinese labor to help complete the Transcontinental Railroad. At the same time, Seward had ambitions to open the markets of Japan and Korea to American trade, the latter of which would be fulfilled by the 1880s.[20]

Seward's quest for empire was not due purely to geopolitical considerations. His ideology was based on an extension of Manifest Destiny. However, instead of creating self-governing states across the North American continent, Seward believed that "Divine Providence" mandated an American empire that dominated Latin America and the Pacific.[21] In a speech given in Madison, Wisconsin, on September 12, 1860, Seward declared that "empire for the last three thousand years ... made its way constantly westward ... until the tides of the renewed and decaying civilizations of the world meet on the shores of the Pacific Ocean."[22] Anglo-Saxonism was clearly the guiding light for his expansionist policy, even when most Americans before and after the Civil War did not care about obtaining more territory.[23] Seward adopted an attitude of paternalism that he laid out in American foreign policy. He saw China as having been "under the spells of superstition and caste," only to be roused by the blessings of American trade.[24] The United States would serve as a "tutor" to China in the arts of Western civilization, which presaged the idea of the "White Man's Burden."[25]

For all his ambition, Seward's contemporaries dismissed his vision for the United States, particularly his purchase of Alaska from Russia. The country's unwillingness to expand the navy was a stumbling block for Seward, which would only be rectified long after he had left office in 1869. In retrospect, however, Seward could be seen as a transition from the pre–Civil War ideology of non-interference to the ideaology of imperial expansion. A new generation of policymakers in the State Department and the Navy would fulfill his plans in the years between 1890 and the First World War with the Open Door Policy in China and the acquisition of the Virgin Islands in the Caribbean. Seward anticipated the rise of the United States as a global economic power, and the Anglo-Saxonists would be the ones standing on his shoulders.[26]

Changes in American Society

In the years after Seward's departure from the State Department, the United States began to break away from its traditional disengagement from international affairs. There were a number of factors that were behind this shift to a more aggressive foreign policy. One reason was a changing population. Between 1870 and 1890, the population grew from thirty-nine million to sixty-three million.[27] Immigration was a significant contributor to population growth. Between 1880 and 1920, the "New

Immigrants" from southern and eastern Europe were outnumbering the "old stock" immigrants from northern and western Europe. By 1910, one-third of Americans were either foreign-born themselves or had at least one parent who was born in another country. Immigrants constituted significant proportions of major metropolitan areas and provided the labor for factories in the booming economy.[28]

The major shifts in population caused some to think about the direction of American society. The closing of the frontier marked a turning point in the social history of the United States. Historian Frederick Jackson Turner postulated in his "frontier thesis" in 1893 that the expansion and settlement of the frontier played a role in shaping American character and molded American democracy, which distinguished the United States from the cramped nations of Europe.[29] Other intellectuals of the time grabbed onto Turner's frontier thesis by arguing that the closing of the frontier, with no other outlet for expansion, would be detrimental for American manhood. Without the free air of the West, they feared that industrialization and urbanization would weaken American men and diminish their taste for war, unlike the previous generation who had fought in the Civil War. The United States would then be torn into the class conflicts and revolutions that had so plagued Europe throughout the nineteenth century. Jingoists of the 1890s proposed a new frontier of colonies and markets beyond America's shores where American masculinity could flower through the crucible of war.[30]

The changing landscape of international relations of the late nineteenth century also influenced the development of a more aggressive American foreign policy. Starting in the 1880s, the European powers, particularly Britain and France, had been partitioning the continent of Africa into colonies and protectorates. Asia was also divided into colonies, and China, the biggest prize in Asia, was carved into spheres of influence by Britain and France. Additionally, there were new contenders, which altered the geopolitical balance of power. For the first time, a unified Germany arose and unsettled the traditional Concert of Europe, which had previously maintained the peace since the end of the Napoleonic Wars. In Asia, Japan escaped European domination through extensive reform and industrialization, and it became an imperialist power in its own right, having subdued China in the Sino-Japanese War 1895.[31] To many Americans of the period, the United States could no longer afford to cling to the sentimentality of George Washington's Farewell Address. As a rising industrial power, the United States had to join the European powers in dominating the non-industrial world for markets and resources, or else it would risk falling behind the European powers in gaining access to markets in Asia, thus failing to fulfill its own destiny of dominion over the Western Hemisphere.[32]

By the end of the 1880s, a new generation of elite policymakers had emerged in Washington. Unlike their predecessors, they were well connected through their travels to Europe and relationships with the European aristocracy. While previous generations may have eschewed any admiration of European, particularly British, culture, these White Anglo-Saxon Protestant elites were ready to proclaim their affinity with the Anglo-Saxon community.[33] In their paradigm, the pinnacle of humanity was the Anglo-Saxon race, to which the United States belonged through its connections with Great Britain, Germany, and Scandinavia. The rise of this new WASP elite coincided with the emergence of late nineteenth century Anglo-Saxonism, which was based on the application of Darwin's theory of natural selection on human society. Social Darwinists saw the world in terms of limited resources, wherein the race that made the most effective use of those resources was destined to rule, while "inferior" races should accept "benign" subjugation. It was therefore incumbent upon them that the Anglo-Saxon nations, particularly the United States and Great Britain, should work in concert, if not enter into a full-fledged alliance.[34] Theodore Roosevelt, Henry Cabot Lodge, and Alfred Thayer Mahan were the most prominent among the many individuals most closely associated with Anglo-Saxonism who applied its principles to American foreign policy. This new generation's policies would lead the United States upon a new course in its world outlook, taking its place among the industrialized powers by shouldering the "White Man's Burden."[35]

Alfred Thayer Mahan and the New Navy

In order for the United States to achieve its destiny of domination, it needed to have the necessary tools, most importantly a navy that ranked among that of the major European powers. After the Civil War, the United States Navy had greatly deteriorated. By 1880, the navy, which had helped secured Union victory less than twenty years earlier, was mostly derelict and obsolete. Out of 1,942 vessels, only forty-eight were in fighting condition. The same insular attitude that discouraged any interest beyond America's shores had contributed to the decline of the United States Navy during the 1870s.[36] However, by the 1880s, the growing realization of access to markets in Asia and dominance of the Western Hemisphere made both political and military leaders reconsider the importance of a modern, world-class navy. In 1881, Secretary of the Navy William Hunt established a naval board that would be up to date on the latest naval developments, culminating into the creation of the Naval War College of 1884, thus setting the stage for a modern navy.[37]

Congressman William McAdoo of New Jersey and diplomat John Kasson pled the case for the modernization of the United States Navy. They argued that American citizens and economic interests in areas as far flung as the Samoas had the right to be protected by an adequate navy. In 1883, Congress authorized spending for four steel vessels, laying the foundation for the "New Navy." Between 1885 and 1889, Congress authorized the construction of thirty more vessels. However, the ships to be constructed were only lightly-armored cruisers that targeted commerce ships, not offensive battleships for domination of the seas. Nevertheless, the creation of the "New Navy" during the 1880s became a starting point upon which Anglo-Saxonists could formulate a new aggressive foreign policy for the 1890s.[38]

One of the most significant contributors to this change in American foreign policy at the beginning of the twentieth century was Alfred Thayer Mahan. Mahan's entire life revolved around service to his country: he was born on September 27, 1840, on the grounds of the U.S. Military Academy at West Point, and he died on December 1, 1914, at the Naval Hospital in Washington, D.C. Mahan's father, Dennis Hart Mahan, was the professor of civil and military engineering at West Point.[39] Alfred Thayer Mahan graduated from the U.S. Naval Academy in Annapolis in 1859 and devoted the rest of his life to the Navy. Even though he served the Union during the Civil War, because of his family's roots in Virginia, Mahan held the same prejudices regarding African-Americans as "inferior" to whites, which would influence his worldview.[40]

Mahan combined the ideology of Anglo-Saxonism with a practical means of applying it: the use of the Navy as a tool of foreign policy. In particular, Mahan emphasized the social-darwinistic dimension of Anglo-Saxonism, which rested on the assumption that the world was a battleground in which the races of humanity competed for limited resources. Thus, the nation, or people, that could best utilize those resources was to Mahan the nation that was "the fittest" and best suited to survive in such an environment. In this worldview, Mahan saw a natural partnership between the United States and Great Britain because of their shared values, particularly the love of liberty and the rule of law, which were considered to be the foundations of self-government, the cornerstone of Anglo-

Saxonism. He envisioned the history of the United States as one in which the Anglo-Saxon ideals of the United States spread across the North American continent, assimilating everyone in a manner similar to that of ancient Rome. Mahan therefore saw overseas expansion to the Pacific as a natural and necessary outlet for the United States, since Latin America in the south consisted of an "alien people" with strange values, while Canada in the north shared similar Anglo-Saxon values, which would not tolerate foreign occupation.[41]

Mahan would be best known for his seminal book, *The Influence of Sea Power upon History*. Originally part of his lectures on naval history, *The Influence of Sea Power upon History* covered the rise of the British navy between 1660 and 1783. Mahan began with the statement, "The History of Sea Power is largely, though by no means solely, a narrative of contests between nations, of mutual rivalries, of violence frequently culminating in war."[42] Mahan listed the conditions that determined whether a country became a sea power: geographical location, physical area, population, and political institutions.[43] He therefore concluded that Britain satisfied these conditions, which allowed it to become a global empire by the eighteenth century. In his work, Mahan analyzed Britain's wars against France, Holland, and Spain and concluded that Britain's success as a commercial and world empire lay in the fact that it used sea power more effectively than its neighbors. Mahan explained that the command of the sea was predicated on the following criteria: destroying the enemy's navy in pitched battles, acquiring its colonies, blockading its ports, and blocking its access to strategic trade routes.[44] By holding Britain as a model for national greatness, Mahan implied that the United States could also become a great power by following the British example of building a great navy to protect its commercial interests.

Mahan's work was widely read among the foreign policy establishment of the 1890s and beyond, and it influenced the course of American foreign policy. *The Influence of Sea Power upon History* was a textbook for American foreign policy makers who desired to see the United States take its place among the major powers of the late nineteenth century. Mahan's ideas coincided with the desire to have access to markets in the late nineteenth century, declaring that

> foreign necessaries or luxuries must be brought to [a nation's] ports, either in its own or in foreign ships, which will return, bearing in exchange the products of the country, whether they be fruits of the earth or the works of men's hands, and it is the wish of every nation that this shipping business be done by its own vessels. The ships that thus sail to and fro must have secure ports to which to return, and

must, as far as possible, be followed by the protection of their country throughout the voyage.⁴⁵

On the necessity of a navy, Mahan argued:

> [The need for a navy] springs from the existence of peaceful shipping and disappears with it, except in the case of a nation, which has aggressive tendencies and keeps up a navy merely as a branch of the military department. As the United States has at present no aggressive purposes, and as its merchant service has disappeared, the dwindling of the armed fleet and general lack of interest in it are strictly logical consequences.⁴⁶

The Influence of Sea Power in History thus regenerated an interest in the navy, which had been allowed to deteriorate in the decades after the Civil War. Mahan's work injected a sense of purpose to a new generation of naval officers, who tied the nation's well-being to trade. Therefore, in order to protect trade, a large navy was deemed necessary. Thus, the United States would need to establish its naval presence in the Caribbean, Hawaii, and other strategic locations to protect its trade.⁴⁷ As a result, the curriculum at the Naval Academy in Annapolis began to reflect the teachings of Mahan, albeit slowly, to include "modern" subjects such as economics and political science.⁴⁸

Mahan was part of a new generation of "navalists" who pleaded the case for a "large policy," and a powerful navy to enforce it. He was considered a "prophet" of a new age, one in which the United States was a major player in the geopolitical maneuverings of the great powers of the late nineteenth century; his reading public went beyond the naval establishment, all of whom waited for his pronouncements on the military and diplomatic questions of the day.⁴⁹

Theodore Roosevelt was among the "navalists" who identified very closely to Mahan's vision. To Roosevelt, simply having a defensive military was clearly insufficient for the global diplomatic realities of the late nineteenth century. His review of *The Influence of Sea Power upon History* reiterated the necessity for a navy that would be able to stand against that of a major European power. Roosevelt stated most explicitly that

> forts alone could not prevent the occupation of any town or territory outside the ranging of their guns or the general wasting of the seaboard.... We need a large navy, composed not merely of cruisers, but containing also a full proportion of powerful battleships, able to meet those of any nation. It is not economy—it is niggardly and foolish shortsightedness—to cramp our naval expenditures, while squandering money right and left on everything else, from pensions to public buildings.⁵⁰

In his article "The United States Looking Outward," Mahan reiterated the importance of markets and highlighted the fact that the United States in the late nineteenth century was in the unique position of being both an Atlantic and a Pacific power.[51] Mahan saw the rise of another newcomer, Germany, as a threat to the long-term interests of the United States in the Pacific, which he believed to be a future battleground of the great naval powers:

> All over the world German commercial and colonial push is coming into collision with other nations: witness the affair of the Caroline Islands with Spain; the partition of New Guinea with England; ... the Samoa affair; the conflict between German control and American interests in the islands of the western Pacific; and the alleged progress of German influence in Central and South America. It is noteworthy that while these various contentions are sustained with the aggressive military spirit characteristic of the German Empire, they are credibly said to arise from the national temper more than from the deliberate policy of the government ... a condition much more formidable.[52]

Mahan in this article further made the connection that economic rivalry would inevitably lead to political and military conflict. It was in the best interests of the United States to build up its navy in order to embark upon the new policy of what Foster Rhea Dulles called "mercantile imperialism," the idea that a nation must have overseas bases beyond its home shores in order protect its commerce abroad.[53]

It was not surprising then that Mahan considered himself an anglophile, having written about the rise of the Royal Navy as an example for the United States to emulate. Amid the Anglo-American *rapprochement* of the late nineteenth and early twentieth century, Mahan supported a "cordial understanding" with Great Britain rather than a formal alliance. This new relationship would be based on the shared national interests of both countries in a world in which continents were being partitioned for their markets and resources.[54] Mahan anticipated the eventuality that war would erupt between Great Britain and Germany. In such a war, he believed that the United States would side with Britain. He argued, therefore, that the United States should not adhere to a strict definition of neutrality, which dated back to the War of 1812, and should adopt the British maritime practice of seizing contraband during wartime.[55]

In pushing the United States to take a more strident position in world affairs, Mahan continued to press for greater cooperation between Great Britain and the United States. In his article "An Anglo-American Reunion," Mahan called upon the shared kinship of the American and British peoples. He believed that the fundamental similarities in language and heritage were breaking down the traditional enmity between both countries that had existed since the American Revolution.[56] This article was part of a compilation of his writings, titled *The Interest of America in Sea Power, Present and Future*, which he began in 1897. The timing for this work could not have been more striking. During this time, the crisis in Cuba was compelling leaders in the United States to intervene on behalf of the Cuban people's struggle against Spain. Additionally, there were mounting pressures for the United States to annex Hawaii. Mahan persuaded the publishers Little, Brown, & Co. to market his book to a military audience in order to influence policy makers in Washington and advance a "broader policy" for the United States, and, working in concert with Great Britain, against Germany, a country Mahan perceived to be a shared threat.[57]

Mahan's Influence on U.S. Foreign Policy

Mahan's influence on foreign policy had become extensive among the policy makers in the State and War Departments by the beginning of the twentieth century. Mahan encouraged the growing *rapprochement* between the United States and Great Britain in the early years of the twentieth century by drawing upon Anglo-Saxonism as the basis of global cooperation against common threats like Germany. He noted that despite waves of immigration, the United States still remained "English" in its political traditions and ethnic makeup; thus despite the growth of the United States into a major world power, the similarities between both countries in Anglo-Saxon values, such as the ideals of self-government and the rule of law, meant that Great Britain did not see the United States as a threat to its strategic interests.[58] In 1906, Mahan persuaded President Theodore Roosevelt and Secretary of War Elihu Root to abandon traditional American neutrality rights, which was one of the causes of the War of 1812.[59] Mahan's flock of "navalists" had grown within the policy-making organs of Washington, which stressed the importance of continued Anglo-American cooperation and sought to adapt his teachings to the new foreign policy of the United States.[60]

A direct application of Mahan's writings could be found in the policy of acquiring bases in the aftermath of the Spanish–American War. The necessity for bases was compatible with Seward's social darwinistic perceptions, which structured the world as a battleground where the fittest nations survived. Mahan expressed this sentiment in an article on Asia in *Harper's Weekly*:

> The first law of states, as of men, is self-preservation—a term which cannot be narrowed to the bare tenure of a stationary round of existence. Growth is a property

of healthful life, which does not, it is true, necessarily imply increase of size for nations, any more than it does for individuals, with whom bodily, and still more mental, development progresses long after stature has reached its limit; but it does involve the right to insure by just means whatsoever contributes to national progress, and correlatively to combat injurious action taken by an outside agency, if the latter overpass its own lawful sphere.[61]

Using history as a guide, Mahan referred to the decision made by the Roman Republic to occupy Messina in Sicily, which was the first instance in which Rome extended its influence beyond the Italian peninsula, ultimately transforming its destiny from a landlocked republic into a Mediterranean empire.[62] Likewise, Great Britain provided a template for the United States to chart its course into the unknown waters of being a global power. Mahan cited Great Britain's extensive networks of naval bases stretching from Gibraltar to India, as well as British possessions in the North Atlantic and the Caribbean, which also lay at the basis for its global empire.[63] According to Mahan, it was not sheer seamanship alone that established Britain's global pre-eminence by the late nineteenth century. Rather, it was the Anglo-Saxonist qualities of self-government and the love of liberty throughout England's history that allowed Britain to rise from an insignificant island among the nations of Europe to the pre-eminent global power by the nineteenth century. During the age of exploration under Elizabeth I, Mahan credited the initiative of "buccaneers" like Sir Francis Drake and Sir Walter Raleigh who added to England's wealth by plundering Spain's treasures since they were not hindered by unnecessary regulations of a bloated bureaucracy.[64] Thus, in staking out its claim in the New World, which he described as "the brawl of nations," what seemed to be a disadvantage in not conquering "half-civilized" peoples like the Aztecs and Incas, the British people instead planted the seeds of self-government, seeds that grew unhindered and ultimately became the United States. These were the lessons that Mahan hoped to impart upon his readers.[65]

Though considered laughable during Seward's time, the need to establish an American military and economic presence overseas gave the navy a sense of urgency. In 1900, the General Board of the Navy was created to list the priorities of the navy, particularly the locations for potential naval bases. There were two areas of interest to the United States Navy: the Caribbean and Asia. The General Board desired to make the Caribbean Sea an "American lake," with an isthmian canal as its crown jewel. The Spanish–American War had given Puerto Rico and Cuba to the United States. The Board considered additional sites such as Almirante

Bay and Chiriqui Lagoon in Panama, Port Elena in Nicaragua, the Galapagos Islands off the coast of Ecuador, and even as far as Bahia Hondo in Brazil.[66] By the first decade of the twentieth century, the navy became the foundation for American imperialism in the Caribbean and in Latin America. It was instrumental in the transformation of Cuba into an American protectorate, through numerous interventions into its domestic affairs. The importance of the Panama Canal, as well as other American economic interests, also required interventions into the governments of Central America by maintaining dictatorships in Guatemala and Nicaragua that were friendly with the United States.[67]

The increasing importance of Chinese markets necessitated an American presence in East Asia by the end of the nineteenth century. As in Latin America, there were strong recommendations from both the army and the navy to establish coaling bases either on or near the Chinese mainland. This would complete the "insular empire" of the United States, which extended from Hawaii to the Philippines.[68] Accessibility to China's markets led the United States government to follow the Open Door Policy, ensuring that it would not be left out as China was increasingly held at the mercy of European spheres of influence, a reality made even more evident with the crushing of the Boxer Rebellion by a multinational force of Europeans, Americans, and Japanese.[69] In the event that the Open Door Policy had failed and China was open for partition, the Navy was willing to consider gaining a concession at Tianjin and bases at the Chusan Islands, which were part of Mahan's August 1898 recommendations. Ultimately, such plans never materialized because they would have contradicted the ideals of the Open Door Policy and posed a potential risk of the major powers intervening against the United States.[70]

By the end of the nineteenth century, Mahan, who had become the acknowledged authority on foreign policy, was called upon to give his analysis of the role of the United States in Asia in *Harper's Monthly*. In a three-part article titled "The Problem of Asia," Mahan acknowledged the fact that the acquisition of the Philippines after the Spanish–American War had placed the United States into the position of an "Asiatic Power," and, as such, it could no longer afford to remain aloof from international affairs.[71] Mahan concluded that Asia would be the focus of international events in the twentieth century. He stated this most succinctly with the following:

> For the problem of Asia is a world problem, which has come upon the world in an age when, through the rapidity of communication, it is wide awake and sensible as never before, and by electrical touch, to every stirring in its members, and to the tendency thereof.[72]

Theodore Roosevelt expressed complete agreement with Mahan's analysis of conditions in Asia, which required the attention of the United States and Great Britain. In a letter penned in response to Mahan's article, Roosevelt stated the following:

> I feel that the United States and England should so far as possible work together in China, and that their cooperation and the effective use of sea power on behalf of civilization and progress which this cooperation would mean in the valley of the Yangtze [River], is of the utmost importance for the future of Asia, and therefore of the whole world.[73]

In his further study of Asia, Mahan acknowledged Japan as an emerging power as a result of the modernization efforts undertaken during the Meiji Restoration, joining the ranks of the European powers, though considered to be the "Yellow Peril." However, rather than focusing on the coastlines, Mahan saw Central Asia between the thirtieth and fortieth parallels, from Asia Minor to the Korean Peninsula, as a future battleground among the major powers, with the "Slavic peoples," (i.e., Russia) as the chief rival to the Anglo-Saxon race.[74] Because of its geographic limitations, Russia would have no choice but to expand southward toward the goal of obtaining a warm water port. Mahan concluded that Russia would then collide with maritime powers such as Great Britain. The concern over Russia as a potential rival in Asia would also be shared by other elites in the foreign policy establishments in both the United States and Great Britain. Anglo-Saxonists would thus again have a sense of purpose.[75]

Theodore Roosevelt

Among the foreign policy makers of the early twentieth century, none would be as influential as Theodore Roosevelt. His ascendance to power coincided with the rise of the United States as a world power; Roosevelt embodied the vigor of an emerging industrial power that was willing to play a more aggressive role in international politics. Roosevelt's personal transformation from a sickly child into a larger-than-life figure was a personal statement of the kind of masculinity that the United States required as it began to chart the unknown waters of the twentieth century. Roosevelt's aristocratic background and his sense of purpose was a testament to the Anglo-Saxonism of the early twentieth century, showing that the United States, by virtue of its Anglo-Saxon heritage, had a responsibility to spread the light of civilization.[76]

For Theodore Roosevelt, Anglo-Saxonism and foreign policy were

III. Anglo-Saxonism in the Foreign Policy Establishment

one and the same. Like other Anglo-Saxonists of the early twentieth century, Roosevelt was a firm believer in the "White Man's Burden." Like the European powers, the United States, to Roosevelt, had to take charge in civilizing its new conquests in the tropics, particularly the Philippines and Puerto Rico. Roosevelt believed that only the United States and other Anglo-Saxon peoples could teach "inferior" peoples about good government. To place such people in charge over their own fate, to him, would be irresponsible.[77] As the United States took on the responsibilities of colonial rule at the beginning of the twentieth century, Anglo-Saxonists like Roosevelt could look to the British Empire as a template. The self-governing dominions of Australia, Canada, New Zealand, and South Africa were peopled mainly by Anglo-Saxons from the British Isles and were located in temperate zones. However, in the tropical zones, such as Africa and Asia, the British government maintained direct rule. This example taught American Anglo-Saxonists that the United States must maintain dominance over its tropical possessions in the Caribbean and the Pacific.[78]

The application of Roosevelt's Anglo-Saxonism into policy can be seen in his letter to Secretary of State John Hay supporting President William McKinley's nomination of Major General Leonard Wood for command in Cuba and Major General Francis V. Greene for command in the Philippines. Roosevelt's letter stated concern for the challenges the United States was facing as it inaugurated its governance of the former Spanish colonies, the failure of which "might mean the definite abandonment of the course upon which we have embarked—the only course I think fit for a really great nation."[79] Hay also shared the view that the United States had an "obligation" to annex the Philippines, which trumped the objections raised by the Anti-Imperialists who opposed the acquisition of Spain's last colonies. Of the opposition, Hay recounted the following to Whitelaw Reid, one of the American commissioners to the Philippines:

> There is a wild and frantic attack now going on in the press against the whole Philippine transaction. Andrew Carnegie really seems to be off his head.... He says the [McKinley] Administration will fall in irretrievable ruin the moment it shoots down one insurgent Filipino. He does not some to reflect that the Government is in a somewhat robust condition even after shooting down American citizens in his interest at Homestead. But all this confusion of tongues will go its way. The country will applaud the resolution that has been reached, and you will return in the role of conquering heroes, with your "brows bound with oak."[80]

Roosevelt's letter to Hay expressed the need for the United States to have able administrators for its newly acquired colonies:

> In Cuba we may lay up for ourselves infinite trouble if we do not handle the people with a proper mixture of firmness, courtesy, and tact. In the Philippines we are certain to invite disaster unless we send ample forces, and what is even more important, unless we put these forces under some first-class man. Both in Cuba and in the Philippines what we obviously need, and need at once, is to have some man put in supreme command in whom we can absolutely trust and to whom we give the widest liberty of action.[81]

At no point in the letter did Roosevelt even discuss the wishes of either the Cuban or Filipino people. Roosevelt's letter clearly indicated that the United States knew exactly what was in the best interests of the peoples it had acquired from Spain, and that what they required were strong-minded men who had the will to bring forth civilization. Particularly relevant was his recommendation of Greene to stop the growing guerrilla war; Roosevelt said Greene would "smash the insurgents in every way until they are literally beaten into peace; entertaining no proposition whatever from them save that of unconditional surrender."[82] Roosevelt, in his praise of Wood, compared him to British colonial officials, who served as models for the United States in undertaking the "White Man's Burden."[83]

Roosevelt's impact on American foreign policy of the early twentieth century had significant consequences. When he assumed the presidency in 1901, Roosevelt applied Mahan's policy of modernizing the navy in the era of the *Dreadnought*. Between 1901 and 1909, Roosevelt allocated funding for a modern navy that would place the United States on par with major naval powers such as Great Britain and Germany. During Roosevelt's first term, ten battleships were constructed, each at a cost of between $6.6 million and $7.5 million. Unlike the smaller warships that saw action at the Battle of Manila Bay in 1898, these larger battleships were sixteen thousand tons, traveled at eighteen knots, and boasted twelve-inch guns as their main batteries and eight-inch guns as secondary batteries.[84] In 1906, the Royal Navy unveiled the *Dreadnought*, which had a single battery of twelve-inch guns, displaced eighteen-thousand tons and could travel at twenty-one knots on oil-fueled turbines, rendering the rest of the world's navies obsolete. The United States Navy followed suit by producing a series of battleships: the *Florida Utah* in 1908, which displaced twenty-two thousand tons and had ten twelve-inch guns; the *Wyoming* and *Arkansas* in 1909, which were twenty-six thousand tons and had twelve twelve-inch guns; and then the *New York, Nevada, Pennsylvania,* and *California* in 1910, which displaced between twenty-seven thousand and thirty-two thousand tons and had ten to twelve fourteen-inch guns. Despite Mahan's objections at the increasing size and expense of these

III. Anglo-Saxonism in the Foreign Policy Establishment 93

new battleships, the General Board recommended the naval build-up as early as 1902 and 1903: this move gained a sense of urgency in the aftermath of the Japanese victory in the Battle of Tsushima during the Russo-Japanese War, which was decided by *Dreadnought*-type battleships that were larger and more powerful than their predecessors.[85]

Roosevelt had justification for the expansion of the U.S. Navy. The Spanish–American War had shown that naval power was crucial in implementing foreign policy, when he remarked, rather casually, to his friend William Wingate Sewall on the destruction of the Spanish fleet at Manila Bay by Commodore George Dewey.[86] As Secretary of the Navy, he emphasized accuracy in naval gunnery, readiness for combat, and modernization of the fleet.[87] Roosevelt's interest in the navy continued to be a major priority in his administration. In his letter to Secretary of the Navy Paul Morton, Roosevelt declared that the U.S. Navy should be a major national priority. Roosevelt's close watch over the navy can be reflected in a letter in which he pointed out the improvements made under Morton's predecessor, William Henry Moody. Roosevelt appraised Moody's tenure as Secretary of the Navy thusly:

> He has understood clearly that there are two sides to the work of the Department. There is, in the first place, the industrial efficiency of the navy; that is, the building of ships, engines and ordnance, the provision of equipment and stores, the purchase and inspection of material, the employment of laborers and mechanics, the care of dockyards, and many similar details. All of this is of the utmost importance, but to do it implies in the Secretary simply such qualities as are shown in the administration of a great private manufacturing establishment.[88]

Roosevelt continued to reiterate the importance of the navy in the larger realm of international relations, saying that it should be in "a state of constant preparedness for war." He dismissed opponents of his naval policy as "unprogressive inert men" whom he considered a threat to national security. As Roosevelt wrote the above letter, he was especially concerned about the clash between Russia and Japan over control of Korea in the Russo-Japanese War, particularly the aftermath of the Battle of Tsushima, in which the Japanese navy dealt a surprising blow to the Russian navy, a development that could potentially change the balance of power in the Pacific.[89]

At the beginning of the twentieth century, it appeared that Russia was a potential rival to the Anglo-Saxon powers in East Asia. Between 1898 and 1904, the Russian government had designs on dominating northern China, planning to use it as a springboard to the Pacific as part of its long-range goal of securing a warm-water port. In 1898, St. Petersburg wrested a concession at Port Arthur from the Chinese government and secured first preference for a railroad through Manchuria. In 1900, fifty thousand Russian troops occupied Manchuria in order to demand further concessions from Beijing, with the goal of possibly directly annexing Manchuria.[90] In 1899, Roosevelt conveyed the threat of Russian domination over Asia to his friend, British diplomat Cecil Spring Rice. As with his other correspondences, Roosevelt's perceptions of race were evident, wherein he saw the United States and Great Britain as part of an Anglo-Saxon family struggling against the Slavs. Roosevelt considered Russian domination of Asia to be a calamity for Anglo-Saxondom, but he believed that an American presence in Asia would be a benefit to the British in India.[91] While assuaging Spring Rice of his fears of the Russian threat, Roosevelt expressed another chief concern:

> The diminishing birth rate among the old native American stock, especially in the north east, with all that that implies, I should consider the worst. But we have also tremendous problems in the way of the relations of labor and capital to solve. My own belief is that we shall have to pay far more attention to this than to any question of expansion for the next fifty years, and this although I am an expansionist and believe that we can go on and take our place among the nations of the world, by dealing with the outside problems without in any way neglecting those of our internal administration.[92]

Roosevelt's fear over the shrinking birthrates of the "old stock" Americans was shared by other Anglo-Saxonists of the late nineteenth and early twentieth centuries: this was part of the greater fear of the decline of American "manliness" due to the increasing industrialization and urbanization of American society and the growing rift between the capitalist and working classes. Anglo-Saxonists like Roosevelt worried that the decline of the traditional elites and the dilution of American stock by immigration from eastern and southern Europe, along with the growing "feminization" of politics, would render the United States unfit to assume its destined leadership in the international arena.[93]

Just as the United States was a newcomer in international politics, Japan, too, was an emerging power in Asia. The fast-paced modernization that followed the Meiji Restoration in 1868 spared Japan from the fate of European domination that occurred during the late nineteenth century throughout Asia, most notably in China, so much so that Japan was competing with Russia over China.[94] The Russo-Japanese War provided an opportunity for Roosevelt to mediate as a peacemaker between the belligerent parties, while at the same time protecting the interests of the United States in Asia. On the one hand, Roosevelt was impressed with the

Japanese people for having modernized fairly quickly. In a letter to Spring Rice, Roosevelt said he was a "firm believer in the Japanese people ... and believed that Japan would simply take her place from now on, among the great civilized nations." However, he was also concerned that if Japan were to defeat Russia and continued to rise in power, a future conflict with the United States lay on the horizon.[95] Thus, in a subsequent letter to Hay, Roosevelt realized the necessity of balancing the interests of the United States versus that of Japan or Russia as they competed for control of East Asia.[96]

Roosevelt took the opportunity to mediate the peace between Japan and Russia at Portsmouth, New Hampshire, in 1905, four months after Japan's victory at the Battle of Tsushima. The naval yard at Portsmouth was chosen as the site for the talks between the two belligerents because Washington, D.C., would have been too hot for the summer, when the talks were scheduled, and also so that both the Russians and the Japanese would have been made mindful of America's military might during their negotiations.[97] The upset resulting from Japan's victory at Tsushima caused a great deal of excitement from Roosevelt: he wrote as much to Spring Rice, treating the Japanese people as "honorary" Anglo-Saxons with his praise for the results of their modernization:

> What wonderful people the Japanese are! They are quite as remarkable industrially as in warfare.... The industrial growth of the nation is as marvelous as its military growth. It is now a great power and will be a greater power.... I believe that Japan will take its place as a great civilized power of a formidable type, and with motives and ways of thought which are not quite those of the powers of our race.[98]

The Anglo-American Rapprochement of the 1890s and its Impact on U.S. Foreign Policy

The rise of the United States as a major power in the 1890s coincided with its diplomatic *rapprochement* with Great Britain. The ideology of Anglo-Saxonism provided the final piece to the Anglo-American *rapprochement*, upon which American and British foreign policy elites could establish a common purpose. The addition of the United States as a possible partner in imperial affairs partially offset Britain's relative decline, as it dealt with new challenges in European diplomacy.[99]

In the late nineteenth century, Britain grew increasingly isolated by the new diplomatic realities taking shape in Europe. After experiencing several decades of unquestioned leadership, the British faced foreign policy challenges from different areas of the globe, such as Russia's encroachment towards India and presence in China, along with colonial disputes with France in Asia and Africa. Also in 1894, France and Russia signed the *Entente Cordial,* which caused much alarm in London. Meanwhile, Germany rose as the leading military power, becoming home to the largest army in Europe.[100] Then, in 1890, Kaiser Wilhelm dismissed Bismarck as chancellor and introduced a new foreign policy based on direct competition with Britain in the acquisition of colonies and the enlargement of Germany's navy.[101]

The overwhelming lead Britain had enjoyed in industrial capacity and naval size steadily eroded in the nineteenth century's closing years. A chief reason for this development was the spread of industrialization throughout Europe and the United States.[102] One of the stark realities challenging Britain was a united Germany, whose population and industrial capacity was growing steadily after 1870. For example, German coal production grew from under ninety million tons in 1890 to just under two hundred eighty million tons in 1914 as opposed to Britain's at over two hundred ninety million tons.[103] In the last two decades of the nineteenth century, Britain's industrial and commercial pre-eminence shrank. In 1880, Britain commanded about twenty-three percent of world manufacturing and world trade. By 1913, that share had dropped to fourteen percent. Between 1820 and 1840, Britain's annual productivity was four percent: this shrank to three percent between 1840 and 1870 and decreased even further to about two percent between 1875 and 1894. While its traditional industries of coal, textiles, and ironware continued to increase production, Britain lost its lead in the newer industries of the late nineteenth century, such as steel, chemicals, machine tools, and electrical products. These industrial statistics alarmed the British government because of their diplomatic ramifications.[104]

This trend of decline did not go unnoticed by the British leadership. Prime Minister Lord Salisbury saw the need for Britain to end its traditional isolationist policy. In 1898 Lord Salisbury addressed the House of Lords on the dire situation in British foreign policy. By the late nineteenth century, Britain had acquired extensive colonial holdings in Africa and Asia, raising the envy of various European powers, notably Germany. Salisbury argued that the acquisitive policy of the late nineteenth century left Britain in a vulnerable position since it might incite the hostility of other nations, as well as leaving Britain spread out too thinly, thereby putting a burden upon its resources.[105] By 1898, various sectors of the British leadership called for an alliance between Great Britain and the United

III. Anglo-Saxonism in the Foreign Policy Establishment 97

States. Joseph Chamberlain, the colonial secretary, was one of the most ardent supporters for closer ties between Britain and the United States. Chamberlain succinctly analyzed Britain's isolation as follows:

> Since the Crimean War nearly 50 years ago, the policy of this country has been a policy of strict isolation. We have had no allies—I am afraid we have had no friends.... As long as the other Great Powers of Europe were also working for their own hand were separately engaged, I think the policy [of isolationism] we have pursued ... was undoubtedly right for this country.... But now in recent years, a different complexion has been placed upon the matter.... All the powerful states of Europe have made alliances, and as long as we keep outside these alliances, we are envied by all and suspected by all.[106]

Chamberlain was one of a growing number of voices clamoring for a *rapprochement* and a formal alliance between the United States and Great Britain. Realizing Britain's isolation, Chamberlain reached out to the United States as the best place to look for an alliance due to its cultural similarities and compatible worldviews.[107]

In light of Britain's imperial overextension, the foreign policy establishment in Washington sought to establish the hegemony of the United States over Latin America, ending Britain's economic supremacy over the Western Hemisphere. Crucial to this aim was the renegotiation of the Clayton-Bulwer Treaty, signed in 1850, in which it was originally planned that both countries would share custody over an isthmian canal.[108] Imperialists in the foreign policy establishment wanted the United States to have sole control over a future isthmian canal. During the Spanish–American War, Commodore Dewey's fleet had to make the months-long journey around the Straits of Magellan to reach the Spanish fleet in Manila, which could have been dramatically shortened by an isthmian canal. Negotiations with the British government began in 1898, with the State Department calling for changes in the Clayton-Bulwer Treaty. McKinley argued before Congress that an American-controlled canal was crucial to the economic interests of the United States, especially since Hawaii had been annexed that year.[109]

An obstacle to the renegotiation of the Clayton-Bulwer Treaty was the controversy surrounding the border between Alaska and Canada, due to vague wording in a treaty between Britain and Russia, Alaska's former occupier. The British government wanted to link the fate of an isthmian canal with the settling of Alaska's boundary with Canada, which had been a bane in Anglo-American relations throughout the nineteenth century.[110] Secretary of State John Hay, in a letter to U.S. Ambassador Henry White, found it "deplorable" that the British insisted on linking the issue of the canal with the issue of Canada. He claimed that British public opinion supported an American-controlled canal and would be a benefit to the global community. Nevertheless, he remained confident that the United States and Britain would come to an equitable agreement.[111] Ultimately, the Clayton-Bulwer Treaty lapsed and was replaced by the Hay-Pauncefote Treaty, which was signed in 1901 and established American hegemony over the Western Hemisphere, assuring the British government that the United States would not become a problem. As a result of the treaty, the Anglo-American *rapprochement* that had begun in the 1890s became the foundation for the "Special Relationship" of the twentieth century.[112]

The continuing evolution of Anglo-Saxonism was crucial to the flowering of the Anglo-American *rapprochement* of the 1890s. The foreign policy elites of the United States and Great Britain saw Anglo-Saxonism as a common worldview that provided a purpose for their respective countries. As the United States took on the responsibilities of empire, Great Britain saw a potential partner acting in concert that would hold back more hostile world powers such as Germany or Russia. In the aftermath of the Spanish–American War, British Anglo-Saxonists welcomed the debut of the United States as a world power. British commentators like Geoffrey Seed and Professor Edward Dicey saw the victory of the United States over Spain as proof of Anglo-Saxon "superiority" in the perpetual struggle among the races for survival and dominance.[113] In an article in the *North American Review*, American professor of archaeology and strong supporter of the Anglo-American *rapprochement* Charles Waldstein praised the potential benefits of Anglo-American partnership. In his article, Waldstein did not point to the ethnic school of Anglo-Saxonism as the basis for the *rapprochement* between the growing friendship between the United States and Great Britain: this was because of the ethnic diversity of the United States, as well as the diversity of peoples that formed Great Britain, which he found problematic. Rather, Waldstein considered the English language to be what tied both countries together.[114] I his article, Waldstein actually objected to the racial and ethnic chauvinism that pervaded Continental powers, particularly Germany, which he traced to a reaction to Napoleon Bonaparte's armies in the early nineteenth century, later to be channeled by Otto von Bismarck in his unification of the German states in 1871. Thus, Waldstein felt that reducing the *rapprochement* between the United States and Great Britain to mere ethnic solidarity cheapened its potential.[115]

Waldstein pointed to the shared culture of the American and British peoples as what bound them together, regardless of the countries' ethnic make-up. As examples, he used British monuments like Westminster Abbey, which memorialized statesmen and poets, to inspire and provide a sense of familiarity to Americans regardless of their ethnicity. Secondly, Waldstein used English literature, citing authors like William Shakespeare and Sir Walter Scott as common sources of unity for both countries on either side of the Atlantic.[116] Waldstein best explained the role of language in how British and American travelers understood the world:

> At every step while the Englishman or American travels abroad, even in the most civilized countries, he meets with administrative enactments, privileges, restrictions, injunctions and directions, sent from the summits of government into the busy plains of ordinary daily life, which are foreign to him and which evoke a sense of criticism, if not of irritation and revolt. The same feeling of strangeness and of foreignness constantly comes over him, if he attempts to follow their political life, whether the American consider the legislative and administrative proceedings of a European republic, or the Englishman study the laws and enactments of some other constitutional monarchy. On the other hand, every Englishman becomes readily familiar with the political system of the United States and feels at home under its rule, as the American lives happily under the laws of Great Britain and can follow with interest the work of the House of Commons.[117]

Overall, Waldstein believed that the *rapprochement* between the United States and Great Britain, which he considered "an English-speaking brotherhood," to possess inherent qualities not found in any other European power. He declared that by working together, the United States and Great Britain could be the leaders of human civilization because of their commitments to constitutional and representative government. He did not consider the American War of Independence of 1776 to be a disaster, but rather an affirmation of the Thirteen Colonies' commitment to self-government, a continuation of the arc of early English history that started with the Magna Carta and the English Civil War.[118] Waldstein also reminded his readers that the Monroe Doctrine in 1823 originated as a joint statement between the American and British governments, in their commitment to protect the newly independent nations of Latin America against an invasion by the Continental powers, foreshadowing the *rapprochement* of the 1890s. He closed his article with a plea for both governments to remember that it was deep cultural bonds, rather than ethnic chauvinism, that should tie the American and British peoples together, a bond through which they could improve humanity.[119]

One tangible result of the Anglo-American *rapprochement* was the unchallenged dominance of the United States in the Western Hemisphere. The diplomatic realities of the late nineteenth century convinced the British government to relinquish control of the Western Hemisphere to the United States in order to deal with the rise of Germany as a competitor, instead of having to fight against both countries.[120] Seeing that American hegemony over Latin America was far more preferable to German dominance, the British Foreign Office and press encouraged the United States to assert its "moral superiority" over Central and South America, which Theodore Roosevelt happily did through his corollary to the Monroe Doctrine, thus becoming another vehicle applying the ideology of Anglo-Saxonism at the beginning of the twentieth century.[121]

In a 1912 article in the *American Political Science Review*, Phillip Brown, the former minister to Honduras, analyzed the role of the United States in Central America and how the Monroe Doctrine could be best applied to achieving the objectives of American foreign policy, giving the reader insight into an American diplomat's challenges in dealing with the governments of Central America, namely Guatemala, El Salvador, Honduras, Nicaragua, and Costa Rica. It was very clear from the beginning of the article that Brown approached the relationship between the United States and the nations of Central America from an Anglo-Saxonist perspective. First, he described the cultures of the peoples of Central America as anathema to the values of Anglo-Saxonism represented by the United States. In addition to making a comparison between the federal system of the United States and the unitary systems of the nations of Central America, the virtue of self-government, the cornerstone of an Anglo-Saxon society like the United States, was according to Brown, "a concept dimly comprehended" in Central America. Brown noted that respect for the rule of law, while highly regarded in Anglo-Saxon countries like the United States, was completely reversed in Central America, which tended to favor whoever was in power.[122]

Secondly, the way Brown described the role of the American diplomat followed the script of Rudyard Kipling's "The White Man's Burden." He noted the natural apprehension of Central Americans to the motives of the United States, citing the taking of California during Mexican War, the imposition of the Platt Amendment on Cuba after the Spanish-American War, the occupation of Puerto Rico, the wresting of Panama from Colombia in 1903, and the handling of the foreign debts of the Dominican Republic. However, Brown justified such actions by the United States as ultimately out of benevolent intentions.[123] Thus, he used words like "ungrateful" and "onerous" in his dealings with the governments of Central America, which he likened to that of a petulant student who resents his wise old tutor. Brown best illustrated the dilemma of the American diplomat thusly:

If he is what is popularly termed a "sidestepper," in trying to avoid unpleasant diplomatic issues with the local government and at the same time satisfy his aggrieved compatriots, not to mention his own government, he usually falls between the two stools. If, on the other hand, he is normally conscientious, he finds he must either incur the hatred of the complainants who may be able to cause him serious annoyance, or he must in cases deserving diplomatic action, make unpleasant representations without the certainty of receiving the approval and support of Washington.[124]

Brown also pointed out why it was important for the United States to have such a strong hand in Central America and the Caribbean: the short distance between Central America and the United States; the Panama Canal; and the necessity to prevent Central America from falling under European influence due to the "enforced feebleness" of the peoples of the region.[125]

Brown interpreted the Monroe Doctrine as a means to advance Anglo-Saxon concepts of civilization into Central America. He portrayed the role of the United States as that of an "older brother" caring for his younger siblings; he even cited a line from the Gilbert & Sullivan operetta *HMS Pinafore* to reiterate the idea of the United States as the policeman of the Western Hemisphere. Brown cited instances in which the United States had to intervene in conflicts between the various Central American states. For example, in 1906, President Theodore Roosevelt and President Porfirio Diaz of Mexico mediated in a conflict involving Guatemala, Honduras, and Nicaragua, which was resolved on the gunboat *Marblehead*. Also, in 1907 when war again threatened to break out between Guatemala and Honduras, Roosevelt mediated by inviting delegates from the Central American republics to a peace conference.[126] However, such overtures of peace, Brown argued, needed to be balanced by the use of force: he cited instances in 1909 and 1911 when American and British forces landed in Nicaragua to restore order and to prevent a wider conflict from breaking out.[127] Brown concluded his article by restating the importance of the Monroe Doctrine, which was to help the people of Latin America attain civilization and self-government, the true foundation on which Anglo-Saxon nations, like the United States, were based.[128]

The Experience of the Philippines and Anglo-Saxonism

The one arena where policy makers could apply the ideals of Anglo-Saxonism was the Philippines, which the United States acquired by the

Treaty of Paris, ending the Spanish–American War. One of the arguments in the debate for acquiring the last of Spain's colonies, most notably the Philippines, was so that the United States would assume its responsibility like the other European powers and bring "civilization," (Protestant) Christianity, and "progress." Having taken on the task of governing the Philippines, American policy makers sought to apply the ideals of Anglo-Saxonism, particularly imparting "self-government" to the Filipino people. While it was one thing for Boston patricians to boast of the past glories of the Anglo-Saxon race, it was another thing to apply the credos of Anglo-Saxonism in the new situation that was unfolding in the Philippines. Politicians could no longer talk about the *potential* benefits of American rule, but of how to bring "civilization" to the Philippines. As the United States began to establish the foundations of colonial rule in the Philippines, ideas of race (particularly Anglo-Saxonism) based upon precedents established well before the Spanish–American War played a significant role in determining the relationships between American administrators and the Filipino people, whether through the grueling realities of the guerrilla war against the insurgents or through the actual business of colonial government.[129]

For future American colonial administrators, there was no question that Great Britain would be the model for governing the Philippines. At an annual meeting of the American Academy of Social and Political Science in May 1899, the question of the best way for the United States to establish colonial control over the Philippines was discussed by academics and politicians alike. The opening remarks given by Theodore S. Woolsey, a professor of international law at Yale University, compared the Dutch colonial system to the British colonial system. He concluded that the British colonial system was worth emulating because of its Anglo-Saxon ideals of self-government, as evidenced by the dominions of Canada, Australia, and New Zealand; in comparison, he referred to the East Indies as little more than "a sort of huge farm by the government of the Netherlands."[130]

Woolsey cited British rule over India as a model for how the United States should rule the Philippines. He based his entire assumption upon the premise that the Filipino people were incapable of self-government and must therefore rely on the tutelage of the United States government. With regard to India, Woolsey professed his admiration for the British civil service because of its use of young British men, "the flower of the race," to take upon the "White Man's Burden." He commended the British for having made a study in the governance of "dependent races." Therefore

III. Anglo-Saxonism in the Foreign Policy Establishment 103

the result, according to Wolsey, was that the British in India had kept the peace, preserved order, built roads, railroads and irrigation works, brought justice to the humblest, lessened famine and pestilence, introduced state education, sanitation and dispensaries, freed trade from many burdens, simplified taxation, and had begun to introduce local self-government.[131]

Taking a cue from the British model, Woolsey summarized the goals of the United States in its management of the Philippines: to exercise religious toleration among the Christian and Muslim populations, to "educate" the "civilized" half of the Philippines in the arts of self-government, to expand communication and public works, and to raise revenue.[132] The challenge in establishing self-government in the Philippines was reflected in the accounts of Theodore Roosevelt, Jr., who served as governor-general of the Philippines. He blamed the "backwardness" of the Philippines on Spanish colonial rule, which, he argued, introduced feudalism to the Philippines and was reinforced by the Roman Catholic Church.[133] However, Woolsey introduced a paradox that would hang over the United States when grappling with the reality of colonial rule over the Philippines. In establishing "order" and "civilization" in the Philippines, Woolsey believed that it would be unthinkable for the United States to grant self-government to a "half-civilized" nation such as the Philippines. Doing so, he argued, would lead to chaos. Thus, Woolsey likened the relationship between the United States and the Philippines to that between a guardian and a ward who must be kept on the tight leash of military rule.[134]

Regardless of the academic debates, the American experience of governing the Philippines was born in the crucible of the Filipino insurrection that followed almost immediately after the conclusion of the Spanish–American War. Much to the surprise of the Americans, the "insurgents" had the utter temerity and audacity to demand the independence that Dewey had promised Aguinaldo in Singapore. On February 4, 1899, barely two months from the Treaty of Paris, troops under Aguinaldo's command fired upon an American unit in Manila, thus inaugurating the Philippine–American War, which cost $170 million (plus hundreds of millions more in pensions), four thousand American casualties, and hundreds of thousands in Filipino lives.[135]

In an address on October 7, 1899, Secretary of War Elihu Root justified America's role in the insurrection and the actions of the military. He argued that because the United States was the only civilizing force in the Philippines, the region would fall into the anarchy of tribal warfare should the Filipino people be left to their own devices. Root described Aguinaldo's forces as "men who prefer a life of brigandage to a life of industry" and painted Aguinaldo as a "military dictator ... who has attained supreme power by the assassination of his rival, and who maintains it by the arrest and punishment of every one who favors the United States, and the murder of every one whom he can reach who aids her."[136] In the same breath, Root extolled the Anglo-Saxon virtues of the American soldiers in the Philippines, even though he did not mention Anglo-Saxonism by name. To him, the American soldier

> ...carries with him not the traditions of a military empire, but the traditions of a self-governing people. He comes from a land where public discussion has educated every citizen in the art of self-government ... where the affairs of city and county and town and village, have made the art of government the alphabet of life for every citizen, where every citizen has learned that obedience to law, and respect for the results of popular elections is a part of the order of nature.[137]

In imposing another brand of colonialism upon the Philippines, the first duty of the United States was to impose order by suppressing the "insurrection." Unlike the war against the Spanish, which utilized conventional military tactics, the Philippine–American War was a guerrilla war, a conflict that blurred the line between soldier and civilian as American troops moved outside Manila.[138] Brute force, however, was not the only means the United States employed in suppressing the guerrilla war. As the occupation of Manila began, McKinley gave express orders that the army would treat the Filipinos as humanely as possible in order to match American actions with American desires for the well being of the Philippines, providing Anglo-Saxon "civilization" and ideally winning over the Filipino people to the cause of American colonialism. The military government would continue to allow Spanish law to remain in force with justice administered by officials already in place, provided that those officials accept American authority. Private property would also be respected.[139] One of the army's first duties during the occupation of Manila was to provide health and sanitation facilities, which were previously woefully inadequate under the Spanish and had been destroyed by war. The Board of Health was created under the direction of Chief Surgeon Major Frank S. Bourns. The Board of Health instituted health regulations; inspected homes, markets, and other establishments that could affect public health; ran the leper hospital; and provided smallpox vaccinations.[140] It should be noted, however, that such services became unevenly distributed outside Manila and into the countryside.[141]

As the guerrilla war continued, the question over whether to keep the Philippines intensified among Americans. In Congress, there was an intense debate between Senator Albert Beveridge of Indiana and Senator

George Hoar of Massachusetts. Beveridge had introduced a resolution calling for the United States to retain the Philippines and to stay the course in putting down the insurgency; Hoar denounced this measure. In defending his resolution, Beveridge questioned the ability of the Filipino people to govern themselves:

> The great majority of the natives of the islands ... were incapable of understanding even the simplest form of self-government. Decades would be necessary to instruct them in the rudiments of administration as it was understood in America.... As a rule they were indolent, and their methods of the most primitive nature. They must be dealt with as children by a strong and simple government.[142]

Hoar, however, responded from the constitutional perspective by asking, "Where did the United States get the right to buy and sell people like sheep?" He countered Beveridge's claims by arguing that the Philippines already had an established government with courts, schools, governments, and churches. Thus, to Hoar, in maintaining its grip on the Philippines, the United States would be responsible for smothering the sovereign entity of the Philippine Republic that had been proclaimed in the struggle against the Spanish.[143]

The Philippine Commissions

With the capture of Aguinaldo in 1901 and other revolutionary leaders subsequently thereafter, the United States proceeded to follow McKinley's mandate of "uplifting," "civilizing," and "Christianizing" the Philippines. On In the midst of the guerrilla war, there had been debates over what form of civil government in the Philippines would be established. The question of the relationship the Philippines would have the United States—whether as a state, territory, or colony—hung over Congress. The Insular Cases of May 1901 resolved that question by granting limited rights to Filipinos and other subject peoples taken from Spain, under the premise that the Constitution did not fully follow the flag. While the Filipino people were granted the "fundamental rights" of life, liberty, and the pursuit of happiness, they were not necessarily granted "procedural rights," such as trial by jury.[144] American colonial rule in the Philippines was an experiment because for the first time the United States had acquired territory with no intention of incorporating it as state with uniform institutions as could be found on the mainland. Using Anglo-Saxonism as a guide, American administrators of subsequent years would be traversing uncharted waters.[145]

In order to determine what kind of arrangements could be made for the Philippines, in March 1899, as the guerrilla war was commencing, McKinley organized a committee consisting of future president William Howard Taft, Dean C. Worcester, Luke E. Wright, Henry C. Ide, and Bernard Moses, and committee leader Jacob Schurman, the president of Cornell University. After a tour of the islands, the Philippine Commission, also known as the Schurman Commission, concluded that the Philippines was unprepared for self-rule despite the government established under Aguinaldo. In an article in the *Times of London,* a Filipino committee protested that the Schurman Commission did not make any efforts to cooperate with Aguinaldo's government, arguing that "it is impossible for a commission sitting only at Manila and unaided by friendly cooperation on the part of the national Government, to arrive at a proper understanding of the actual condition of affairs in the Philippines, the unanimity and aspirations of the people, and their capability of self-government."[146] The Schurman Commission operated on cultural biases and had contact only with members of the elite, who were seeking to maintain existing class prerogatives with the new American order. As expected, the Schurman Commission recommended that only American colonial rule was the best safeguard for protecting the welfare of the Philippines, out of concern that the islands would descend into tribal warfare.[147]

In 1900, McKinley ordered a second commission headed by Taft with the purpose of establishing a civil government. Roosevelt wrote to Taft, commending him for having been chosen and saying that he had every confidence in Taft's abilities in heading the commission.[148] The report by the Taft Commission began by generalizing the majority of the Filipino people as "ignorant, credulous, and childlike, and that under any government, the electoral franchise must be much limited, because the large majority will not, for a long time, be capable of intelligently exercising it."[149] However, unlike other Americans who had visited the Philippines, Taft made an effort to become acquainted with the Filipino people beyond two-dimensional caricatures and sought to base civil government upon indigenous traditions.[150] However, Taft, after studying other colonial experiences by the British, concluded that the United States would serve the Philippines better by transplanting American values of freedom and self-rule.[151] The Taft Commission, thus established the founding principles for civil government:

> That no person shall be deprived of life, liberty, or property without due process of law; that private property shall not be taken for public use without just compensation; that in all criminal prosecutions, the accused shall enjoy the right to a

III. Anglo-Saxonism in the Foreign Policy Establishment 107

speedy and public trial ... that excessive bail shall not be required, nor excessive fines imposed, nor cruel and unusual punishment inflicted; that no person shall be put twice in jeopardy for the same offense ... that neither slavery nor involuntary servitude shall exist except as a punishment for crime ... that no law shall be passed abridging freedom of speech or of the press, or the rights of people to peaceably assemble and petition the Government for a redress of grievances; that no law shall be made respecting an establishment of religion, or prohibiting free exercise thereof, and that free exercise and enjoyment of religious profession and worship without discrimination or preference shall forever be allowed.[152]

The Taft Commission began its work on 1 September 1900, establishing civil rule by creating local governments in municipalities and provinces, organizing courts among American lines, and creating the Philippine Civil Service. In his recollections, Worcester, one of the commissioners, encountered initial skepticism from military governor General Arthur MacArthur (father of General Douglas MacArthur), who saw military rule as the only solution and regarded the Taft Commission as an intrusion to that end.[153]

The United States established the Bureau of Insular Affairs (BIA) in 1898 to administer the Philippines, along with the other territories acquired from Spain. Because of the insurgency, the BIA was placed under the jurisdiction of the War Department under Secretary Elihu Root. On August 23, 1898, the operations of the BIA were left to George De Rue Meiklejohn, Assistant Secretary of War, whose position roughly corresponded to that of the British colonial secretary.[154] Upon its founding, the BIA faced two major problems regarding the Philippines. The first problem was how to establish a civil government in the Philippines in the midst of a guerrilla war and, relatedly, whether the military could provide the infrastructure necessary while fighting a war. The second problem was which agencies would claim jurisdiction over the Philippines upon the conclusion of the guerrilla war.[155]

On July 4, 1901, Root ended the military government and appointed Taft as the first civil governor of the Philippines. The administration of the Philippines was divided into four departments that were headed by the members of the Schurman and Taft Commissions: the department of the interior under Worcester; the department of commerce and police under Wright; and the department of public instruction under Moses. In his inaugural address as civil governor to the Philippine Assembly in 1901, Taft stated the goal of the United States: to educate "a people untutored in the methods of free and honest government...."[156] In his reflections as civil governor during a lecture at Yale University in 1906, Taft reiterated that the Filipinos were not ready for independence because they had not been fully trained in the Anglo-Saxon ideals of self-government, heavily underscoring the difference between American and Philippine citizenship and how the Filipino people were not ready to exercise the same constitutional privileges granted to American citizenship.[157]

While grand rhetoric on the "White Man's Burden" was one thing, delivering on the promises of the American government and Anglo-Saxon civilization was another. In implementing its colonial policy, the United States sought to provide law and order for the Philippines, as well as the material benefits of American rule in the form of infrastructure such as roads, sewers, water supply, hospitals, parks, and schools.[158] Nowhere was the inculcation of American Anglo-Saxon values more crucial than in the schools. The goal of the Taft Commission was to provide a public and secular educational system that would teach the arts of civilization to the great majority of the population.[159] In his report to the Taft Commission, David P. Barrows, Superintendent of Education, expressed his concern that limiting education to the children of the elite, at the expense of the children of the peasants, would result in their exploitation because they would not learn the values of self-government and democracy.[160] His aim was to destroy the hold of the landed elite upon the peasantry, and through education create a new class of independent yeoman farmers who would own their own land, setting the foundation for a society based on Anglo-Saxon ideals of liberty and self-government.[161] The Taft Commission recommended that Filipino teachers who were cooperative with the American authorities and who showed an inclination for learning English be trained in the United States where they could be taught the arts of civilization by example.[162] To that end, the Taft Commission ordered that English would be the language of instruction in the schools, rather than the local dialects, with the reasoning that "There is no great advantage in learning to read in a language which offers nothing worth reading to those who have acquired the art.... The limits of the province remain their horizon. They are shut out from the advantages enjoyed by their fellow-countrymen who have had the means to enable them to acquire a language through which may be derived a knowledge of civilized society."[163]

With the establishment of the civil government, the United States commenced its cooperation with the Filipino elite. The elite class that existed in the Philippines owed its origins to Spanish colonialism. When the Spanish first colonized the land that would become the Philippines, they worked with the existing *datus*, or chieftains. By the nineteenth century, this class expanded into the *ilustrado* elite of *mestizos* who had a mixture of either Spanish or Chinese origin. Under Spanish colonial rule, this class of landowners and professionals, many of whom were educated in Europe, gained experience in local politics, but their ambitions for a greater role in governing the Philippines were thwarted by Spain. During the 1890s, a movement for reforms within the colonial government grew among the *ilustrados,* led most notably by José Rizal, but the movement was reluctant to advocate for violent revolution out of fear of unleashing a popular uprising with unpredictable consequences. Nevertheless, as the Philippines became embroiled in the Spanish–American War, the *ilustrados* stood as a natural ruling class that claimed to speak for the Filipino people.[164]

The United States ensured the primacy of the elite through the creation of the Philippine Civil Service. The members of the Taft Commission had hoped that the creation of a civil service in 1901 would eliminate corruption and establish an efficient colonial structure.[165] Through the *pensionado* system, starting in 1903, children from elite families would spend some time in the United States to study and become acculturated to American values; they would then return to the Philippines to take up their posts in the Philippine Civil Service.[166] However, despite the good intentions of the program, the opposite proved to be true. Corruption became rampant in all areas of government as networks of patrons and clients emerged, whereby political bosses handed out offices to their supporters. The vicissitudes of American politics also accelerated the pace at which corruption developed when autonomy was gradually handed over to Manila. Thus in a twist of irony, in its colonial experience, the United States failed its all-important mission: to teach the values of self-government and democracy.[167]

The Boer War: A Crisis in Anglo-Saxonism and the Anglo-American Rapprochement

The *rapprochement* between the United States and the British Empire during the 1890s was interrupted by unraveling events in South Africa, namely the Boer War, which created a crisis among the adherents of Anglo-Saxonism in both countries. Unlike other colonial wars in Africa and Asia, the Boer War was not between European and non-European peoples, but rather two groups of Europeans, the British and the Boers, largely descendants of Dutch settlers who migrated to what is now South Africa during the seventeenth century. The war became a crisis that could have undone the Anglo-American *rapprochement* because the Boers were culturally and linguistically related to the British and Americans. American public opinion empathized with the Boers, who had traveled across the seas and were fighting for their independence against the British, just as the colonists had in the American Revolution. For Anglo-Saxonists, the Boers epitomized the ideals of Anglo-Saxonism by having conquered a wilderness and "inferior peoples"; they also had established a community based on self-government and were fighting to preserve their liberties. These inconsistencies in the narrative of late nineteenth-century Anglo-Saxonism became difficult to reconcile.[168]

The causes of the Boer War originated in 1795 when Britain gained control of Cape Colony (present-day South Africa) from the Dutch Republic during the Napoleonic Wars. The "Boers," however, did not wish to live under British rule. In addition to differences in language and culture, the issue of slavery became the last straw for the Boers, who depended on African slave labor, as the British government abolished the slave trade in 1807 and, in 1833, all slavery in the British Empire.[169] During the 1830s, a few thousand Boers made the "Great Trek" and left Cape Colony and settled in lands along the Vaal and Orange rivers, beyond British jurisdiction, in order to escape further meddling. In 1852, the Sand River Convention established the Transvaal, or the South African Republic, which was recognized by Great Britain. In 1854, Britain recognized the independence of the Orange Free State.[170]

It was not until the 1860s that the British government paid any attention to the Boer republics. Starting with the discovery of diamonds in the 1860s and gold in the 1890s, the Boer republics suddenly became an issue for concern. Overnight, the once thinly-settled Transvaal and Orange Free State became overrun by mainly British prospectors, who were seeking to make their fortunes. The Boer governments, however, resented the presence of the *Uitlanders* (foreigners), who they felt were part of a plot by the British to conquer them; conversely, the miners believed they were not given their rights, such as citizenship and voting, and felt that the government was not responsive to their needs, including sanitation, police, and infrastructure.[171] Tensions exploded in December 1895 during the Jameson Raid, when *Uitlanders* led by Dr. Leander Starr Jameson, an administrator of the British colony of Southern Rhodesia, staged an uprising to overthrow the government of Transvaal under the guise of "liberty." The raid was suppressed in January 1896 by the Transvaal President Paul Kruger. The Jameson Raid confirmed Boer suspicions that Britain sought to add Transvaal and the Orange Free State to its empire, despite protests by the British government condemning the raid. Intransigence on both

III. Anglo-Saxonism in the Foreign Policy Establishment 111

sides ultimately led to the outbreak of hostilities between Britain and the Boer republics.[172]

The Boer War broke out in 1899, a year after the Spanish–American War and the same year as the Samoa Crisis. The conflict was no longer limited to the British and the Boer republics, for it also had international ramifications. Germany also became drawn into the colonial conflict between Great Britain and the Boer republics. Despite Bismarck's reluctance, powerful lobbying groups pressed for German colonial expansion in Africa in the years following unification in 1871 in order to enhance Germany's standing among the European powers. Ernst von Weber, a proponent of German colonial expansion, argued for intervention in the Boer conflict as part of a strategy allowing Germany to expand into southern Africa with the Boer republics serving as an agricultural base. He also argued that the Boer and the German peoples were part of a larger Teutonic family who had a mutual interest in repelling the English invaders.[173] After Bismarck's retirement in 1890, Kaiser Wilhelm II adopted a more active foreign policy with the goal of aggrandizing Germany's international position. In the aftermath of the Jameson raid, Wilhelm II sent a telegram to President Paul Kruger of Transvaal congratulating him for resisting foreign encroachment of his territory, a move that aroused the anger of the British government, which saw Wilhelm II interfering in a purely colonial affair.[174] For the British government, the Boer conflict had the potential to expand into an international conflict and was symptomatic of the reality that the "splendid isolation" enjoyed by Britain for much of the nineteenth century could no longer be sustained with the rise of Germany, Russia, Japan, and the United States as challengers to its supremacy.[175]

The Boer War had direct consequences for the United States. By the late nineteenth century, South Africa had great economic potential. The discovery of gold showed Americans that South Africa was a potential market for American products, for both white and black consumers. It was therefore in the interest of American policy makers that Great Britain be successful in establishing its dominance over the Boers. South Africa under direct British rule would be profitable for many reasons. The British government would open South Africa to American trade and investment, which the agrarian Boer governments strongly opposed. Anglo-Saxonists in the American foreign policy establishment naturally expected direct British rule over South Africa to be more efficient than that of the Boers. More importantly, since the British would impose English as the primary language of South Africa, American companies would have a far greater advantage than that of other European continental powers, especially Germany.[176]

Reaction to the conflict between the Boers and the British government was divided in all levels of American society. A significant proportion of the U.S. Senate was sympathetic to the Boer struggle. Senator A. O. Bacon of Georgia, a Democrat, compared the Boer conflict to previous nationalist movements of the nineteenth century, of peoples struggling for liberty against powerful empires. He used examples such as the Greek War of Independence against the Ottoman Empire during the 1820s and the Hungarian Uprising against the Austrian Empire in 1848, and he cited the precedent of the United States stating its moral support in those struggles. Thus, he argued, that expressing support for nationalist movements was not the same as a "foreign entanglement" in those struggles themselves.[177] Significant sectors of the American public were also sympathetic to the Boers, most notably Americans of Irish, German, or Dutch descent. Theodore Roosevelt, due to his Dutch ancestry, saw much to be admired in the Boers, who he suggested were an embodiment of Anglo-Saxonism:

> The Boers are belated Cromwellians with many fine traits. They deeply and earnestly believe in their cause, and they attract the sympathy which always goes to the small nation…. The Boers are marvelous fighters, and the change in the conditions of warfare during the past forty years has been such as to give peculiar play to their qualities…. In our congested city life of today the military qualities cannot flourish as in a mounted pastoral population, where every male is accustomed to bearing arms, and, what is quite as important, is accustomed from his youth to act under a rough but effective military organization.[178]

The "yellow journalists" Hearst and Pulitzer printed articles that were favorable to the Boers. So it was no stretch of the imagination for average Americans to equate the Boer conflict with the American Revolution. Prominent Americans, including former President Benjamin Harrison, industrialist Andrew Carnegie, the German-American politician Carl Schurz, philosopher Henry Adams, and the lawyer Clarence Darrow, all voiced their support for the Boers.[179] The Boer republican governments, who were familiar with the sympathies of American public opinion toward their plight, sought to court American foreign policy makers and transfer their support from the British. In 1900, a Boer delegation came to the United States to rally Boer support in Washington. However, division among the pro–Boer organizations and the entrenched anglophilia brought upon by the Anglo-American *rapprochement* rendered this mission a failure.[180]

The foreign policy makers in the United States were placed in a delicate position. The Boer War broke out amidst the *rapprochement* between the United States and Great Britain, as both powers were in the midst of negotiating their final outstanding disputes in the Western Hemisphere, namely the Alaska Boundary Dispute and the renegotiation of the Clayton-Bulwer Treaty; the British government had gone to great lengths to ensure American neutrality by making significant concessions in these disputes and essentially handing control of the Western Hemisphere to the United States.[181] So despite the sentimental rhetoric, the foreign policy establishment, particularly John Hay and Theodore Roosevelt, sided with Great Britain, since a British victory would be more beneficial to American long-term economic interests in South Africa. During the conflict, American trade between with South Africa and Great Britain increased, as exports grew from $16 million in 1899 to $20 million in 1900, which included sales of boots, gunpowder, and firearms.[182] The response of the United States to the Boer conflict resembled that of Great Britain during the Spanish–American War. During the Spanish–American War, the continental powers, particularly, Germany, showed sympathy with Spain, yet Great Britain, in spite of its official neutrality, gave much moral and material support to the United States. In the Boer War, it was the United States that sided with Great Britain, despite opposition from the other European powers.[183]

The Boer War was a challenge for the proponents of Anglo-Saxonism. Unlike other previous colonial conflicts, the Boer war did not involve Africans, but rather a people of European descent, specifically Dutch descent, who were ethnically and linguistically akin to the English-speaking peoples. Theodore Roosevelt expressed his ambivalence in a letter to an Australian on March 9, 1900. He expressed his affinity with the Boers because of his Dutch descent, and he considered it a tragedy that there should be conflict between the British and the Boers. However, Roosevelt cast his loyalty with the English-speaking peoples. Roosevelt concluded, therefore, that the ultimate destiny of the Boers lay with Great Britain, and that the greatest benefit for Africa would be a union of the British and Boer peoples, similar to the mixture of Dutch and English in the United States, or of the Irish and English in Australia.[184]

Anglo-Saxonists who opposed Britain's actions saw the Boers as another branch of Anglo-Saxons in South Africa. In this narrative, like their cousins in Great Britain and the United States, the Boers had left their ancestral homeland in the Netherlands for Africa, where they tamed the wilderness and carved out their farms and homes, later establishing their own free societies that became the Boer republics of the Transvaal and the Orange Free State.¹⁸⁵ In an article of the *North American Review*, Dr. F. V. Engelenburg, the editor of the *Pretoria Volkstem*, delivered the case of the Boer peoples. His article read like an Anglo-Saxon narrative, of a people who had traveled across the seas to settle in a wilderness and create a thriving society. He described South Africa, when the first Europeans arrived in the seventeenth century, as "a poor country" with scant rainfall and periodic plagues of locusts and other insects that was devoid of natural amenities, such as navigable rivers and harbors. However, despite such disadvantages, Engelenburg noted that the Boer had been able to survive and would continue to survive long after the gold and diamond mines had been exhausted.¹⁸⁶

Engelenburg described the relationship between the British and the Boer peoples as one of continual encroachment by the British, with the Boers desperately clinging to their way of life. He also turned the narrative of Anglo-Saxonism against the British, painting them as an effete people who thrived on luxury and gave up at the first sign of hardship and instead casting the Boers as a hardy people, capable of self-government and fortitude. Engelenburg vividly described:

> This population is dependent on the outside world, not merely for the products of technical industry, but also for those of agriculture.... Every week sees numerous steamers arriving from all parts of the world, laden with every conceivable kind of goods, to supply the limited South African community with many necessaries of life. Should this means of supply ever be cut off, a large portion of our white and other population would simply starve, or at any rate be deprived of the comforts of life. Only the Boers, who eke out a frugal existence on their secluded farms, and have not yet become dependent on frozen meat, European butter, American meal and Australian potatoes? Only the Boers, who, with rare endurance, the heritage of their hardy race, boldly face years of drought, rinder pest, locusts and fever, could survive such a collapse of the economic machinery of a country so severely dealt with by nature. The remaining Europeans would gradually disappear, just as the Phoenicians and the Arabs disappeared in the days long past.¹⁸⁷

Another way Engelenburg contrasted his people to the *Uitlander* was to cast the Boers as farmers, while the British miners and capitalists were those who had no desire other than to plunder and enrich themselves. Engelenburg used biblical analogy to describe the Boers of the inland areas as agriculturalists who "work by the sweat of his brow," watering their fields against odds from locusts to Hottentots, who would ultimately save civilization. On the other hand, he described those who lived along the Cape of Good Hope individuals who amassed their fortunes through trade with India and who lived in luxurious ease.¹⁸⁸ Ultimately, Engelenburg blamed the interference of the British administrators in the Cape

III. Anglo-Saxonism in the Foreign Policy Establishment

Colony for the cause of the conflict. He stated that the conflict arose from the gradual infringement of the rights of the Boers through "negrophilistic" policies regarding the treatment of African slave labor; the imposition of the English, rather than the Dutch, in the courts and bureaucracy; British attempts to annex the Boer republics; and the dominance of British speculators, whom he regarded as alien to the Boer agricultural way of life and "unworthy of the Anglo-Saxon nation."[189]

The Boer War thus exposed a vulnerability in relations between Great Britain and the United States that the *rapprochement* of the 1890s had not completely eradicated, namely American anglophobia. Memories from the American Revolution and the War of 1812 continued to be evoked every Fourth of July, and these memories were thus exploited by politicians who did not support the growing closeness between Great Britain and the United States. The Anti-Imperialist movement conflated both the Boer War and the Philippine Insurrection, exposing the inconsistencies of Anglo-Saxonism by showing that it was unethical for a free people to impose their will upon alien peoples, which was supposed to be the very antithesis of the principles of Anglo-Saxonism.[190] Senator Augustus Bacon from Georgia, who was not among those caught up in the fever of Anglophilia, surmised British colonialism thusly when he wrote, "…only with the sword and the gun can millions of the semi-civilized be kept in subjection" as a lesson for the United States, which was contemplating following Britain's example.[191]

An example that expressed the ambivalence of many Americans regarding the Boer War was a work called *Between Briton and Boer* by Edward Stratemeyer, who would later be known for *The Hardy Boys'* mysteries under the pseudonym Franklin Dixon. *Between Briton and Boer* was written as a boys' adventure, which was a popular genre in the late nineteenth and early twentieth centuries. The construction of the story is itself a reflection of Anglo-Saxonism, as well as an allegory of the Boer War. The story begins with two English brothers, Martin and Ralph Nelson, who part ways. Martin settles in a ranch in Texas, while Ralph establishes his ranch in South Africa.[192] The brothers' two sons, Dave, the American, and Will, the Briton, finally meet as circumstances force Martin to leave Texas for South Africa: much of the story shows how Dave and Will's instant friendship blooms and details their adventures that follow due to their common English forebears.[193] When the Boer War breaks out in South Africa, Will, despite having been born in South Africa, automatically declares his loyalty to Britain and is confident of the outcome, while Dave shows some skepticism.[194] The following conversation between Will and Dave encapsulates American ambivalence toward the Boer War:

> "Pooh, Dave, you don't imagine [the Boers] can whip us?," demanded his cousin.
> "Certainly not—if England sends out a big enough army; but [the Boers] must be fighting with a lot of pluck."
> "I dare say they are—since their homes are here; but this war won't last—take my word for it."
> "I think it will last a good bit longer than many suppose. Unless I am mistaken, the Boers will fight to the last ditch. They are sure that they are in the right and that God is with them."
> "And we are sure they are wrong—and there you are."
> "Yes there you are, Will; but that doesn't settle the matter."
> "No, that must settle itself, if you are going to put it that way." The English lad looked at his American cousin questioningly. "Dave Nelson, I believe you about half side with the Boers."
> "I don't deny it Will, for they are fighting for what they consider their natural right—Liberty. You must remember that we Americans fought for the same thing during the Revolution. For myself, I am sorry this matter wasn't patched up without an appeal to arms."[195]

The story expresses the tensions of the meaning of the war. For the British, as expressed by Will, the war is clearly about establishing the authority of the British Empire in the African Veldt, regardless of the intransigence of the Boers. The Boers were cast as the villains in the story, for not having the foresight to understand the benefits of British rule, and they viewed the Americans with suspicion due to their closeness with England. In a conversation with Boer soldiers, for instance, Dave is astounded at their insistence on defending their lands and their conviction that God was on their side. For Dave, however, he is able to empathize with the Boers because of the similar struggles of the Thirteen Colonies who fought against British oppression.[196] In a sense, the Boer War was not so much a colonial war but rather a civil war within the Anglo-Saxon family because issues central to Anglo-Saxonism were at stake: the desire to rule one's self and to defend one's home from tyranny and despotism.[197]

By the late nineteenth century, Anglo-Saxonism had become an ideology among the American foreign policy elite. Proponents of Anglo-Saxonism were convinced that the United States had to fulfill its destiny and take its place among the European powers. Additionally, because of the social Darwinist element of Anglo-Saxonism, the United States had to compete for markets and resources among the other powers in order to survive. Additionally, the foreign policy makers in Washington justified the surge of American imperialism with the argument of spreading the ideals of self-government inherent in Anglo-Saxonism. These can be seen in the guidelines for naval power, as outlined by Alfred Thayer Mahan, and the examples of American dominance in Latin America and colonial rule in the Philippines. The Anglo-American *rapprochement* of the late nineteenth and early twentieth century showed a way in which the United States and Great Britain could merge their own respective interests. The Boer War presented a unique challenge to Anglo-Saxonism. The belligerents, the British and the Boers, were similar not simply because of their ethnic and linguistic makeup. Like the British people, the Boers also believed in self-rule, which they accomplished by trekking across the veldt to establish their own societies. When their societies were infringed by a distant government, they fought back to preserve their own way of life. American foreign policy makers found themselves in a dilemma because they were torn between their growing friendship with Great Britain—which justified its actions by arguing it was spreading "civilization"—but sympathized with the struggles with the Boers, struggles that were similar to the ideals of the American Revolution. Ultimately, economic and geopolitical interests would prevail over sentiment.

CHAPTER IV

Anglo-Saxonism in the First World War

In August 1914, the outbreak of hostilities between the Entente and Central Powers, the United States automatically declared its neutrality in keeping with the traditional policy of staying out of European wars, which the American people saw as the usual "family quarrels" among the crowned heads of Europe. However, in sentiment, President Woodrow Wilson and his cabinet, with the exception of Secretary of State William Jennings Bryan, were on the side of the Allies, most notably the British government, due to the close ties that had been cultivated twenty years earlier in the *rapprochement* between both countries. Even in a private capacity, the United States provided significant financial and material assistance to the Allied powers throughout the war, much to the consternation of the German government. In addition to the traditional aversion to European wars over the balance of power, any further involvement by the United States would not have been realistic at the beginning of the war due to the high proportions of Americans of German and Irish descent, who, in many cases, still retained close ties with their respective homelands, neither of which were particularly friendly to Great Britain.

In order to sway public opinion effectively to the Allied cause, Anglo-Saxonism was once again reinterpreted to suit the *zeitgeist* of the First World War. As had been shown previously, Anglo-Saxonism had been slowly evolving to suit the needs of the time, which served as a source of shared identity for the English-speaking peoples, by appropriating certain values such as virtue, self-reliance, and "self-government." By the turn of the century, Anglo-Saxonism was further cemented with a racial component due to the pseudo-scientific and social Darwinist assumptions of the time. The First World War, however, presented a new dilemma for proponents of Anglo-Saxonism, both in the United States and Great Britain.

IV. Anglo-Saxonism in the First World War

Similar to the conundrum posed by the Boer War over how to place the Dutch settlers within the narrative of Anglo-Saxonism, the issue now was Germany. In the decades before the Great War, Anglo-Saxonists considered the German people to be racially close relatives to the Anglo-Saxon peoples; Germany was even declared to be the primordial birthplace of all Anglo-Saxon peoples, though this came with some reservations, especially with the unification of Germany under Prussian hegemony in 1871. Nonetheless, it became difficult to reconcile the affinity between the German and Anglo-Saxon peoples, an affinity that still held in the United States at the beginning of hostilities, with the idea of a fratricidal war that broke out in 1914.

With the progression of the war, a growing divergence took place within Anglo-Saxonism. As the war became more entrenched, the idea of "Teutonism" developed in the presses of Great Britain and the United States. This idea held that the Germans simply could not be part of the Anglo-Saxon peoples because they had developed into a warlike state and did not adopt self-governing institutions like the representative governments of the Anglo-Saxon peoples of the United States and the British Empire. This was evidenced by the conservative government under the Hohenzollern monarchy, which claimed to rule by divine right and extolled the ideology of Prussian militarism and *"Kultur."* Meanwhile, the ideals of self-government and "civilization" had become ingrained foundations of Anglo-Saxonism in the United States and Great Britain, and these ideals had become exclusively claimed by both English-speaking nations upon the outbreak of the First World War. To push the argument for war among significant Irish- and German-American populations, a steady stream of atrocity stories persuaded the American public to turn against the German government and people. By the time Wilson asked Congress for a declaration of war against Germany, all pretense of the German people's membership in the Anglo-Saxon family was removed due to a propaganda machine that asserted that Germany's development into a warrior state, and its inherent barbarity, made it unsuitable to be among the ranks of the "real" Anglo-Saxons who developed democracy and "civilization." Thus, the ideals of "civilization" and "self-government," which had earlier been monopolized by proponents of Anglo-Saxonism, had become universal values extolled by Wilson as he made the case for war. Once those values became identified with a wider segment of the American people, it then became acceptable to take up arms against Germany.

"War, as Practised by Germany," *Western Mail*, August 21, 1914. This cartoon refers to German atrocities committed at the Belgian town of Linsmeau, which included the bayoneting of infants and wholesale massacres of civilian men and women. Such "atrocity stories" would turn American public opinion against Germany.

American Neutrality

When the guns roared in August 1914 following the July Crisis between Austria and Serbia that flared in the aftermath of Archduke Franz Ferdinand's assassination, all the major European powers were dragged to war and the United States reflexively declared its neutrality. On July 27th, as Austria mobilized against Serbia and British Foreign Secretary Sir Edward Grey proposed a conference to defuse the crisis, Wilson replied that the United States would not take part in events beyond the Western Hemisphere.[1] In a speech on August 19, 1914, Wilson warned the American people against following their passions and taking sides in the European conflict, suggesting that those who incited such passions "will assume a heavy responsibility" for causing divisiveness within American society. He further pleaded this point:

> The United States must be neutral in fact as well as in name during these days that are to try men's souls. We must be impartial in thought as well as in action, must put a curb upon our sentiments as well as upon every transaction that might be construed as a preference of one party to the struggle before another.[2]

To the American people, the outbreak of the Great War was yet another of the constant quarrels among the peoples of Europe, which they and their forebears had sought to escape. Secretary of State William Jennings Bryan reflected his contempt at the actions of the European powers that led to the outbreak of hostilities in August 1914, and his synopsis to Wilson of the July Crisis gave a rather comical tone to the opening of the most devastating war in human history:

> ...Each one declares he is opposed to war and anxious to avoid it and then lays the blame upon someone else. The German Ambassador this morning blamed Russia and congratulates his country that the [German] Emperor did what he could to avoid war. He also commends the efforts of France and Great Britain to avoid war, but the Czar is charged with being the cause, his offense being the mobilization of his army after Austria had assured him that the integrity of [Serbia] would not be disturbed.[3]

Bryan's synopsis appeared to justify the long-standing American policy of staying aloof from the international power politics of European diplomacy. The decades between the end of the Franco-Prussian War in 1870 and August 1914 showed simmering nationalist tensions and the arming of Europe through the growth of alliances, which made difficult any understanding of the causes of the outbreak of war. The "domino effect" of the aftermath of Archduke Franz Ferdinand's assassination exposed the inherent weakness of the European alliance system, of which that Bryan appeared to be glad that the United States was not a part.[4]

In the early stages of the war, American opinion was still even-handed toward the German government and people, owing to the late nineteenth century association of the Germans as closely related to the Anglo-Saxon peoples. An editorial in *The Independent* compared the justifications used by both Great Britain and Germany in waging war. The article made references to America's cultural debt to Germany, as it weighed the German government's appeal for the sympathy of the American people, which drew on shared Teutonic affinities, in justifying its war against Russia, described by German Chancellor Bethman-Hollweg as "a half-Asiatic and semi-civilized barbarism." Though the editorial ultimately sided with Great Britain, it still considered Germany a "good and powerful friend."[5] Theodore Roosevelt's book *America and the World War*, a critique on the Wilson administration's policy of neutrality, published in 1915 is another

"A Despicable Beggar," *Western Mail*, August 27, 1914. The United States declared its neutrality at the outset of the Great War. In this cartoon, Kaiser Wilhelm II tries to elicit the sympathies of the American people by sending Count Bernstorff, despite reports of German atrocities in Belgium.

such example. Rather than blaming Germany for starting the Great War, as the Treaty of Versailles would do in 1919, Roosevelt placed the blame squarely on the Serbian government for allowing secret societies to carry out the assassination of Franz Ferdinand on the basis of nationalist irredentism, setting off the cataclysm that would engulf the major European powers.[6] Of the German people, and particularly Kaiser Wilhelm II, Roosevelt considered them just and honorable, and he condemned the notion that Germany was inherently evil.[7] Quite the contrary, Roosevelt saw calls for the destruction of Germany as a grave mistake, and he again drew upon the similarities between the American and German peoples, alluding to the Teutonic school of Anglo-Saxonism from the late nineteenth century:

> The Germans are not merely brothers; they are largely ourselves. The debt we owe to German blood is great; the debt we owe to German thought and to German

example, not only in governmental administration but in all the practical work of life is even greater. Every generous heart and every far-seeing mind throughout the world should rejoice in the existence of a stable, united, and powerful Germany, too strong to fear aggression and too just to be a source of fear to its neighbors.[8]

Roosevelt reiterated his regard for Germany in a letter to Edmund Robert Otto von Mach, a German-born Harvard graduate and art historian, who wrote a series of books defending Germany's reasons for war, by declaring that it is from Germany that "the United States has most to learn." Roosevelt reassured von Mach that, even though he condemned Germany's actions against Belgium, he did not have any personal animosity toward the German people. Roosevelt indirectly reaffirmed Germany's ties to the Anglo-Saxon peoples by saying that "if Mexico governed herself as well as Canada, she would not have any more to fear from us than has Canada," referring to the political instability in Mexico due to the revolution sparked in 1910. Roosevelt believed that the German people, through their ties with the Anglo-Saxon peoples, also represented civilization and good government, which he hoped that countries like Cuba and the Philippines would attain under American tutelage. He concluded his letter by saying that it would be "a world calamity if the German Empire were shattered or dismembered."[9]

Nevertheless, Roosevelt faulted the German government for its violation of Belgium's neutrality, insofar as it was a part of policy and not out of pure malice, while again stressing his Germanic ancestry and his affinity with the German people.[10] In a letter to British historian Arthur Hamilton Lee two weeks after the outbreak of the Great War, Roosevelt reiterated his respect for Germany and acknowledged the German people's contribution to American society, as well as referencing his own Germanic ancestry. However, in the letter, Roosevelt had already begun to distance himself from the government of Kaiser Wilhelm II; this distance portended the ultimate separation between the Anglo-Saxon and Teutonic peoples, which Roosevelt believed contributed to the igniting of the conflict:

> ...the Government of Prussianized Germany for the last forty-three years has behaved in such fashion as inevitably to make almost every nation with which it came in to act its foe, because it has convinced everybody except Austria that it has no regard for anything except its own interest, and that it will enter instantly on any career of aggression with cynical brutality and bad faith if it thinks its interest requires such action.[11]

However, regarding the conduct of the British, Roosevelt praised the government's decision to come to the aid of the Belgian people, which he held up in order to shame the Wilson administration for what he saw as a lack of action.[12] Roosevelt's letter to Lee condemned the violation of Belgian neutrality and squarely placed the blame on Germany, writing, "...I do not know whether I would be acting right if I were president or not, but it seems to me that if I were President, I should register a very emphatic protest, a protest that would mean something, against the levy of the huge war contributions on Belgium."[13] Roosevelt made note of the motives of the British people, including the dominions of Australia, Canada, and South Africa, who became involved to protect civilization and liberty, ideals appropriated as the hallmarks of Anglo-Saxonism, foreshadowing the anti-German sentiment that would emerge in the later years of the war.[14]

Additionally, Americans in 1914 generally had a parochial view of the world, which added to their contempt of European power politics.

"A Crime Unmatchable," *Western Mail*, December 24, 1914. This cartoon refers to German atrocities committed during its occupation of Belgium. The lines come from a scene in William Shakespeare's play *King John*. The author ties the death of the character in the play, Prince Arthur, with the "rape of Belgium" and the solidarity of the Allied nations: Britain, France, and Russia.

The British journalist Sydney Brooks, in his analysis of American public opinion during the first year of the war, criticized the lack of interest by Americans in the cataclysm unfolding across the Atlantic, despite the direct effects it had on American trade, such as the loss of trade revenue, unemployment, and contraction of the economy.[15] Because of the unique position of the United States in the international stage due to its long-standing aversion to European conflicts, Brooks believed that that position made the United States an "impartial" observer to whom the Allies and the Central Powers could present their case, based on the assumptions that American public opinion would not support a war that was not just; also, American economic assistance in the event of war would tilt the balance.[16] Brooks's observation of the results of the 1914 midterm election, which was generally a Republican victory, reinforced the belief that Americans were far more interested in domestic affairs, such as the reduction of the tariff, with none of the candidates discussing the European war at length.[17] Brooks best explained American attitudes by reminding his British audience of the following:

> American foreign policy, therefore, so far as it is concerned with the affairs of Europe and Asia, proceeds without any reasoned and consistent backing of popular knowledge or interest, and very largely, in consequence, turns on the personality and opinions of particular Presidents or particular Secretaries of State. It is altogether natural that this should be so. The United States is remote, unconquerable, huge, without hostile neighbors or any neighbors at all of anything like her own strength, and lives exempt in an almost unvexed tranquility from the contentions and animosities and the ceaseless pressure and counter-pressure that distract the close-packed older world. Inevitably, therefore, a sober, sustained, and well-informed interest in foreign affairs is a luxury with which the ordinary American citizen feels he can dispense.[18]

Despite this lament over American insularity, Brooks concluded his article by highlighting the fact that the majority of the American public remained sympathetic to the Allied cause, associating it with "civilization" and democracy. Brooks noted, however, that Prussian militarism was a long-term threat that not even American neutrality could tolerate.[19]

As Ambassador to the United States throughout the First World War, Cecil Spring Rice reported on American public opinion to his superiors at Whitehall, notably Foreign Secretary Sir Edward Grey, as well as friends and family. In a letter to his nephew, Spring Rice gave his appraisal of American society:

> The US has ceased to be a whole—that is, a uniform population moved by feelings of patriotism ... while Germany was gradually getting all the elements in the nation to think alike in national terms [Britain] and the US were encouraging our people

to think only in terms of *personal* not national advantage; we care for the honey, not the hive.[20]

Spring Rice further added in his observations on the regional mindset of Americans:

> For instance, in California there is a complete contempt for the affairs not only of Europe, but of the middle and eastern States. The middle States think in terms of wheat and the southern States in terms of cotton, just as the Welsh miners think in terms of wages. What is a government to do under these circumstances? Just to act as the majority desire, and the majority desire is to make money and not to make war.[21]

Spring Rice was especially concerned about the German government's influence on American public opinion, which encouraged Americans to stay out of the European conflict, and he further worried that the Wilson administration would ultimately be swayed by it. Spring Rice wrote to his colleague, British journalist and diplomat Sir Valentine Chirol, that "Everyone who has had the slightest connection with Germany either in business, science, or literature ... receives special copies of pamphlets and personal appeals signed by distinguished men of letters and scientists."[22] Spring Rice noted that German sympathy was strong in the Midwest, as was anti–British sentiment. He also observed that the German government seemed to have strong connections with Jewish bankers in New York and accused the bankers of collaborating with the Germans before the outbreak of the war. Spring Rice also surmised that even though the Wilson administration was strongly pro–British, it had to tread very carefully to make sure that neutrality was maintained and would not have the appearance of siding with the Allies.[23]

In the aftermath of the sinking of the *Lusitania*, Spring Rice expressed his frustration to his former colleague, Lord Onslow, over the neutrality of the United States through the lens of Anglo-Saxonism, praising the British dominions which rushed to the aid of the mother country, thus criticizing the inaction of Wilson's administration:

> The U.S. was regarded as the eldest child of liberty, the principal incarnation of the Anglo-Saxon idea of independence and self-sufficiency, and of the hostility to outside control. In Australia and Canada, for instance, it was taken for granted that the occupation of Belgium and the triumph of German militarism in Europe would arouse the unanimous condemnation of the American government and people. But the government was silent and inculcated in the people 'neutrality in thought as well as deed'—that is, an absolute complete and systematic indifference to what most people regard as one of the greatest crimes in history.... England now, and not the U.S., is fighting for the cause of liberty and the U.S. and not England is holding aloof. The result is that the natural hegemony of the free

English-speaking world falls to England and the free colonies are fighting on her side as bound together in the common cause of freedom.²⁴

For many Americans, the First World War was just another "family squabble" among the monarchs of Europe, and it was in the national interest of the United States to distance itself as much as possible, just as it had sought to do during the Napoleonic Wars a century earlier, putting it in a position to conduct trade with belligerents on both sides.²⁵ Wilson best expressed that hope in a speech he gave in the first weeks of the war. He noted the diversity of the American people, many of whom originated from the nations involved in the Great War. However, Wilson believed that "the people of the United States, whose love of their country and whose loyalty to its Government should unite them as Americans all...,"

"The Power of the Mighty Dollar," *Western Mail*, January 7, 1915. Theodore Roosevelt was the most vocal critic of Woodrow Wilson's policy of neutrality. In this cartoon, the United States shows no emotion to the various atrocities committed during Germany's occupation of Belgium. However, it is only when the British blockade begins to interfere with American trade that the United States government protests.

and he foresaw such a nation would be in the best position to mediate peace in Europe, with his exhortation to the American people to "be neutral in fact as well as in name...."[26]

Nevertheless, Wilson's neutrality policy was criticized for its inconsistency. From the outbreak of the war, Senator Henry Cabot Lodge clearly supported the Allies and believed that it was in the interest of the United States for the Allies to defeat Germany, which contrasted Wilson's position that the United States should not have a stake in either side, so that he could appear as a more impartial mediator.[27] Lodge and Theodore Roosevelt found it ironic that Wilson should protest British violation of neutrality rights, while being silent on other issues regarding the war, such as Germany's violation of Belgian neutrality, the encroachment of Chinese sovereignty by Great Britain and Japan, and the violation of the Hague Conventions, which seemed to undermine his role as the mediator between the Allies and the Central Powers.[28]

"A Whiff of the Kaiser's Gas," *Western Mail*, July 13, 1915. Brother Jonathan, the symbol of the United States, tries to protect himself from German propaganda while maintaining neutrality. Even though other countries had used poison gas, Germany used massive amounts of it at the Second Battle of Ypres on April 22, 1915, which was forbidden by the Hague Convention in 1907.

During his brief tenure as Secretary of State, William Jennings Bryan's main priority was to maintain the neutrality of the United States. If the United States was to have a role at all in the Great War, it was to play the role of mediator to stop the carnage. Wilson offered to be the mediator between the Allies and Central Powers at the inception of hostilities, based on the argument that the United States, as a major neutral power, would have the credibility to broker a settlement that would be equitable to the belligerent powers.[29] In the first months of the war, Bryan strenuously advocated for a mediator's role for the United States. In a letter to Wilson on December 1, 1914, he laid out the arguments for mediation. Firstly, he argued that the war was having a negative impact on the economy through the disruption of trade with Europe. Secondly, he believed that the United States could take a leadership role among the neutral powers that were also suffering from the effects of the conflict between the Allies and the Central Powers. He stated succinctly that, "other neutral nations are complaining of the act of belligerents in interfering with neutral commerce—the friction and irritation are increasing. These neutral nations look to us to represent the third party—'the bystanders' who, though innocent, suffer while the combatants fight."[30]

William Jennings Bryan vs. Robert Lansing

During the first year of the war, there were two men who competed for Wilson's attention regarding the war in Europe: Secretary of State William Jennings Bryan and State Department Counselor Robert Lansing, who would succeed Bryan as secretary of state on June 8, 1915. The competition between Bryan and Lansing reflected the evolving policy of the United States throughout the war and the changing nature of Anglo-Saxonism that would ultimately lead to the entry of the United States into the conflict in 1917. While Bryan wanted to remain strictly wedded to the principles of neutrality, Lansing believed that an armed confrontation with Germany was inevitable because a German victory would be opposed to the interests of the Anglo-Saxon powers. Lansing believed in Anglo-Saxonism, itself, feeling that the principles of "civilization" and "self-government" were associated only with the Anglo-Saxon peoples, which behooved the United States to side with Great Britain.

These two men's differing backgrounds and philosophies influenced the policy directions of the United States, from the strict neutrality declared in 1914 to the declaration of war against Germany in 1917. Bryan, best known for his "Cross of Gold" speech as the Populist Party candidate, was chosen by Wilson as Secretary of State for his large following among ordinary Americans. Unlike many secretaries of state before or since, Bryan took pride in his simplicity, a contrast with the refined Washington establishment.[31] His Christian beliefs were adamantly manifested in how he conducted American foreign policy between 1913 and 1915. Bryan saw war as an abomination upon Christian civilization and therefore sought to prevent it as much as possible through arbitration. As early as 1905 during the Russo-Japanese War, Bryan proposed a treaty in which all international disputes would be settled by an international tribunal. The treaty gained the support of the Inter-parliamentary Union in London in 1906 and the International Peace Conference in New York in 1908, including President William Howard Taft and British Prime Minister Sir Henry Campbell-Bannerman. Bryan continued to push his proposal after his appointment as Secretary of State in 1913 by gaining international support; by September 1914, only Germany, Austria-Hungary, and Italy were not signatories.[32]

Lansing, however, was the complete opposite of Bryan. While Bryan was known as the "Great Commoner," Lansing came from a distinguished New York family and had training in international law. He had traveled abroad in his youth and had practical experience in settling international agreements. Among those agreements were the Bering Sea Claims Commission in 1896, the 1903 Alaska Boundary Tribunal, the North Atlantic Fisheries Arbitration from 1908–1910, and the North Atlantic Fisheries and Fur Seals Conference in 1911.[33] On 27 March 1914, Lansing was appointed Counselor to the State Department, making him second only to the Secretary of State. This position gave Lansing an opportunity to take part in the decision-making process. Lansing's extensive experience in international law complemented Bryan's inexperience; at times, Lansing would fill in when Bryan was away on his lecture circuits.[34] Unlike Bryan, Lansing was a realist in international affairs. Even though he believed in the principles of democracy and was devout in his Presbyterian faith, Lansing held no illusions about the perfectibility of humanity and understood that conflict was part of the interactions among nations; Lansing felt that to rely on naiveté was detrimental in conducting foreign policy. Instead, he wanted to temper the innate idealism of the American worldview with pragmatism in foreign policy.[35]

Unlike Bryan, Lansing was sympathetic to the Allied cause, particularly that of the British, from the outset of hostilities in 1914. As part of the WASP elite, Lansing's support was echoed by others in the foreign policy establishment. Lansing reflected in his memoirs that, despite the *rapprochement* between Britain and the United States in the previous two decades before the war, public opinion, buttressed by teachings in the public school system, held the British to be a "hereditary foe" to the American people: such "prejudice" against the British Empire had prevented earlier interventions in the war. Additionally, he noted that a significant proportion of Americans who opposed the entry of the United States into the conflict were naturalized citizens of German and Austrian descent, as well as Americans of Irish descent, who despaired of British–oppression of Ireland. Lansing was especially suspicious of German-language newspapers that supported Germany's cause and criticized Allied war policy, particularly the British blockade of Germany, but expressed his indigna-

"Bombarding the World," *Western Mail*, November 3, 1914. Germany wages a propaganda war, according to this cartoon, by bombarding the world with blatantly false information in order to deflect criticism of atrocities committed in its occupation of Belgium. It is worth noting that the Allies also disseminated their own propaganda.

tion when these newspapers were also under the employ of the German government, with the purpose of disseminating propaganda for the Central Powers.[36]

For example, in a memorandum to Wilson on December 9, 1914, Lansing denounced a letter written by German psychologist Hugo Munsterberg, which objected to the preferential treatment given by the Wilson administration to the Allies, while German-Americans faced discrimination. Lansing concluded that because Munsterberg was German, he was naturally an agent of the Kaiser on the mission to spread German propaganda throughout the United States, and, further. that their goal was to "separate American citizens of German nativity or descent from the general body of the American people, to impress upon them that they are a distinct group of society ... and to make them feel that they are first of all Germans," and to "use this great body of German origin as a political machine with which to threaten the Administration into showing special favors to Germany and Austria in the performance of the neutral duties of this government."[37] Lansing furthermore dismissed British violations of neutrality as part of the realities of the war, simply because the British navy had command of the seas and Germany did not. Thus, were Germany to have naval superiority, Britain and France would be cut off from world trade.[38]

Lansing often complained that the long-standing animosity against Great Britain, generated from the American Revolution and the War of 1812, was reinforced in history textbooks that continued to engender antagonism among many Americans, which was confirmed by British violations of neutrality rights, notably American shipping. Thus, it became incumbent upon Lansing to influence American public opinion by stressing the dangers of German hegemony, should Germany win the war.[39]

The sinking of the Lusitania was an example of the divide between Bryan and Lansing. Bryan, in a letter to Wilson, was careful to maintain neutrality by condemning British violations of neutrality as well as German submarine warfare. He was also quick to remind Wilson that the *Lusitania* was flagged by the German government as an enemy vessel, and that the Americans on board were traveling at their own risk. He continued to exhort Wilson to play the role of the mediator, pleading as follows:

> As the well-wisher of all we should act; as the leader in the peace propaganda we should act; as the greatest Christian nation we should act—we cannot avoid the responsibility. The loss of one American, who might have avoided death, is as nothing compared with the tens of thousands who are dying daily in this 'causeless war.' Is it not better to try to bring peace for the benefit of the whole world than to risk the provoking of war on account of one man?[40]

Lansing, however, in a letter to Bryan, was quick to condemn the German government for the sinking of the *Lusitania*. He considered the warnings posted by the German government not to travel on British vessels to be insufficient. Rather, Lansing argued, "it is a more flagrant violation of neutral rights on the high seas, and indicates that the German naval policy is one of wanton and indiscriminate destruction of vessels regardless of nationality."[41] Lansing believed that war with Germany was inevitable, if not immediately, then soon after.[42] Lansing's memorandum to Wilson, dated July 11, 1915, regarding the sinking of the *Lusitania* declared that

> ...the German Government is utterly hostile to all nations with democratic institutions because those who compose it see in democracy a menace to absolutism and the defeat of the German ambition for world domination. Everywhere, German agents are plotting and intriguing to accomplish the supreme purpose of their government.[43]

Lansing wanted the United States to take a stronger stance toward Germany in light of the sinking of the *Lusitania*. He demanded that Bryan declare that the sinking of the *Lusitania* by Germany was an "indefensible action," which called for "strict accountability" on part of the German government, and that the United States would take "steps necessary" to safeguard American lives and property.[44] However, Bryan maintained in his letter to Wilson that the *Lusitania* was carrying ammunition valued at $152,400 and argued that "Germany has a right to prevent contraband going to the allies and a ship carrying contraband should not rely upon passengers to protect her from attack—it would be like putting women and children in front of an army."[45]

Whereas Bryan saw the war on moralistic terms, Lansing saw the conflict in terms of the traditional European balance of power and felt it was a redefinition of the ideals of Anglo-Saxonism that placed Germany on the wrong side of history. For Lansing, a German victory would be a threat to the interests of the United States. As events in the late nineteenth century had shown, imperial Germany had expressed a desire to expand its influence in the Pacific and in the Caribbean, areas where the United States had economic and political interests. Lansing's memorandum cited "plots and intrigues" by German agents to undermine American influence in Latin America, such as fomenting anti–Americanism in Mexico, Haiti, and the Dominican Republic.[46] Therefore, to Lansing, Great Britain represented the forces of liberal democracy, while Germany was the incarnation of militarism and autocracy. As the carnage of the Western Front was proof of the stalemate between the Allied and Central Powers, Lansing

"Outside the Pale," *News of the World*, May 16, 1915. Germany, in the form of Kaiser Wilhelm II, is pushed beyond the limits of civilization as a result of the sinking of the *Lusitania*, on May 7, 1915, by a German submarine, which killed over 1,100 civilians, including 128 Americans.

believed that it was just a matter of time before the United States would have to intervene.[47]

Bryan did not share the same view. Unlike Lansing, who wanted to give full support to the Allies, Bryan held to a belief in strict neutrality. On the issue of private banks loaning money to either side, Bryan argued that it would drag the United States into the war, violating its neutrality. As the conflict began, Bryan and Lansing held opposite viewpoints. In a letter to Wilson on August 10, 1914, Bryan noted that Lansing had no problems with the Morgan Company of New York loaning money to the French Government:

> If we approved of a loan to France, we could not, of course, object to a loan to Great Britain, Germany, Russia, Austria, or to any other country, and if loans were made to these countries our citizens would be divided into groups, each group loaning money to the country it favors.... All of this influence would make it all the more difficult for us to main neutrality, as our action on various questions that would arise would affect one side or another and powerful interest would be thrown into the balance.[48]

Lansing had a more pragmatic approach. In a memorandum dated October 23, 1914, he reminded Wilson that the United States owed money to various European countries. He informed Wilson that there had been European demand for American products. He then warned Wilson that not doing business with the belligerent countries would have a disastrous effect on American foreign trade.[49] The issue of Britain's violation of neutral rights was a clear difference between Bryan and Lansing. While Bryan objected strenuously to British violations of neutrality by interfering with the rights of neutral nations to engage in trade during times of war, Lansing, in essence, chose not to pursue the issue with the British government. He based this position on the assumption that it would only be a matter of time before the United States would side with Great Britain and declare war against Germany, which was, to him, the greater threat to international security. Lansing frankly stated that to condemn the British government would have tied the hands of the United States in the eventuality it entered the war, as other neutral nations would accuse the American government of hypocrisy, should the United States also engage in the practice of intercepting neutral shipping. Ultimately, the increasingly pro–Entente stance by Wilson and his cabinet would compel Bryan to resign as secretary of state.[50]

The Role of the American Clergy in the First World War

Aside from the State Department, other institutions came out to support the Britain and the Entente nation and marginalize Germany and the Central Powers well before 1917. The Protestant clergy played a significant role in molding public opinion against Germany by anticipating the arguments of Anglo-Saxonists, who declared the war to be a "just war" for the causes of "civilization" and "self-government." Since the days of the American Revolution, Protestant churches had galvanized Americans using patriotism and nationalism from the pulpit.[51] In their sermons, New England clergymen from varied denominations such as the Congregationalist, Baptist, and Lutheran churches were the most vocal in their support of American independence. Thus, the American Revolution was transcended from a dispute over the taxation to that of a holy struggle between the forces of liberty and tyranny.[52] During the Civil War, both the Union and the Confederacy claimed to have God on their side, as clergy in the North and the South presented arguments for and against secession and the morality of slavery.[53] In the war against Spain in 1898, Protestant clergymen again claimed to have God on their side because the United States was fighting for Cuba's liberty against a Catholic tyrannical Spain.[54] By the early years of the twentieth century, there was a growing peace movement that had ecumenical support among Catholic, Protestant, and Jewish organizations, which sought to persuade nations to abolish the art of war. This movement had the support of prominent people such as William Jennings Bryan and Andrew Carnegie. However, such calls for peace fell on deaf ears in August 1914, when Europe once again marched to war.[55]

American preachers sounded the call for war one again. This time, Germany was cast as a demonic monster that threatened to destroy civilization. This coincided with the "Teutonism" belief that Germany could not be part of the Anglo-Saxon peoples because of their conservatism and militarism. Therefore, the cause of the Entente was a just war because of Germany's invasion of Belgium and the "atrocity stories" that reinforced the alleged barbarities committed by the Germans in the territories that they occupied.[56] In the early years of the war, the peace movement, which had been in vogue in the early twentieth century, was lamented as having been futile in preventing war. The focus, then, was to prepare the United States against a German invasion, out of fear of the repetition of the abuses that were carried out against the Belgians.[57] One such clergyman was the Rev. Dr. Charles Henry Parkhurst, pastor of the Madison Square Church in New York City. He was no ordinary preacher, for his flock consisted of the Manhattan elite, which served as his power base in his forays into politics.[58] As early as August 23, 1914, he placed the sole blame of the war upon Germany, likening Kaiser Wilhelm II to a "rabid dog" and called upon the Entente to

> ...deal with him exactly as Germany dealt with Poland at the time of the partition (even though there was no united Germany during the eighteenth century partitions of Poland) ... deal with him as Germany meant to deal with France in the [Franco-Prussian] war of [1870] when she intended to impose a war indemnity so heavy, and so to cripple her military means of offense and defense s to crush her as a military power and render Germany invulnerable from the aide of France.[59]

As soon as the United States declared war on Germany, almost every Protestant denomination, the Catholic Church, and the Jews preached on the themes of patriotism and that of a "holy war." The United States, in their eyes, was undoubtedly in the right and had God's approval. Those who had previously been pacifists, such as William Jennings Bryan and attorney Clarence Darrow, had been converted to the cause of war.[60] Clergymen, such as Newell Dwight Hillis of the Plymouth Congregational Church organized drives for war bonds and preached that the United States had an obligation to support Britain, "the motherland" and France because of its support during the Revolutionary War against "German invaders."[61]

As the United States became more heavily involved in the war effort, preachers went beyond instilling patriotism, but rather helped fuel a climate of war hysteria. German atrocity stories, depicting German soldiers raping French and Belgian women were repeated in every sermon. The nature of the war changed from a war against Prussian autocracy and absolutism, but to a war against the German people, itself. The Kaiser was not merely a warmonger, but the devil, himself.[62] The result, then, was a virulent strain of hatred and antagonism to the German people and culture, which had hitherto been admired by many Americans. The teaching of the German language in schools was forbidden in fourteen states. States such as Iowa prohibited any public meeting to be conducted in languages other than English. German operas were banned from concert halls.[63] More substantively, clergymen encouraged the formation of vigilante groups that hunted for spies, purportedly to be lurking behind every corner, with the support of government agencies, such as the Bureau of Investigation (the predecessor of the Federal Bureau of Investigation) and the Justice Department, which threatened the very democracy that Wilson promoting when he asked Congress for a declaration of war.[64]

The British and American Propaganda Machines

One cannot discount the impact of newspapers and government propaganda machines in molding American public opinion during the First World War. Before war was declared on April 4, 1917, British propagandists vigorously courted the United States with the purpose of turning the American public against Germany. The British government used censorship to provide American readers with the British perspective of the war. Under the Defense of the Realm Act, the British government had control over "all statements intended or likely to prejudice His Majesty's relations with foreign powers."[65] The British propaganda machine, Wellington House, circulated reports of German atrocities in Belgium. The Central Committee for National Patriotic Organizations published a series of pamphlets written by members of the Oxford Faculty of Modern History titled, *Why We are at War: Great Britain's Case*.[66] While the British and French aimed for American involvement, the Germans aimed for preserving American neutrality. The German government made attempts to refute the charges of barbarism. German propaganda showed pictures of German soldiers feeding Belgian and French children. In the final analysis, however, the Germans proved to be less adept at swaying the American public to support its cause because the British and French were much more effective in provoking American outrage.[67]

The British government succeeded in portraying Germany as a savage nation whose army paid no regard to the rules of warfare. In doing so, it secured America's sympathies. British newspapers had warned the American public in the early stages of the war that the collapse of the British Empire would be detrimental to American interests.[68] Put it simply, the British propaganda machine portrayed the war as simply a crusade, a war of civilization against the forces of darkness. Therefore, the Allies were

"The German Peril," *Western Mail*, August 5, 1915. This cartoon is an update of an 1895 painting by German Hermann Knackfuss, called "The Yellow Peril." Instead of Asia being portrayed as the greatest threat to European civilization, the cartoon shifts the focus on the danger of Germany.

on the side of good. The British propagandists had the fortune of calling upon the cultural similarities between the American and British peoples and marginalizing the Germans as the "other." The German people were often portrayed as "power hungry," "impatient," and unfit for the duties of being a great nation.[69]

In 1915, the British government published the *Report of the Committee on Alleged German Outrages*, more popularly known as the "Bryce Report" because the prominent scholar Lord James Bryce headed it. The report was a collection of German atrocities in Belgium. Upon its publication, the Bryce report incensed the British and American public with horrific tales of German brutality.[70] Brutality committed against children was common throughout the Bryce report. One such account by a Belgian soldier read:

> I was at Hofstadter, the Germans were retreating, and we were advancing near the headquarters of the Gendarmerie. I saw a woman about 45 years old and a boy of about 9 who had been struck with a bayonet several times, both in the face and in the body, both the boy's hands were cut off at the wrist, he was kneeling on the ground, one hand cut off was on the ground, the other hanging by a bit of skin.[71]

A recurring theme in the Bryce Report was the destruction of property by German soldiers. A Belgian professor testified as follows:

> ...All the civilians had fled and the Germans were in possession of the town. I saw some of the soldiers breaking open private houses in the principal square. The whole town was looted ... [The German officer] and his men were lighting matches and setting them to the curtains. The excuse given for this and the burning of the houses was that a German officer of high rank had been killed in the house of the mayor ... [A German soldier] stated that he regretted the kind of warfare that the Germans were carrying on, but said that they had been fired on by civilians and that what they had done was done by orders.[72]

Sexual violence was also prevalent throughout the Bryce report. A Belgian soldier testified to witnessing the corpse of a man with his genitals slashed off and a woman with "clear marks of violation." Such stories titillated, as well as outraged, the British and American public.[73]

The testimonies gathered by the Bryce Report were merely accumulated and not analyzed. Much of the testimonies were incomplete and based on second- and third-hand information. The stories that were printed were based upon the assumption that they were true until proven otherwise.[74] Despite these gaps of credibility, the Bryce Report bore a great deal of credence among the American public. Bryce was an eminent scholar whose work, *The American Commonwealth*, had laid the foundations for Anglo-American friendship in the late nineteenth century. As ambassador to the United States, Bryce had a reputation as a great friend to the United States. It was therefore, not difficult to suspend disbelief and skepticism over the report's description of atrocities committed by the Germans.[75]

American newspapers were all too eager to print German atrocities. The sinking of the *Lusitania* was grist for anti–German propaganda mills. Despite claims by the German government that the ocean liner was carrying arms bound for Britain, the sinking of the *Lusitania* coincided with the publication of the Bryce Report.[76] *The New York Times* reported that the *Lusitania* was unarmed and "defenseless as a ferryboat" and flatly denied that it carried any arms.[77] The deaths of more than 1,000 people, of which 128 were American, earned Germany a new level of infamy because of its use of submarine warfare. In a compilation of editorials by newspapers from all over New York City published on May 8, 1915, *The*

"The Arch-Hypocrite," *Western Mail*, April 18, 1916. Kaiser Wilhelm II is condemned here as a hypocrite who mourned the deaths that resulted from the sinking of the *Titanic* in 1912, but yet he smiles gleefully as German submarines sink civilian vessels, killing many aboard.

New York Times called the sinking of the *Lusitania* "murder" and piracy and posed the question, "What advantage will it be to [Germany] to be left without a friend or a well-wisher in the world?" Therefore, the article showed that the verdict clearly cast the German government as guilty of such an infamous outrage.[78]

Major American newspapers concluded that the German people were an inherently savage people, based on Allied atrocity propaganda. From the beginning of the war, the German people had been stricken from the Anglo-Saxon family. They were, at best, relegated to the "Teutonic" race; at worst, they were labeled as "Huns" in a reference to Kaiser Wilhelm's speech during the Boxer Rebellion, wherein he exhorted his soldiers to imitate the actions of Attila the Hun.[79] Using nineteenth century phrenology, Allied newspapers cited "scientific" findings that showed that Germans were predisposed to psychopathic behavior due to the size of the German brain.[80] The sinking of the *Lusitania* added fodder as the *St. Louis Republic* in its opinion section accused the German government of not only reversing the progress of international law, but the very tenets of Christianity, itself.[81]

Prominent Americans, including William Skaggs, a southern progressive, added to the anti–German hysteria. His book *German Conspiracies in America,* traced the history of German treachery from Hessian mercenaries during the American Revolution to the destruction of the *Lusitania*, describing Germany as "a nation of ruthless destroyers," rhetoric clearly intended to incite his reading public.[82] His book reinterpreted history by describing the American Revolution as a struggle between a free Anglo-Saxon people and a despotic German king in the form of George III, who was also the elector of the German state of Hannover. Skaggs argued that it was only the influence of three generations of English liberalism that reformed the British royal family by the beginning of the reign of Queen Victoria.[83]

A few months after the sinking of the *Lusitania,* an even greater outrage was the arrest and subsequent execution of an English nurse, Edith Cavell. Cavell was charged with having aided English and French prisoners of war by hiding them and helping them escape to France. As with the *Lusitania,* the German government justified her execution by claiming that she was a spy, not a nurse. Brand Whitlock, the Minister in Belgium wrote to General Moritz von Bissing, the German Governor General in Belgium, imploring him to spare Cavell from death by describing her as having "spent her life in tending the sufferings of others" and having "lavished her care upon German soldiers" as well as Allied prisoners of war.[84]

Cavell's execution stirred the American public on a level that equaled the sinking of the *Lusitania* because of her gender and her profession, which should have spared her from the brutality of war.[85] Whitlock reported in his letter to Bryan that coverage of the case of Cavell's execution was extremely upsetting to the German government. He wrote that he had to meet several times with German officials "to prevent serious complications," which referred to their objection to having a Belgian citizen on the staff of the Legation.[86] After having been informed of Cavell's execution, Whitlock wrote Walter Page, the Ambassador to Great Britain that he considered the failure to save her life a blow on the part of the American Legation in Belgium:

> Although the German Authorities did not inform me when the sentence had actually been passed I learned through an unofficial source that judgment had been delivered and that Miss Cavell was to be executed during the night. I immediately sent Mr. Gibson, the Secretary of Legation, to present to [German civil governor] Baron von der Lancken my appeal that execution of the sentence should be deferred until the Governor should consider my plea for clemency.[87]

An article by James M. Beck, the former Assistant Attorney General of the United States, also protested Cavell's execution, claiming that she was not given a fair trial. Beck differentiated German from American and English concepts of "justice," emphasizing that the German form of justice consisted only in the following of procedure, rather than the concept of "inalienable rights" and the presumption of innocence under English common law.[88] He argued as follows:

> Miss Cavell's fate only differs from that of hundreds of Belgian women and children in that she had the pretense of a trial and presumably had trespassed against military law, while other victims of the rape of Belgium were ruthlessly killed in order to effect a speedy subjugation of the territory. The question of the guilt or innocence of each individual was a matter of no importance. Hostages were taken and shot for the alleged wrongs of others.[89]

The execution of Edith Cavell and its coverage by British and American newspapers continued to resonate throughout the war, convincing the American public to sympathize with the Entente and that Germany was capable of any gross violation of human decency.[90]

The final straw that eliminated any shred of sympathy for Germany was the publication of the Zimmerman Note in 1917, in which, in the event of war between Germany and the United States, Germany promised Mexico the states of Texas, New Mexico, and Arizona in exchange for an alliance against the United States. To the American public, the publication of the Zimmerman Note was a culmination of German villainy from the atrocity stories in the Bryce Report to the execution of Edith Cavell.[91] *The New York Times* connected the Zimmerman Note to suspected German movements in Mexico and Mexico's supposed attempt to cause friction in relations between the United States and Japan.[92] Despite the fact that Zimmerman was within his duties as foreign minister to secure Germany's interests, he was still roundly condemned as a villain by the American public. The course was thus set for war between Germany and the United States.[93]

After three years of neutrality and propaganda by the British, the groundwork had been laid for an American propaganda machine. Wilson established the Committee of Public Information (CPI) through an executive order eight days after the declaration of war. The Committee consisted of the Secretary of War and the Secretary of the Navy, and was chaired by George Creel, a civilian journalist.[94] In a report given to Wilson on June 1, 1919, Creel stated that the purpose of the CPI "was to drive home the absolute justice of America's cause, the absolute selflessness of America's aims."[95] In his book concerning his work in the CPI, Creel describes the function of the CPI as a vehicle to project American ideals and to maintain Allied morale by using all forms of media—telegraph cable, motion pictures, radios, and print.[96] Between 1917 and 1919, the CPI received more than $6.8 million in funding from Wilson's office and Congress. During those two years, the CPI received more than $2.8 million in receipts from the sale of publications and movie tickets for its films. Between 1917 and 1919, the CPI spent more than $7.9 million.[97] In his own words, Creel defended his work:

> In no degree was the Committee an agency of censorship, a machinery of concealment or repression. Its emphasis throughout was on the open and the positive. At no point did it seek or exercise authorities under those war laws that limited the freedom of speech and press."[98]

Despite such assertions, the CPI waged an extensive campaign to maintain war morale and to remind the American public of the righteousness of their cause. One such example was the Four Minute Men, which was an organization of speakers who toured the country making speeches. About 75,000 people gave speeches of no more than four minutes specific topics, such as arguing for the selective service, selling Liberty Bonds, and the reasons for fighting Germany.[99] As with the Protestant clergy previously mentioned, the CPI contributed to the war hysteria and censorship that resulted after the declaration of war with Germany.[100]

As a result of the constant barrage of propaganda, the effects of anti–German sentiment would be manifested in various ways. Though originating before the declaration of war, the "Americanism movement" gained full force by stressing enthusiastic and uniform support for the war. German-Americans, who had lived with their neighbors in peace, were considered an enemy that had to be stamped out within American society. Since German-Americans had maintained strong cultural connections to the Fatherland in the decades before the war, Americanists sought to eradicate any vestige of German culture. Some examples included dropping the German language from public school curricula, the closing of German language newspapers, the Anglicization of German names, the banning of German opera and music, and the renaming of sauerkraut to "liberty cabbage."[101]

The Anglo-American Connection

Despite President Wilson's intentions, it would prove to be all but impossible for the United States to remain completely impartial over the events in Europe. In the two decades preceding the outbreak of the Great War, Great Britain had been cultivating friendship with the United States by eliminating the last remaining controversies between both countries in the Western Hemisphere. The Washington foreign policy establishment, for the most part, was unabashedly Anglophile. Lodge, despite being an Anglophobe early in his political career, became more of an Anglophile due to his Boston origins; this affinity was reflected in his constant travel to Britain, his fashions, his admiration for the British Empire, and his support for the *rapprochement* between the United States and Great Britain during the 1890s.[102] Wilson depended upon a small circle of advisors on foreign policy: Robert Lansing, the Counselor to the State Department; Walter Page, the Ambassador to Great Britain; and William Jennings Bryan, the Secretary of State. Only Bryan was adamant in maintaining the strictest American neutrality.[103]

Additionally, the intricate economic connections between the United States and Great Britain made neutrality and complete impartiality rather impossible. British banks and investment had financed the development of the American economy throughout the nineteenth century, particularly its railroad expansion. Britain had been a market for American agricultural products, particularly southern cotton. Even though the United States had become an industrial giant at the beginning of the twentieth century, it still depended on the British to navigate the complex waters of global finance.[104]

"Dealing with the Huns," *Western Mail*, January 6, 1917. This cartoon is another example of shaming President Woodrow Wilson for his continued stance of neutrality in the face of Germany's resumption of unrestricted submarine warfare.

As war in Europe progressed, the American and British economies would become more inextricably linked. As early as September 1914, the British government sent agents on behalf of the War Office to the United States to fill orders for munitions in anticipation of a more protracted conflict with Germany. Despite protests from the Irish-American community, the State Department declared that belligerents from both sides had the right to purchase munitions from neutral countries like the United States.[105] By late 1914, the War Office sent Lieutenant B. C. Smyth-Pigott to make arrangements with American firms such as Remington and Winchester for the purchase of rifles to meet the demands of Britain's growing army, which was projected to be at nearly 1.2 million by July 1915.[106] It was not just for munitions that the British were turning to the United States, but rather any industry, material, or commodity that could be of use to the Allied war machine. As a result, a mad dash of agents from private firms came to the United States, claiming to act on the authority of the

British government, to secure deals that they would then sell to the War Office, plus a ten percent commission.[107]

On January 1915, the firm of J. P. Morgan & Co. became the British government's sole purchasing agent, upon the suggestion of Cecil Spring Rice, the British ambassador. Spring Rice believed that Morgan would be the best person with whom to do business since the firm of J. P. Morgan & Co. was the largest and most powerful bank in the United States. Additionally, Morgan owned a substantial portion of the shipping industry, which would deliver goods to the Allies easily.[108] In Spring Rice's letter to Foreign Secretary Sir Edward Grey, he expressed the utmost confidence in Morgan's abilities as the chief purchaser for the British government in the United States; he alluded to an earlier confusion that pre-dated Morgan's appointment, which he believed was a marked improvement.[109] J. P. Morgan had strong personal ties to Britain. He spent half the year in England and was well connected with high society. His niece, Mary Burns, was married to the first Viscount Harourt. As a strong believer in the Allied cause, Morgan donated his country house to be used as a hospital up on the outbreak of hostilities. With Morgan as the chief purchaser, the British government could be assured that the most powerful bank in the United States would not have any dealings with Germany.[110]

The British government was especially eager to garner American support. In the twenty years preceding the Great War, it had cultivated a *rapprochement* with the United States to the point of relinquishing Britain's control of the Western Hemisphere. With the outbreak of the First World War, the Foreign Office hoped its efforts would yield a return in the form of American cooperation, while keeping in mind the sensitivities of American public opinion against intervention in Europe. As his experience with Americans, as his friendship with Theodore Roosevelt had shown, Spring Rice gave his insight on the nuances of American public opinion:

> Roosevelt writes (and I agree with him that that everyone must be impressed by the very friendly feeling of [the United States] towards England and its anti–German sentiment ... but there are other elements and the influence of the Germans and especially the German Jews is very great, and in parts of the country is supreme. We must not count on American sympathy as assured to us. A little incident might change it, and there are the cleverest people in the world at work with large sums at their back who will let no opportunity pass to do [Britain] mischief.[111]

Likewise, Spring Rice, in his communications with Grey, emphasized the fact that Germany's actions regarding the invasion and occupation of Belgium showed that it was beyond the pale as a civilized nation, which necessitated action.

I venture to enclose for your information the paraphrase of a telegram from [Foreign Secretary] Sir Edward Grey in answer to a telegram of mine reporting an accusation circulated in the press to the effect that England was opposed to peace and demanding exorbitant terms. I enclose this telegram not, of course, with any idea of influencing your policy but merely as the statement of a point of view which I am sure you will be interested to know.[112]

Grey replied to Spring Rice as follows:

...Germany planned this war and chose her own time for forcing it on Europe. No one was in the same state of military preparation as Germany was when war began.... A series of able writers, instructors of Germany, from [German nationalist historian] Heinrich von Treitschke, has openly taught under the sanction of the Government that the main object of German policy must be to crush Great Britain and to destroy the British Empire.... A cruel wrong has been done to Belgium; wanton destruction has been inflicted on her and her resistance has been punished by wholesale acts of cruelty and vandalism. Is Germany prepared to make reparation for these acts?[113]

Theodore Roosevelt, throughout his correspondences to his British friends, trumpeted his support for the British cause, which had come to the aid of the Belgian people; he used this to express his dissatisfaction with the Wilson administration's policy of neutrality. In a letter to Spring Rice on February 5, 1915, Roosevelt expressed the belief that a war between Great Britain and the United States over the violation of neutrality rights would have been a disaster that would have worked to Germany's advantage; he used the Civil War as an analogy, in which Lincoln wisely prevented a war with either Britain or France, while simultaneously preserving the Union.[114] In another letter, written to John St. Loe Strachey, British journalist and editor of *The Spectator*, Roosevelt reiterated his pro–British views after, in an article of *The Spectator*, Strachey insinuated that Roosevelt did not appear to be strongly behind Britain. Roosevelt's defense was that, regardless of his affections for Britain, he was an American first. Nevertheless, Roosevelt reiterated his support:

I emphatically stated that England was right; and that England had made all peace lovers her debtors by her action toward Belgium; but I thought it very unwise to indulge in hysterics in the matter.... Next to my own country I put England first; I am in closest sympathy with her.[115]

Roosevelt argued further:

Surely you must realize, if only from the bitterness expressed toward me by the Germans, that I have unequivocally expressed my sympathies with the Allies and my denunciation of Germany and my abhorrence of a neutrality which is neutral between right and wrong.... I have distinctly stated that in what England did for Belgium she has set the right example for the United States. I have spoken in the highest terms of your Army and Navy of the attitude of the upper classes and of large sections of your people. I have explicitly stated that you have done better than we would have done. I have held you up as being better compared to us.[116]

Anglo-Saxonism and the First World War

The outbreak of the First World War unleashed the next step in the evolution of Anglo-Saxonism with the exclusion of the German people from the Anglo-Saxon family, particularly from the midst of the English-speaking peoples from both sides of the Atlantic. In the decades before the war, even though British intellectuals such as James Bryce were not closely aligned to their German counterparts, they did, in some ways, consider German universities superior to British higher education. British academics routinely visited German universities to learn the latest ideas.[117] After the war began, however, British academics made great effort to divorce themselves, intellectually and philosophically, from Germany. For example, three weeks after the war began, historians at Oxford University such as L. G. Wickham Legg, H.W.C. Davis, C.R.L Fletcher, Arthur Hassall, and F. Morgan wrote published *Why We Are At War: Great Britain's Case*, to justify the British position. *Why We Are At War* was the first of a series of "Oxford pamphlets" that reiterated the reasons Britain went to war. These historians highlighted the plight of Belgium, as its neutrality was violated by Germany, thus giving Britain the moral high ground of protecting an innocent and weaker nation from a stronger aggressor.[118] Without mentioning Anglo-Saxonism directly, the Oxford historians ascribed to the British cause the qualities of humanity and civilization, while defining Germany as the "enemy of humanity." However, most damning to the Germans was the argument that in coming to the aid of the Belgian people, Great Britain, as the Anglo-Saxon power, disregarded any ties to Teutonic militarism, and that "the call to right" was far higher than "the call of blood."[119]

The racial and Social Darwinist element had been part of the ideology of Anglo-Saxonism in the two decades before the First World War, which held that the Anglo-Saxons and their descendants in Britain and the United States were destined to rule. This coincided neatly with the WASP elite, justifying their dominance in the social, economic, and political spheres of American society.[120] In the decades before the war, Anglo-Saxonists like Theodore Roosevelt railed against "hyphenism," or the remaining bonds that immigrants continued to hold for their countries of origin, and called for a purer definition of being an American in reac-

"Household Refuse," *Western Mail*, June 28, 1917. Many British aristocratic families like the Battenbergs anglicized their names in order to promote their British identities and thus renounce their German heritage.

tion to the waves of immigrants from eastern and southern Europe, as well as the Irish- and German-Americans.[121] When the Great War began, Anglo-Saxonists embarked upon the policy of "Americanism," in order to instill loyalty among immigrant populations for the American way of life, by diluting "hyphenism," which was a source of discomfort for the WASP elite in the latter decades of the nineteenth century. In doing so, the WASP elite established that the Anglo-Saxon was the American ideal. This was best exemplified in a speech Wilson gave to the Daughters of the American Revolution in October 1915, which reflected the evolution of Anglo-Saxonism,

> The American Revolution was the birth of a nation; it was the creation of a great free republic based upon traditions of personal liberty, which theretofore had been confined to a single little island, but which it was purposed should spread to all mankind.[122]

Critics of "Americanization" pointed out that the WASPs were the most blatantly hyphenated Americans, emphasizing their English origins, which were manifested in the Wilson Administration's condoning of Britain's violations of neutral nations on the high seas.[123]

Despite generations of assimilation and making contributions to American society, German-Americans became suspect to charges of "disloyalty" and being "un-American," charged with being more devoted to the Kaiser than to the principles of liberty. Propaganda stories of German atrocities in Belgium, Germany's submarine campaign, and sabotage attempts at factories fueled anti-German sentiment across the United States, convincing many that their German-American neighbors could be agents of the Reich itself.[124] Spring Rice reported the following to his colleague Sir Valentine Chirol on the sentiment toward German-Americans::

> It is curious to see the violent tone adopted by the German press [in the United States] against the American public, on the ground that they are Anglo-maniac. Their tone is almost friendly to France and Russia, but nothing is too bad for England, and they are almost inarticulate with hate. A great danger here is racial feeling, and if this were to break out the task of the government would be difficult. I think the Government is really afraid of it. There is a distinct feeling of fear that if the Allies are beaten the turn of America would come next and come soon. Twelve million Germans in one's belly is rather a severe weight for a nation which has to fight seventy millions outside. And that is the situation here.[125]

Wilson was concerned that, since German-Americans were among the most organized white minorities in the country, they might somehow foment social or political disturbances across the country where German-American leaders would seek to use the numbers of German-Americans to influence Wilson to maintain a policy of neutrality.[126]

From the beginning of the war, the Allied propagandists sought to define the aims of the conflict, and most importantly, to define the "enemy," specifically Germany. The British and later American governments appropriated the values of self-government, liberty, and "civilization" and associated them with Anglo-Saxonism on one hand, while on the other conflating Germany's *"Kultur"* with Prussian militarism, the preponderance of the state over the individual, and "barbarism," resulting in the atrocities committed by the German army in its occupation of Belgium, for example. After the sinking of the *Lusitania*, public opinion clearly condemned Germany, and leaders like Lodge were convinced that the Anglo-

Saxon powers, such as Britain and the United States, as well as France, represented democracy and liberty against "Prussian militarism."[127] Indeed, for German intellectuals the outbreak of the war was seen as a seminal moment for German national consciousness. By eschewing French and British ideals of democracy and capitalism, they held up the warrior ethos, which contrasted the materialism of British capitalism, and they saw themselves as "defenders" of Europe and Western Civilization from "Slavic barbarism," which came to be known as *Kultur*.[128] Ironically, in the June 1915 issue of the *Irish Quarterly Review*, which presented a more neutral perspective on the war, Germany's political and economic philosophy was summed up in the abject worship of the state, dominated by a military elite, which is not subject to any external authority: the more its power grew, the more it became a threat to the liberties of other peoples.[129]

While nativism did not sprout during the First World War, the anti–German hysteria of the First World War was unprecedented in its magnitude, which reflected the evolution of Anglo-Saxonism as one of the factors behind the increasing sympathy in the United States for the British cause. The most tangible result of the *rapprochement* between Great Britain and the United States during the 1890s was a pro–British element in the foreign policy establishment. Despite the country's stated official neutrality, Wilson and almost all of his cabinet were unabashed Anglophiles and made every accommodation to the British government, especially in the trading of contraband.[130]

For the foreign policy establishment, however, having drunk from the same well of Anglo-Saxonism before the war, had to separate Germany from the Anglo-Saxon tradition. Only English-speaking peoples of Great Britain and the United States could be considered true Anglo-Saxons because of their devotion to liberty and civilization. Therefore, only the Anglo-Saxons, who held elements of British influence, could be considered true Americans. The "Teutonic" peoples, then, of whom the Germans were a part, were clearly inherently different from the Anglo-Saxons and therefore, not American. In the eyes of the policy makers in Washington, D.C., this was the most effective way to sway public opinion toward the side of the Allies in a war, which otherwise the great majority of Americans would have opposed.[131] After the entry of the United States in 1917, this new definition of Anglo-Saxonism would be applied to the "100 percent Americanism" campaign to root out "hyphenism," differentiating the "true Americans" from the Teutonic elements (i.e., German-Americans), banning the teaching of the German language in the curriculum of schools and universities and resulting in the lynching of German-Americans. The federal government, in the name of "Americanism," would enact measures to limit free speech through the Sedition Act, and would go as far as denaturalization for American citizens of German descent.[132] Wilson's attack on "hyphenism" can best be exemplified in his address to Congress on December 7, 1915, in which he warned of citizens of other nations who, despite being welcomed by the United States, had either spread dissension, sabotage, or conspired against the government that gave them the privilege of citizenship. It was, of course, a thinly-disguised reference to German-Americans, whose loyalty was becoming increasingly in doubt, as these American and were being perceived as closely associated with the German government.[133] Thus, Wilson called on Congress to act:

> To enact such laws at the earliest possible moment and feel that in doing so I am urging you to do nothing less than save the honor and self-respect of the nation. Such creatures of passion, disloyalty, and anarchy must be crushed out. They are not many, but they are infinitely malignant, and the hand of our power should close over them at once. They have formed plots to destroy property, they have entered into conspiracies against the neutrality of the Government, they have sought to pry into every confidential transaction of the Government in order to serve interests alien to our own.[134]

Lodge had a similar reaction to those he called "hyphenates," people who did not conform fully to the American ideal. He saw even naturalized German-Americans as a potential fifth column that could subvert the political system of the United States, which he had long believed to be part of Anglo-Saxon civilization and associated with republican self-government and individual liberty. Additionally, Lodge believed all of the English-speaking peoples, including Great Britain and its dominions, shared the same genius for establishing self-governing societies out in the wilderness.[135] As the war began, Lodge's Anglo-Saxonism crystallized; he saw a conflict between Anglo-Saxon civilization and "Teutonism," and thus identified the interests of Great Britain as similar to those of the United States.[136] Lodge's hostility toward "hyphenism" was evident in a letter he wrote to Roosevelt describing a Senate Foreign Relations Committee meeting, in which he resented being lectured by a German-American immigrant about patriotism and Americanism. Lodge described the account thusly:

> The German-American propaganda has become pretty bad. We had them before the Foreign Relations Committee the other day on the question of prohibiting the export of munitions of war, when a man from the Lutheran Theological Seminary in St. Louis named Bente, addressed us.... He had an accent so strong that you could stumble over it, and he proceeded to lecture us on Americanism, patriotism,

what true Americanism was and what the opinions of George Washington were. Some of us are not hyphenates—we are just plain Americans.... They are now engaged in telling us how loyal they are to the United States.[137]

Both Lodge and Roosevelt were of the same mind, perceiving the Wilson administration to be incompetent and playing into German hands through its policy of neutrality, which they believed to be far too passive; they likened Wilson to Thomas Jefferson a century earlier when the United States was at the mercy of Britain and France during the Napoleonic Wars.[138] Roosevelt described Wilson and Bryan as the worst men in their positions, for allowing the United States to be a state of "unpreparedness," like the Jefferson and Madison administrations on the eve of the War of 1812.[139] In a letter to British scholar James Bryce, Roosevelt reiterated his belief that Wilson was intimidated by the German-American vote; Roosevelt also accused American pacifists like Henry Ford and Andrew Carnegie of playing into the hands of the German government by opposing military preparedness for the United States and encouraging the Wilson administration to maintain strict neutrality, despite the atrocities committed by the Germans in Belgium.[140]

If the American public had to be convinced of supporting the Allied cause, the media was the means by which to do it. The first step would be to alienate the American public against the German cause. In the decades leading up to the First World War, there had been a great affinity between the American and German peoples. Germans made up a significant proportion of American immigrants during the mid-nineteenth century, when they escaped the chaos of revolution and saw the United States as a beacon of democracy. Americans, in turn, looked to Germany as a model of social progress. American progressives of the early twentieth century, such as Randolph Bourne, marveled at German innovations in social legislation.[141] However, as the war progressed, even American intellectuals who were once solid supporters of Germany joined the rhetoric of cutting off Germany from the Anglo-Saxon family. The economist Thorsten Veblen, most known for his *Theory of the Leisure Class*, stressed the incompatibility of the German imperial system with capitalism and liberal democracy.[142]

For generations, Americans retained perceptions of their government's disinterest and impartiality during the first three years of the First World War—this changed only when Germany declared unrestricted submarine warfare. Such perceptions, however contradicted the reality that American political and business elites deemed it in their best interests to support the forces of the Entente and gradually alienate the larger public from the Central Powers.¹⁴³ Prominent members of American society devoted much of their time and talents toward persuading the American public to support the cause of the Entente, by exploiting atrocity stories revolving the German occupation of northern France and Belgium. Additionally, official German policies, such as the use of submarine warfare, played into the hands of British and American propagandists, who were more adroit in the demonization of Germany.¹⁴⁴

One of the methods of persuading the American public to side with the Entente powers was to emphasize the fundamental difference between the Anglo-Saxon and "Teutonic" peoples, particularly the inherent militarism in German culture. Less than a decade before the outbreak of the war, when Germany and the United States were rising powers in competition, the abhorrence of standing armies was considered to be one of the virtues of the original Anglo-Saxon peoples. The Anglo-Saxons supposedly mobilized for battle only reluctantly and in self-defense, not to glory in war for its own sake, as opposed to other war-like continental powers, most notably the Germans from Prussia.¹⁴⁵ British journalist Arnold White

"Were Germany to Win," *News of the World*, **January 30, 1916. This propaganda cartoon reinforces the image of Germany as the enemy of "civilization," and it calls on the United States and China to intervene.**

saw Germany as a threat to world peace a decade before the war. In particular, he saw Prussian militarism as a cause of the next world war for several reasons. For example, in his article "Germany's Aim in Foreign Politics," Arnold analyzed Germany's increasing desire for continental hegemony, as seen in ambitionssuch as conquering the Netherlands, which would greatly enhance its colonial empire with the addition of Dutch colonies in the East Indies and the Caribbean.[146] Also, the inherent militarism of German society, in Arnold's view, would make prolonged peace impossible because of the fear of falling into "decadence," even so far as to describe a proposal to erect a military-style barracks for the poor in major towns and cities. Because of this slavish devotion to the Kaiser and the military, Arnold concluded that Germany was no longer a nation of deep intellectual thought, and therefore, on the way to "barbarism."[147]

Likewise, the American intellectual Carlton Hayes cited German militarism as one of the main causes of the outbreak of the First World War. He demonized Germany in his analysis of German history from the mid-nineteenth century to the onset of the war in 1914, through the works of prominent Germans like the politician Prince Bernard von Bülow, General Friederich von Bernhardi, and the German-American psychologist Hugo Muensterburg. Hayes argued that Prussian militarism was incompatible with the rise of liberalism in the aftermath of the French Revolution and the Napoleonic Wars. He cited examples from the failure of the Frankfurt Assembly in 1849 to unify the German people under a democratic government to the rigid conservatism of the Hohenzollern monarchy, reinforced by the reactionary East Prussian Junker aristocracy that would not "pick up a crown from the gutter," when offered a chance at German leadership.[148] Rather, it was Bismarck's "blood and iron" through three wars in the 1860s that united the German states into the German Reich. Thus, to Hayes, what made the unified Germany of 1871 unique was that the army was its core, and that the apparatus of the state was simply grafted onto it, which he described as follows:

> In the new Germany a huge national army was superimposed upon a hierarchical civil service, and ballot-boxes were rendered ornamental rather than useful.... With such a state, liberal government after a British or French model would be clearly incompatible; under liberal institutions neither the civil bureaucracy nor the military machine could be maintained at the proper pitch of efficiency. Nor would liberalism suit the German genius. "In the German view," says Professor Münsterberg, "the state is not for the individuals, but the individuals for the state."[149]

Hayes's article painted a picture of Germany in the years following unification that was the antithesis of the Anglo-Saxon powers, which valued self-government and democracy. For example, Hayes described Chancellor von Bülow as "a good conservative, a landowner and a bureaucrat, he evinces much impatience with the Reichstag, its opposing parties and its dilatory actions. He has no comprehension of the operation of parliamentary government. He indicts the whole party-system, and his judgments on political parties turn largely upon their several attitudes toward armaments."[150] This explained his automatic revulsion to the British party system, especially in his unwillingness to work with the Social Democratic Party, saying that, "the more English the tendency of a party, the more he assails it." Hayes argued further that the German electorate shared a similar view.[151] Hayes also attributed the dominance of militarism to the influences on German intellectual thought of the late nineteenth century, particularly the chauvinist and jingoistic influence of the German philosopher Heinrich von Treitschke. Hayes asserted that Treitschke's sole purpose was to "unite national history and Darwinism." He summarized Treitschke's writings as an attempt to show the evolution and the inevitable triumph of the German state; thus, Treitschke became known as "the national historian" for the German people. Hayes connected Treitschke's ideas with the development of German foreign policy of the late nineteenth century, going so far as to count how many times politicians like von Bülow cited Treitschke in their writings and gave credit to him for their policies in the two decades leading to the First World War.[152] Thus, to Hayes, Treitschke's ideas became the framework for Germany's foreign policy after Bismarck's dismissal in 1890, which inaugurated the "world policy" of Kaiser Wilhelm II and his chancellors, emphasizing the enlargement of the German navy, the acquisition of colonies, and Germany's overall aggressive posturing in international diplomacy—all factors that contributed to the outbreak of the First World War in 1914.[153]

Hayes appraised Chancellor von Bülow using von Bülow's own words:

> Billow sounds the keynote of his policy, both domestic and foreign, in the ringing words: " It is not the duty of the government in the present time to concede new rights to Parliament, but to rouse the political interest of all classes of the nation by means of a vigorous and determined national policy, great in its aims and energetic in the means it employs " (page 341). He denies his willingness or ability to utilize the Fashoda incident or the Russo-Japanese War in order to bring France and Russia into alliance with Germany. He glories in the Agadir incident and claims that it was he himself who inspired the Kaiser to make that melodramatic entry into the Moroccan Question. He exults in the Austrian annexation of Bosnia and Herzegovina and boasts that German threats of war sufficed to secure Russian acquiescence in that high-handed violation of the Treaty of Berlin. But while he takes pride in the German "world policy" of recent times, he remains remarkably oblivious to the danger of Germany's international isolation.[154]

IV. Anglo-Saxonism in the First World War

Despite Hayes's condemnation of German militarism and its contribution to the First World War, he also left some room to single out Anglo-Saxonism, as well, for its contributions to the war. Hayes criticized Ango-Saxonism in all its forms, such as "Anglo-Saxon institutions," "the manifest destiny of the Anglo-Saxon race," and the "White Man's Burden," as examples of British hypernationalism and imperialism extolled by British writers like Henry Spencer and Rudyard Kipling, labeling them but another means to gain public, and most notably American, support for the war.[155] Hayes concluded his essay by arguing that Great Britain and Germany were equally to blame for their actions or inactions that led to the outbreak of the First World War. Thus, to Hayes, not only was Anglo-Saxonism another banner for the war, it was also used as an indictment against the belligerents for the unprecedented death and suffering that came out of the Great war.[156]

To differentiate themselves from the Germans, when hostilities commenced, the reasons for war had been crystallized by the Allies into a war for "civilization" and "liberty"; this justification had been appropriated into the realm of Anglo-Saxonism and thus became a rallying banner, particularly for the Anglo-Saxon peoples of the British Empire and later the United States. Scottish statesman Archibald Colquhoun outlined the reasons Britain and its dominions were fighting the war. He underscored the fact that, despite previous doubts, the British dominions of Australia, Canada, New Zealand, and South Africa enthusiastically joined the war with the mother country without reservation. He noted the Anglo-Saxon bonds that tied Britain and its dominions, which were based on common values and traditions that transcended ethnicity, compared to the German Empire, which was forged by Prussian militarism in 1870.[157] To him, the foremost reason for Britain's involvement was to protect Belgian neutrality, which Germany had violated. Though not purely for altruistic reasons since the conquest of Belgium would have left Britain vulnerable for invasion, Colquhoun used the defense of Belgium to distinguish Anglo-Saxon values of liberty and self-government from Teutonic militarism and the atrocities that issued from it.[158] To reinforce the stark difference between the Anglo-Saxons who loved liberty and the "barbarous" Teutons, Colquhoun reinforced the atrocities committed in Belgium, such as the burning of the medieval library at Louvain, the bombardment of unfortified towns such as Malines, and individual acts of cruelty committed on civilians—all points that he directed to an American audience. He argued that the Germans were more savage than the Huns because, unlike Attila's armies who knew no better, to the German army, the acts were deliberate and part of military policy.¹⁵⁹ While not mentioning Anglo-Saxonism by name, Colquhoun attributed to the British Empire the values at stake in the war associated with Anglo-Saxonism:

> Our partners in this fight have been our foes of old; they may be our rivals in the future, but for the present their cause is ours because Prussian hegemony in Europe would mean the triumph of a crude and brutal militarism. The British Empire is not afraid of nationalism; it views with sympathy the revival of national aspirations in the smaller Slav peoples, and its heart warms to Belgium; but above all we, as a free democracy, are opposed to Teutonism, which is enshrined in a military autocracy and knows no law save its own.¹⁶⁰

Colquhoun concluded by reiterating that, in its fight for liberty, the British Empire was in a struggle against German militarism. He believed that a German victory would set humanity back to a social darwinian world in which "nature is red in tooth and claw," in which any sort of barbarity was encouraged, especially in wartime, contrasting of course, to how Britain and its dominions observe the rule of law, even in wartime. Thus, he considered Germany to be far worse than previous enemies, including Napoleon Bonaparte.¹⁶¹

The difference between the values of self-government and liberty, represented by Anglo-Saxonism, and Teutonic militarism, represented by Germany, can be best described in an article of the *Journal of International Ethics* by the anarchist Victor S. Yarros. His comparisons between the Anglo-Saxon Allies and Germany are based on the role of the state. Unlike his contemporaries, who condemned Germany purely out of jingoism, Yarros's analysis of the conflicting values of Anglo-Saxonism and Teutonism was more subtle and nuanced. He remained consistent with other critics in their assessment of the German government, which was dominated by a militarist elite and ruled by a Kaiser who based his authority on divine right. Because of the way Bismarck formed the German Empire in 1870, any hopes of liberalism taking root were dashed by the preponderance of Prussian militarism. However, Yarros diverged from other critics in pointing out that the German constitution still checked the power of the Kaiser through the budget, and thus Germany could not be a true "absolute monarchy."¹⁶² As part of the larger political spectrum, however, Yarros considered the juggernaut of the German state to be a greater threat to civilization because, unlike the Anglo-Saxon democracies of Great Britain and the United States, the individual accounted for nothing and could be disposed of at will. In fact, Yarros's critique of the compromise between the supremacy of the state and elements of democracy made Germany even more unstable:

"Hun Justice," *Western Mail*, September 28, 1917. This cartoon portrays Germany as the modern-day "Hun," who pillaged Belgium.

Of course, a half divine dynastic state cannot consent to submit its decisions to any parliament or referendum. Of course, in a political sense a half divine state is "irresponsible"—that is, responsible to God alone. Such a state is, in truth, of infinitely more value than all its subjects taken together. It may order them to fight foreigners or one another, and it may keep up the fighting indefinitely, with-out condescending to give reasons. But the question is whether, rhetoric and loose writing aside, any educated German can seriously maintain that the constitution of the Teutonic empire expressly or by necessary implication recognizes the sacrosanct and divine nature of the state, or the insignificance of the individual.[163]

On the other hand, Yarros analyzed in detail the political systems of the United States and Great Britain and how they differed from the government of the Hohenzollerns in Germany. He explained the British parliamentary system as a balance between the sovereign and Parliament, particularly emphasizing the House of Commons, which was intended to speak for the majority of the people. Yarros, however, criticized the British political system, which had historically been dominated by the landowning elite for the interests of the landowning elite. Nevertheless, he still believed that, when compared to Germany, Great Britain still stood for the Anglo-Saxon ideals of democracy and self-government, arguing that "Democracy is assuredly better and safer than any of the superseded forms of government, and democracy has long meant, and still means, the rule of the majority—at least within certain constitutional bounds."[164] Yarros noted the trends in British politics toward democratization in the decades before the outbreak of the Great War, with the enfranchisement of the working classes, the diminishment of the powers of the House of Lords, from holding veto power to merely a suspension of legislation, and the inevitable suffrage of women voters.[165]

Regarding the United States, Yarros emphasized the system of checks and balances in the Constitution, as well as constitutional protections of civil liberties, thus protecting both majorities and minorities from a tyrannical government. He also alluded to trends from the political reforms of the Progressive Era, such as the initiative, referendum, and recall that led toward direct democracy giving political power to the people themselves, rather than lawmakers in either state or federal governments.[166]

As an anarchist, Yarros's bias would paint both the Allies and Germany with the same brush in which the state is supreme over the individual. However, he made a distinction from his fellow contemporary anarchists who believed all governments to be tyrannical. Despite his anarchist leanings, Yarros believed in the Allied cause. To Yarros, what was at stake in the war against Germany was autocracy, the embodiment of the state in either the form of the Kaiser or the Prussian military elite, versus democracy through majority rule. Yarros believed that the days of autocratic government as embodied by Germany were numbered, and he felt that the democratic governments epitomized by the Anglo-Saxon countries, such as Great Britain and the United States, were the wave of the future.[167] Yarros most eloquently criticized his fellow anarchists when he stated the following:

> The fight for democracy is a fight for the very conditions of growth—for free discussion, local autonomy, individual and group rights under the law. The anarchist who says that all governments are alike, that tyranny is tyranny, and that the war

IV. Anglo-Saxonism in the First World War

"A Timely Removal," *Western Mail*, July 19, 1917. In 1917, the British monarchy changed its name from the House of Saxe-Coburg-Gotha to the House of Windsor, rejecting a German lineage that dated to the Hannoverians, of which George V was a descendant. In a royal proclamation, George V repudiated all of the German titles associated with the British monarchy, thus severing Germany from the British Anglo-Saxon royal family.

does not concern him—and, alas, there are not a few who say this—simply reveals his ignorance of the course and conditions of human evolution. Progress there has been, and progress there will continue to be—if societies and states preserve their freedom and society is not rebarbarized by the Prussian type of government. The anarchist who assumes that institutions can be suddenly changed, and that whole nations can lift themselves by their boot-straps, needs an elementary course in political science and political history. But such a course, coupled perhaps with a few advanced lectures, would also greatly benefit those who write and talk superficially about the difference in kind between the German view of the sovereign state and the Anglo-Saxon view.[168]

Among Anglo-Saxonists, Theodore Roosevelt was among the most outspoken public figures of his day. As president, he guided a more aggressive foreign policy and was instrumental in making Americans more comfortable with their country's new role as a world power, while also garnering the Nobel Peace Prize for mediating the end of the Russo-Japanese War.[169] Roosevelt had mildly supported Wilson's declaration of neutrality upon the outbreak of hostilities. However, the end of 1914 convinced Roosevelt that Germany should be confronted for its atrocities in Belgium, and that the United States should ultimately join the Entente to that end.[170]

In a 1915 letter to Arthur Hamilton Lee, Roosevelt's criticism of the Wilson administration's strict neutrality became much sharper. He practically accused Wilson of cowardice, describing him as "an entirely cold-blooded seeking man ... anxious at all hazards to keep the German-American vote and the pacifist vote,. Roosevelt believed that by not criticizing German atrocities in Belgium as sharply as attacking British violations of neutrality rights, Wilson was giving refuge to the German government. Furthermore, Roosevelt saw German-Americans and pacifist groups as foot soldiers for the German cause, and he thus considered any attack on Britain almost as an attack on the United States, itself. Roosevelt's opinion of Wilson could not be any blunter when he said the following:

> Wilson has permitted the German Embassy to be a center of not only anti–English but of anti–American agitation, which has included the forging of passports, the purchase of newspapers, and even more sinister deeds still, for there can be little doubt that the explosions in American arms and munitions factories and on certain ships have been due to a German propaganda instigated by or connived at and encouraged by the German officials. Of course, if Wilson had any kind of self-respect ... he would have summarily dismissed the German Ambassador and called the German Government to account for this long ago. It has been only the successive brutalities of the Germans which have prevented him from throwing his weight on their side and against the Allies.[171]

Like many Americans, Roosevelt was outraged at the German invasion of Belgium, as stated earlier in his book, *America and the World War*. He spoke of the violation of the sovereignty of Belgium and Luxembourg, the destruction of the medieval town of Louvain, the destruction wrought by airships, and the torment of the Belgian royal family.[172] Despite his protestations for peace, however, Roosevelt denounced the pacifist movements and the movement toward international law of the early twentieth century. He saw the World Court at The Hague as impotent in preventing war and felt that the myriad of arbitration treaties were useless in protecting Belgium.[173]

Ultimately, Roosevelt's book was a thinly veiled criticism of Wilson's policy of neutrality. Like many others, Roosevelt preached for "self-defense." He considered the navy to be the only safeguard for peace, and he believed that the Wilson administration was allowing the navy to deteriorate. Roosevelt ended his book by calling upon the nation to intervene upon Belgium's behalf.[174] Lodge demonstrated full agreement in his appraisal of Roosevelt's critique of the Wilson administration's neutrality policy, particularly on matters such as Bryan's execution of it as secretary of state, as well as disarmament treaties like the Hague Conventions, which Lodge considered, "folly, if not wickedness of making treaties which have no force and no intent of enforcement behind them."[175]

Wilson had no doubt of his sympathies to Britain and the Entente powers, even when he played the role of an honest broker trying to mediate a peace between the belligerents.[176] Additionally, Britain was far more successful in employing methods of persuasion than Germany in winning the sympathies of the American public through its ability to control the flow of news from Europe, thus shaping public opinion.[177] Pro-Entente sentiments abounded in the foreign policy establishment in the opening months of the war. In September 1914, three American ambassadors to France—Myron T. Herrick, the outgoing minister appointed by Taft; Robert Bacon, Herrick's predecessor; and William Graves Sharp, Wilson's appointee—in a special mission to France declared their sympathies with the French cause and promised to persuade American public opinion. In the same month, Henry van Dyke, the ambassador to the Netherlands and Luxembourg, presented Wilson with a clear bias toward the Entente in a letter, declaring the war to be a struggle between democracy and militarism and suggesting that a German victory would be detrimental to the long-term interests of the United States.[178]

Of the senior diplomats in the Wilson administration, Walter Hines Page, the ambassador to Great Britain, devoted his career toward strengthening Anglo-American relations. He not only supported the British on a political basis; he believed that the war was between the English-speaking peoples and German autocracy.[179] While Secretary of State William Jennings Bryan was insistent upon stressing America's freedom of the seas by adhering to the Declaration of London, Page saw the issue as a remnant of the War of 1812 that missed the forest for the trees. Page stressed that the following:

> It is a world-clash of systems of government, a struggle to the extermination of English civilization or of Prussian military autocracy. Let us suppose that we press for a few rights to which the shippers have a theoretical claim. The American people gain nothing and the result is friction with [Great Britain]... If Germany win, will it make any difference what position Great Britain took on the Declaration of London? But suppose England win. We shall then have an ugly academic dispute with her because of this controversy.... As we see the issue here, it is a matter of life and death for English-speaking civilization.[180]

To Page, a German victory was a larger threat than British violations of international law. Page stressed to Wilson the value of America's friendship with Britain, which had been blossoming since the *rapprochement* of the 1890s, and he said that continuing to harass the British would damage long-term Anglo-American relations. Because Page had linked America's destiny so closely with Britain's cause, the Germans could no longer rely upon the United States as a neutral power, but rather as a belligerent in all but name.[181]

On April of 1917, Wilson gave his historic speech to Congress asking for a declaration of war against Germany, which was the culmination of Anglo-Saxonism, though that concept was not expressly mentioned by name. Wilson's arguments for declaring war had universalized the values of liberty and self-government, which had been inherent in Anglo-Saxonism. Events had changed that finally induced Wilson to break off relations with Germany. The announcement of unrestricted submarine warfare meant that even American ships would not be spared, even though the German government had promised in the 1915 *Sussex* Pledge not to engage in indiscriminate sinking of vessels bound for Allied countries.[182] The declaration of unrestricted submarine warfare bore direct economic consequences because the German government had marked the seas around Great Britain, France, and Italy as areas where any ship could be sunk, regardless of whether it was neutral. As a result, American merchants refused to go to sea unless their ships were armed or were escorted by a convoy.[183] Spring Rice reported the effects of unrestricted submarine warfare to Balfour, saying that, "The result is a stoppage of trade, a congestion in the ports, widespread discomfort and even misery on the coast and inland, even bread riots and a coal famine."[184] Even still, Wilson remained reluctant to give up on peace entirely. In the subsequent weeks, German submarines began sinking American ships, which brought the Wilson administration no other alternative but to end American neutrality. Spring Rice wrote:

> Enough has been said and hinted in official circles and in the press to justify the assertion that the die has been cast and that this country has drifted into war. It is

not that the United States wanted it but their hand has been forced by Germany. The President, according to all indications, will not declare war on Germany on April 2 but merely assert that a state of war has existed between the United States and Germany since March 17, or even perhaps March 14, the date of the sinking of the *Algonquin*. Great hopes are entertained that Germany will herself in the interval declare war, consequent upon a probable encounter between the submarines and an armed American ship, two of which should, by now, be entering the area prescribed by Germany.[185]

Germany by 1917 had become associated with the very antithesis of Anglo-Saxonism through its militarism, expressed by the barbarity in how it waged war, and the fact that "self-governing" nations like the United States would take up the struggle. In his April 6, 1917 speech, Wilson outlined the reasons for declaring war against Germany, particularly the repeated violations of American neutrality by the submarine warfare waged by Germany, which he argued had violated international law, using the example of the sinking of hospital ships and other vessels transporting relief to Belgium being sunk by German submarines.[186] Thus, Wilson declared that Germany's policy of unrestricted submarine warfare was

> ...a war against all nations. American ships have been sunk, American lives taken, in ways which it has stirred us very deeply to learn of, but the ships and people of other neutral and friendly nations have been sunk and overwhelmed in the waters in the same way. There is no discrimination. The challenge is to all mankind. Each nation must decide for itself how it will meet it.... Our motive will not be revenge or the victorious assertion of the physical might of the nation, but only the vindication of right, of human right, of which we are only a single champion.[187]

While Wilson's speech to Congress is most well known for its line of "making the world safe for democracy," Wilson also conflated Germany with autocracy and militarism, which were inherently incompatible with the ideals of self-government, ideals espoused in Anglo-Saxonism and embodied by the United States and other free countries. Nevertheless, Wilson declared that the United States was not at war with the German people, nor did the United States harbor any hatred toward the German people, but rather only against the government of Kaiser Wilhelm II that pushed the German people into war without their consent.[188] On the other hand, Wilson declared that "Self-governed nations do not fill their neighbor states with spies or set the course of intrigue to bring about some critical posture of affairs which will given them an opportunity to strike and make conquest. Such designs can be successfully worked out only under cover where no one has the right to ask questions."[189] Perhaps where the speech most highlighted the ideals of Anglo-Saxonism was when Wilson spoke of the incompatibility between Prussian autocracy and the ideals of liberty and self-government as embodied by the United States—an incompatibility that, despite his earlier attempts, he now saw rendered peace-making a hopeless cause from the beginning. At the same time, he ascribed negative qualities of underhanded behavior, such as sabotage, to the Germans, including the Germans' attempt to draw Mexico into a war against the United States through the Zimmerman Telegram. At the same time, given that Russia was part of the Triple Entente, Wilson disregarded the autocracy of the Romanovs, who entered the war, because of the "democratic" nature of the Russian people that had manifested itself during the February Revolution. Thus the American people would not have any ideological qualms about serving with the Russians.[190] Through the context of Anglo-Saxon ideals, Wilson therefore described the war effort's goals in these terms:

> The world must be made safe for democracy. Its peace must be planted upon the tested foundations of political liberty. We have no selfish ends to serve. We desire no conquest, no dominion. We seek no indemnities for ourselves, no material compensation for the sacrifices we shall freely make. We are but one of the champions of mankind. We shall be satisfied when those rights have been made as secure as the faith and the freedom of nations can make them.[191]

The entrance of the United States into the war meant that there would now be a bloc of Anglo-Saxon powers united against German militarism. Spring Rice believed that his role as Ambassador to the United States had been fulfilled by navigating Britain through the mercurial waters of American public opinion. However, he understood that only the United States government should make the decision to declare war on Germany, and only when its interests were endangered. Nevertheless, he was content that the United States and the British Empire were engaged in the same undertaking.[192]

Anglo-Saxonists rejoiced when Wilson asked Congress for a declaration of war against Germany. No longer under the pretense of "neutrality," strict or otherwise, Anglo-Saxonists could openly declare Germany to be an enemy of liberty and therefore not part of the Anglo-Saxon family. Madison Grant, for instance, in his revised edition of *The Passing of the Great Race*, retracted any references to the "Germanic" or "Teutonic" origins of early American settlers. Instead, other Anglo-Saxonists like Henry Fairfield Osborn declared that the German people were actually descended from "Asiatic" peoples, and therefore had no connection to the early Anglo-Saxons who settled in England.[193] George Louis Beer, a history professor at Columbia University, saw the entry of the United States as an opportunity for the Anglo-Saxon peoples to take up the fight for civilization and self-government. It was clear to him that the danger to world peace was the Prussian militarism and autocracy represented by Germany. For the Allies, the goal, then, was to ensure that Germany would never again have the ability to threaten world peace. Beer saw the German state as little changed from its primordial beginnings, when the "Teutonic" warlords had a personal tie to their warriors, compared to democratic countries that had civilian control over the military.[194] He argued that the Prussian military state was incompatible with the values of self-government represented by the Anglo-Saxon Peoples:

> The German people have for generations been so impregnated with the creed of Teutonic racial superiority, they are in large part so thoroughly permeated with the over-weening ambitions of an aggressive *Kulturpolitik* and *Weltpolitik* based upon the doctrines of ascendancy, and they have so widely accepted a materialistic code that rejects all moral considerations in interstate relations, that even the overthrow of an autocracy supported by the army and a subservient bureaucracy would by no means guarantee the liberties of the world and make it safe for peace-loving democracies. The systematic educational drill of two generations cannot be nullified and discredited in a day. But the overthrow of militarism and the establishment of democracy would at least allow the entrance of the light.[195]

"Hurrying Over," *News of the World*, April 7, 1918. On April 2, 1917, the United States declared war on Germany, ending almost three years of neutrality. As part of President Wilson's pledge "to make the world safe for democracy," the United States here sends fresh troops to aid the British and French.

Beer argued that with the entrance of the United States into the war, the unity of the Anglo-Saxon peoples was complete. As Germany represented the values of Teutonic militarism, the United States, Great Britain, and the dominions of the British Empire represented the ideals of self-government, for the dominions of Canada, Australia, New Zealand, and South Africa, were not "colonies" to be subordinated by a mother country, but self-governing polities with democratic institutions.[196] He also ascribed the pioneering qualities of "individual enterprise" in the settlers of the English-speaking dominions, which allowed them to flourish, compared to the militarism of the German Empire and its "contempt" for non-militaristic societies.[197] Additionally, Beer reinterpreted the early leaders of the United States, such as George Washington and Alexander Hamilton, not as rebels to the British crown, but as part of the larger Anglo-Saxon family since the ideals for which they fought during the American Revolution were really part of ideals of Anglo-Saxonism: the right to self-government and liberty.[198] Thus, in Beer's eyes, the British Empire was not a despotism (unlike the German *Reich* of Kaiser Wilhelm II), but rather was a "commonwealth of nations," where elements such as loyalty to the British crown, the parliamentary system, the English language, and not brute force, were the ties that bound the dominions to Great Britain, not as subordinates, but as equals.[199]

The role of the United States throughout the First World War was been complex, to say the least. On the one hand, when the conflict began, Wilson officially declared neutrality and hoped to play a role as a mediator since the United States would be the strongest of all the neutral powers involved. However, that neutrality proved far harder to keep because of the pro–Entente sentiment in the foreign policy establishment in Washington. Politicians like Theodore Roosevelt and Henry Cabot Lodge castigated the Wilson administration for taking too strict a stance on neutrality, especially in light of German atrocities in Belgium and submarine warfare on the high seas. American financiers and companies openly supplied much-needed war materiel, and they loaned significant amounts of money the Allies. While openly condemning Germany's submarine warfare, the Wilson administration, especially following the resignation of William Jennings Bryan as Secretary of State, was not as strenuous in its objections to British violations of neutrality on the high seas.

Despite pro–Allied sympathies among the foreign policy elite, it would have required a great deal of effort to convince American public opinion to enter into the war in support of Great Britain and France. The traditional isolationism in American society would have already made many Americans loath to take part in yet another one of Europe's endless wars, which many of its immigrants had sought to escape since the early years of the United States. Washington's Farewell Address and the Monroe Doctrine had been the cornerstone of American foreign policy since the early days of the republic; this precedent precluded any foreign adventures and had taught Americans to be averse to European affairs. Additionally, through immigration, especially that of the mid nineteenth century, significant proportions of the population consisted of Americans of Irish or German descent, and these groups contributed to the political, economic, social, and intellectual life of the United States. Neither of those groups would have been friendly toward Great Britain even under normal circumstances, and both groups, especially German-Americans, still maintained strong cultural ties to their countries of origin. When the war broke out, German-American groups took great strides to ensure that the United States government maintain the policy of strict neutrality, just as the German government would have preferred. Making a case for war would have been difficult for foreign policy makers.

Thus in order to sway a diverse American populace, Anglo-Saxonism underwent another redefinition. Whereas twenty years earlier Anglo-Saxonism provided the justification for American overseas expansion, Anglo-Saxonism in the First World War became associated with the seemingly "universal" cause of liberty and self-government. Through the joint efforts of American and British propaganda machines, the American public was exposed to a barrage of atrocity stories committed by German occupation forces in Belgium, especially the shooting of an English nurse, Edith Cavell. The sinking of the *Lusitania* also provided the perfect ammunition for the British and American governments to persuade the American public to support action and eventually war against Germany, for it showed that the German government would go so far as to sink unarmed vessels filled with civilians. Such stories would show average Americans that Germany represented the forces of autocracy and barbarism, which could not be reconciled with the Anglo-Saxon values of civilization, liberty, and self-government, characteristics that were instead associated with the Allied cause. Whereas just two decades earlier Anglo-Saxonists acknowledged the German people as "Teutonic" cousins of the Anglo-Saxon family, they completely severed all ties with Germany because Prussian militarism could not possibly bear any resemblance to the ideals of self-government and liberty so espoused by the Anglo-Saxon nations of Great Britain, its dominions, and the United States. Thus, by the time President Wilson argued that the world would be made safe for democracy in April of 1917, it was no longer necessary to trumpet the ideals of Anglo-Saxonism, for, to the American people, the values of Anglo-Saxonism and democracy were already one and the same.

Conclusion

Playwright George Bernard Shaw described the United States and Great Britain as "two countries separated by a common language." Beyond that comparison, he is quite mistaken: in fact, no two countries have ever been closer. Since the end of the Second World War, the "Special Relationship" shared by the United States and Great Britain has been a fact of international diplomacy that has carried both countries in almost every conflict since, including the conflicts in Iraq and Afghanistan during the early twenty-first century. In the shifting sands of international diplomacy, the "Special Relationship" has been considered almost a certainty, with the benefits taken for granted by both English-speaking peoples. No other two countries of such major geopolitical consequence have shared such closeness politically, militarily, economically, and culturally. Additionally, it is the similar worldview shared by both countries that has significantly shaped events of the past century, and the *rapprochement* between Britain and the United States, which established the foundation for the "Special Relationship," has allowed both countries to move beyond old grievances. The first instance of this was during the First World War, when the United States abandoned its traditional reluctance to participate in European wars and entered on the side of the Allies at a very crucial moment. With the availability of American capital, material, and men, the United States turned the balance of the war heavily in favor of the Allies and broke the three-year-long stalemate of the Western Front.

The purpose of this study has been to answer the question of what allowed the United States to break its long tradition of isolationism in global affairs and side with the Allies in the First World War: Anglo-Saxonism provided both English-speaking powers that worldview. Anglo-Saxonism served as the rallying cry for the United States to send its soldiers "over there." In the millennium before the Great War, Anglo-Saxonism had undergone various transformations. In its strictest sense,

Anglo-Saxonism was used as the term for the body of literature in the Anglo-Saxon language that conveyed founding myths of the Germanic peoples who invaded England in the centuries following the end of Roman rule. These myths served to coalesce the disparate groups of Angles, Saxons, Frisians and Jutes, into the English people, who would later distinguish themselves from the Norman conquerors who vanquished King Harold in 1066 at the Battle of Hastings, ushering in feudalism and centralized government. In Anglo-Saxon myths, which form the core of English literature today with legends such as King Arthur and the Round Table, the Anglo-Saxons held the virtues of courage, independence, self-control, and liberty, characteristics that would later be interpreted as "self-government." Over the centuries, English leaders adapted these myths to suit the needs of the time. During the Reformation in the sixteenth century, the Puritans reinterpreted Anglo-Saxon myths to distinguish Protestant England from the corrupt papacy by including the Calvinist doctrine of predestination. By the seventeenth century, Anglo-Saxon myths were mobilized in the struggle between constitutional parliamentary government and an absolute monarchy, with the Whigs casting themselves as the Anglo-Saxons protecting their free institutions against the Normans of their time, the Stuarts, who claimed rule by divine right.

As English settlers crossed the Atlantic toward the New World to establish the thirteen British colonies in North America, Anglo-Saxon myths went with them, which would form the basis of the new American republic. Early leaders commonly referred to as the Founding Fathers, such as John Winthrop, George Washington and Thomas Jefferson, reinterpreted Anglo-Saxon myths to establish the identity of the United States. In the late eighteenth and early nineteenth centuries, it was the Americans who preserved the traditional liberties of the Anglo-Saxons against the feudalistic and tyrannical despotism of the British monarchy. Thomas Jefferson believed that the yeoman farmer was the direct descendant of the Anglo-Saxon citizen-warrior, who was ready to defend his liberty at a moment's notice. Additionally, the New England town hall meeting was seen as a nineteenth-century incarnation of the *"witanagemot,"* the Anglo-Saxon council of elected leaders. Protestantism became part of the American identity as the Puritan settlers believed themselves to be God's "Elect" when they were establishing their "city upon a hill." Thus, the ideals enshrined in the Declaration of Independence, the Constitution, and the Bill of Rights were not so much new ideas but rather a continuation of Anglo-Saxon traditions of liberty. Thus, Americans of the early years of the republic appropriated the Anglo-Saxon values of independence, self-reliance, liberty, rule of law, and self-government.

In the decades following the founding of the republic, the United States expanded westward. As Americans moved west, Anglo-Saxonism also adapted to westward expansion of the antebellum period. With the withdrawal of Spanish influence in the Western Hemisphere, Manifest Destiny provided the justification for the settlement of North America: it was based on the assumption that the entire continent was open for settlement by people of Anglo-Saxon descent. Because only Anglo-Saxons were inherently capable of self-government, other peoples who stood in the way of westward expansion, such as Native Americans and Mexicans, could be swept aside, having been deemed "inferior." At the same time, in the 1840s and 1850s, the Protestant identity of Anglo-Saxonism distinguished nativists from the waves of Irish Catholics who were arriving in the port cities of Boston, New York, and Philadelphia because of the Potato Famine.

In the years following the Civil War, white southerners adapted the Anglo-Saxon narrative to explain their plight. Even though during the Antebellum era they identified with the Norman aristocracy, in the new paradigm of Reconstruction, white southerners saw themselves as the oppressed Anglo-Saxons living under the occupation of the Norman invaders in the aftermath of the Battle of Hastings. White southerners could empathize with the Anglo-Saxons through the loss of self-government as they lived under military occupation and the humiliation of "carpetbagger and Negro rule." Southern intellectuals of the late nineteenth century promoted the study of Anglo-Saxon language and literature as part of their heritage and saw freedmen as inherently incapable of the virtues of self-government, which made Reconstruction an exercise in futility of the most epic proportions.

As the United States moved beyond the scars of the Civil War and Reconstruction, by the end of the nineteenth century Anglo-Saxonism had reached its culmination. The introduction of Charles Darwin's theory of natural selection added a pseudoscientific explanation for the "superiority" of the English-speaking peoples as well as justifying the "inferiority" of other ethnic groups and nationalities. This theory coincided with the rise of the United States as an industrial power, leading to a change in American foreign policy by an elite that was more willing to shed the country's traditional aversion to engagement in global affairs. This White Anglo-Saxon Protestant (WASP) elite was at the top of the political, economic, social, and cultural hierarchy, and they closely identified with the ruling class in Great Britain. Confident, and assured of their place in society, the WASP elite projected the values of Anglo-Saxonism, such as self-control, civic mindedness, and diligence. Whereas Anglo-Saxonism in the United States was, in the early nineteenth century, associated with liberty, by the beginning of the twentieth century it became a justification for colonial rule by the British and American empires, and it served as the basis for the Anglo-American *rapprochement* of the 1890s. The WASP elite, who dominated the foreign policy establishment, began to empathize with the challenges of upholding the "White Man's Burden" carried by the British, as the United States began to administer newly-acquired possessions, such as the Philippines.

The WASP elite vigorously used the social Darwinist element of Anglo-Saxonism to explain their dominance of American society at home and called for a collective unity among all of the Anglo-Saxon peoples abroad, particularly Great Britain and Germany. Anglo-Saxonists of the late nineteenth century made efforts to include the German people in the Anglo-Saxon family through the "Teutonic School," positing that Germany was the primordial birthplace of all Anglo-Saxons, who later migrated to England and the United States. German immigration to the United States went back to the late seventeenth century and also came in waves in the mid-nineteenth century, as Germans sought to escape the upheavals of the Revolutions of 1848. German immigrants and German-Americans made as significant contributions to American political, economic, social, and intellectual life as did the British, and German-Americans comprised a significant proportion of the United States population. After the unification of Germany in 1871 and its subsequent rise as an industrial power, Anglo-Saxonists of the Teutonic School tried to place Germany in the Anglo-Saxon world and wished for some kind of alliance consisting of the United States, Great Britain, and Germany. However, diplomatic realities, namely the rivalry between Britain and Germany, the controversy between Germany and the United States over Samoa, the appearance of German encroachment in the Western Hemisphere, and American ambivalence toward the ideologically conservative and militaristic nature of the Prussian Hohenzollern monarchy, were formidable obstacles in the decade before the First World War.

As the First World War began, despite Woodrow Wilson's profession of strict neutrality, the Wilson administration was far friendlier to the Entente powers than to the Central Powers. American banks loaned billions of dollars to the Allied governments, while American companies supplied munitions and other materiel to the Allies. However, the bloc of

German-American interests, maintaining strong cultural links to the Fatherland, prevented full involvement for the first three years of the conflict. Additionally, American public opinion at the beginning of the war was vehemently opposed to participation in the war because of the country's traditional distaste for European wars. Nevertheless, the foreign policy establishment dominated by the WASP elite once again adapted Anglo-Saxonism by appropriating the values of "civilization," decency, and self-government and associating them with the Anglo-Saxons, and therefore the Allies, relegating "militarism" and "barbarism" to Germany.

Due to the British blockade and command of the seas, the United States provided a captive audience for British propaganda, which constantly disseminated stories of German atrocities in Belgium. Stories of the brutality of German occupying forces in Belgium in the Bryce Report, the execution of English nurse Edith Cavell, and the sinking of the *Lusitania* outraged the American public, who increasingly saw all Germans, including German-Americans, as barbarians with no sense of human decency. Over time, Anglo-Saxonists disqualified Germany from the Anglo-Saxon family because the "true" Anglo-Saxon peoples of Great Britain and the United States had developed systems of representative government and human rights, while Germany remained under warlord rule through the Prussian military state. It was the cultural and political institutions, therefore, of the German Junker elite, particularly militarism and reactionary ideology, that made the German people ineligible to be included among the ranks of the Anglo-Saxons. This was evident in the writings of the Anglo-Saxonists of the period who sought to remove any suggestion that the Teutonic and Anglo-Saxon peoples could bear any kind of similarity.

Thus, by the time Wilson delivered his address to Congress asking for war, a significant portion of the American population was already prepared for war. His argument "to make the world safe for democracy" included the virtues of Anglo-Saxonism, particularly the virtue of "self-government." Wilson's address to Congress carefully distinguished the values of the "self-governing" peoples from the militarism of Germany, which was deemed to be a threat to world peace. It was particularly German government's declaration of unrestricted submarine warfare in 1917 that left Wilson with no other course than to ask Congress for a declaration of war after three years of the role as mediator between the Allies and the Central Powers. At this point, there could be no mistaking the Germans as being part of the Anglo-Saxon family because, by their very nature, they did not share the values of the Anglo-Saxon peoples. When the

United States declared war on Germany, Anglo-Saxonists cheered, for now there was a grand coalition of English-speaking powers consisting of the United States, Great Britain, and its dominions, united toward the noble goal of fighting for the Anglo-Saxon values of liberty and self-government.

Returning to the present day, these next few years will mark the centennial of the outbreak of the "War to end all War." It is now more important than ever to examine the causes of the First World War, a time that, as Earl Grey described, was when "the lights were going out all over Europe" and that twice brought Europeans to the brink of destruction. The century since the "guns of August" has left unresolved issues that continue to plague foreign policy decision makers. I have tried to show the influence of culture on foreign policy by examining the role of Anglo-Saxonism on the American political establishment during the First World War, but more questions arise. Anglo-Saxonism's continuing influence upon American society in the 1920s is also another venue that bears consideration, especially considering the role Anglo-Saxonism played in the resurgence of the Ku Klux Klan. The Ku Klux Klan had its own agenda of "Americanism," which originated during the First World War, as it expanded its mandate from terrorizing African-Americans and preventing them from exercising their rights of citizenship to an anti-immigrant and anti–Catholic platform, which, especially in light of the Russian Revolution in 1917, gained a wide audience, thus bringing the Ku Klux Klan to its highest historical numbers of membership.

The writings of Madison Grant would continue to echo the themes of Anglo-Saxonism by portraying the United States as under siege from the perils of immigration from southern and eastern Europe and "miscegenation;" this would influence policymakers to pass immigration laws in 1921 and 1924 that heavily favored immigrants from northern Europe while severely restricting immigrants from southern and eastern Europe. These immigration policies would bring about significant consequences during the Second World War and the Holocaust. Also, the current debate over immigration reform bears witness to the influence of Anglo-Saxonism: many Americans continue to be uneasy over the changing definition of "American" in light of the Immigration Act of 1965, which removed the previous restrictions of the 1920s, plus the current demographics that suggest a shrinking white majority in the coming decades of the twenty-first century.

The victory of Donald Trump in the 2016 presidential election could be another example of the long reach of Anglo-Saxonism because, throughout his campaign, Trump assiduously courted working-class whites by claiming, in not-so-subtle, racially charged language, that he could help them reclaim their "rightful place" in American society and reverse the forces of diversity and globalization that contributed to their descent in recent decades. The "alt-right movement" or the "white nationalists," who gained prominence as a result of Trump's campaign, reflects the same anxieties of Anglo-Saxonists, who felt threatened by the changing face of American society as it became more diverse through immigration. Like the Anglo-Saxonists of the early twentieth century, working-class whites' senses of having been "left behind" by a globalized economy and their fears of becoming a minority in a country that was growing brown in complexion, in light of having the first African-American president, induced these voters to support Trump.

Having attempted to answer my questions on the origins of the "Special Relationship," I hope to explore the continuing role of Anglo-Saxonism in American and British foreign policy during the interwar period, the Second World War, along with the role of the "Special Relationship" during the Cold War and beyond. The universalist and crusading nature of Wilson's speech to Congress in 1917 also reflects the continuing influence of Anglo-Saxonism in American foreign policy of the twentieth and twenty-first centuries. Almost every president in the past century has repeated Wilson's desire "to make the world safe for democracy" as a justification for the intervention of the United States in subsequent conflicts. The Atlantic Charter, drafted by President Franklin Delano Roosevelt and Prime Minister Winston Churchill, reflected Wilson's ideals and would thus outline the goals of the United States and Great Britain with regard to Europe during the Second World War. The "Special Relationship" can be seen as the fulfillment of the desires of the Anglo-Saxonists of the turn of the twentieth century, as the United States and Great Britain would together face the challenges of the Cold War, with the Soviet Union and communism as the enemy to civilization that must be either contained or eliminated. In the post–Cold War era, the theme of "American exceptionalism" can be seen as another manifestation of Anglo-Saxonism, serving as a justification for neoconservatives to support American intervention in the Middle East and the War on Terror. Perhaps another area that has sparked my curiosity has been the other "special relationships" the United States has with other countries based on shared history or values.

As the global economy becomes further integrated throughout the twenty-first century, the United States and other countries can no longer afford to take refuge in ethnic jingoism such as Anglo-Saxonism and use it to justify aggression, whether in the Middle East, Eastern Europe, or Asia. While Anglo-Saxonism created a purpose and outlet for the United States and the British Empire at the turn of the twentieth century, it came at the expense of the peoples of Latin America, Southeast Asia, the Middle East, and Africa, creating a legacy of bitterness and distrust that continues today. The world must find a new narrative that will foster a common humanity and a fundamental respect for the destinies of all peoples. Only then can Europeans, Americans, and all other peoples of the world escape the fate that befell their counterparts in August of 1914.

Chapter Notes

Introduction

1. Hugh A. MacDougal, *Racial Myth in English History: Trojans, Teutons, and Anglo-Saxons* (Hanover: University Press of New England, 1982), 7.
2. *Ibid.*, 2–3.
3. Gildas, *The Ruin of Britain and Other Works*, Michael Winterbottom, tr. (London: Phillimore & Co., 1978), 22.
4. Nicholas Brooks, *Anglo-Saxon Myths: State and Church 400–1066* (London: Hambledon Press, 2000), 22.
5. Gildas, 23.
6. Don Henson, *The Origins of the Anglo-Saxons* (Hockwold-cum-Wilton, Norfolk: Anglo-Saxon Books, 2006), 58.
7. Brooks, 23–4.
8. Henson, 96–8.
9. *Ibid.*, 106.
10. *Ibid.*, 102.
11. *Beowulf*, Seamus Heaney, tr. (New York: W. W. Norton, 2000), 69.
12. Levom Crossley-Holland, *The Anglo-Saxon World* (Woodbridge, Suffolk: Boydell, 1982), 6–7.
13. Gildas, 17–8.
14. Henson, 103–5.
15. *Ibid.*, 104.
16. C. Warren Hollister, *The Making of England, 55 BC–1399*, 3d ed. (Lexington, MA: D.C. Heath, 1976), 39–40.
17. Bede, *The Ecclesiastical History of the English People*, Judith McClure and Roger Collins, tr. (Oxford: Oxford University Press, 1999), 9–10.
18. *Ibid.*
19. Gildas, 13.
20. George Hardin Brown, *Bede the Venerable* (Boston: Twayne, 1987), 88–9.
21. Bede, 21–2.
22. Gildas, 22–3.
23. *Ibid.*, 25.
24. Bede, 28.
25. *Ibid.*, 27.
26. Brown, 90.
27. *The Anglo-Saxon Chronicle*, M.J. Swanton, tr. (New York: Routledge, 1996), 3.
28. *Ibid.*, 5–9.
29. Janet Thormann, "The Anglo-Saxon Chronicle Poems and the Making of the English Nation," *Anglo-Saxonism and the Construction of Social Identity*, Allen J. Frantzen and John D. Niles, eds. (Gainesville: University of Florida Press, 1997), 64.
30. *The Anglo-Saxon Chronicle*, 13–7.
31. Benedict Anderson, *Imagined Communities: Reflections on the Origin and Spread of Nationalism* (London: Verso, 1983), 6–7.
32. Thormann, 65.
33. Robert Rouse and Cory Rushton, *The Medieval Quest for Arthur* (Stroud, Gloucestershire: Tempus, 2005), 11.
34. Geoffrey of Monmouth, *The History of the Kings of Britain*, Lewis Thorpe, tr. (Middlesex: Penguin, 1966), 53.
35. *Ibid.*, 65.
36. *Ibid.*, 74–5.
37. *Ibid.*, 147.
38. *Ibid.*, 165.
39. Laurie A. Finke and Martin B. Schichtman, *King Arthur and the Myth of History* (Gainesville: University of Florida, 2004), 112.
40. *Ibid.*, 37–8.
41. Allen J. Frantzen, "Bede and Bawdy Bale: Gregory the Great, Angles, and the 'Angli,'" *Anglo-Saxonism and the Construction of Social Identity*, Allen J. Frantzen and John D. Niles, eds. (Gainesville: University Press of Florida, 1997), 25–6.
42. MacDougal, 73–4.

Chapter I

1. Eric P. Kaufmann, *The Rise and Fall of Anglo-America* (Cambridge: Harvard University Press, 2004), 24.
2. David R. Roediger, *The Wages of Whiteness: Race and the Making of the American Working Class* (London: Verso, 1991), 21.
3. Hugh A. MacDougal, *Racial Myth in English History: Trojans, Teutons, and Anglo-Saxons* (Hanover: University Press of New England, 1982), 1–3.
4. Richard Van Alstein, *Genesis of American Nationalism* (Waltham, MA: Blaidswell, 1970), 5.
5. Anderson, 27–8.
6. Kaufman, 47.
7. *Ibid.*, 61.
8. *Ibid.*, 84.
9. Reginald Horsman, "Race and Manifest Destiny: The Origins of American Racial Anglo-Saxonism," *Critical White Studies: Looking Behind the Mirror*, Richard Delgado and Jean Stefancic, eds. (Philadelphia: Temple University Press, 1997), 141–2.
10. Eric P. Kaufmann, *The Rise and Fall of Anglo-America* (Cambridge: Harvard University Press, 2004), 51.
11. *Ibid.*, 51–2.
12. Charles Shattuck, "The True Meaning of the Term 'Liberty' in Those Clauses in the Federal and Stateconstitutions Which Protect [qm]Life, Liberty, and Property," *Harvard Law Review* 4, no. 8 (15 March 1891), 366.
13. *Ibid.*, 369.
14. *Ibid.*, 372.
15. *Ibid.*, 376.
16. *Ibid.*, 383–4.
17. *Ibid.*, 385.
18. *Ibid.*, 368.
19. Anderson, 38.
20. William C. Morey, "The Sources of American Federalism," *Annals of the Academy of American Political Science* 6 (September 1895), 207.
21. *Ibid.*, 208.
22. *Ibid.*, 209.
23. J. R. Hall, "Mid-Nineteenth Century American Anglo-Saxonism," *Anglo-Saxonism and the Construction of Social Identity*, Allen J. Frantzen and John D. Niles, eds. (Gainesville: University Press of Florida, 1997), 133–4.
24. Morey, 213.
25. Dexter A. Hawkins, *The Anglo-Saxon Race: Its History Character and Destiny* (New York: Nelson & Philips, 1875), 25–6.
26. Ritchie Devon Watson, Jr., *Normans and Saxons: Southern Race Mythology and the Intellectual History of the American Civil War* (Baton Rouge: Louisiana State University Press, 2008), 21.
27. *Ibid.*, 169–70.
28. Gregory A. Van Hoosier-Carey, "Byrhtnoth in Dixie: The Emergence of Anglo-Saxon Studies in the Postbellum South," *Anglo-Saxonism and the Construction of Social Identity*, Allen J. Frantzen and John D. Niles, eds. (Gainesville: University Press of Florida, 1997), 157.
29. *Ibid.*, 161.
30. W. P. Trent, "A New South View of Reconstruction," *The Sewanee Review* 9, no. 1 (January 1901), 13.
31. Van Hoosier-Carey, 162.
32. Trent, 16.
33. *Ibid.*, 19.
34. Van Hoosier-Carey, 164.
35. *Ibid.*, 165.
36. *Ibid.*, 169.
37. John Roach Straton, "Will Education Solve the Negro Problem?" *The North American Review* 170, no. 523 (June 1900), 785.
38. *Ibid.*, 786–7.
39. *Ibid.*, 793–4.
40. *Ibid.*, 795–7.
41. *Ibid.*, 798–800.
42. Horsman, 129.
43. Wander, et al., "The Roots of Racial Classification," 31.
44. *Ibid.*, 30–1.
45. *Ibid.*, 31–2.
46. James Hosmer, *A Short History of Anglo-Saxon Freedom: The Polity of the English-Speaking Race* (Boston: Berwick & Smith Printers, 1890), 9–10.
47. Charles Waldstein, "The English-Speaking Brotherhood," *The Living Age* 167 (August 1898), 232.
48. *Ibid.*, 231.
49. Anderson, 37–39.
50. Sir Walter Besant, "The Future of the Anglo-Saxon Race," *North American Review* 376 (August 1896), 129.
51. *Ibid.*, 130.
52. *Ibid.*, 130–1.
53. *Ibid.*, 136.
54. "Are Americans Anglo-Saxon?" *The Spectator*, 30 April 1898, 615.
55. *Ibid.*

56. Reverend George S. Payson, "Anglo-Saxon Supremacy," *Outlook*, 14 March 1896, 11.
57. *Ibid.*
58. "The Anglo-Saxon Race," *Christian Observer*, 6 July 1850, 27.
59. Edward E. Cornwall, M.D., "Are the Americans an Anglo-Saxon People?" *The New York Times*, 14 January 1900, 21.
60. Anderson, 54.
61. Frank Thistlethwaite, *The Anglo-American Connection in the Early Nineteenth Century* (New York: Russel & Russel, 1959), 8.
62. *Ibid.*, 76.
63. Wilkinson, 28.
64. Graeme M. Holmes, *Britain and America: A Comparative Economic History, 1850-1939* (London: David & Charles Publishers Limited, 1976), 9.
65. Thistlethwaite, 40.
66. *Ibid.*, 44-5.
67. Barbara De Wolfe, "Introduction," *Discoveries of America: Personal Accounts of British Emigrants to North America During the Revolutionary Era*, Barbara De Wolfe, ed. (Cambridge: Cambridge University Press, 1997), 3-4.
68. Alexander Thomson, 16 August 1773, "News from America," *Discoveries of America: Personal Accounts of British Emigrants to North America During the Revolutionary Era*, Barbara De Wolfe, ed. (Cambridge: Cambridge University Press, 1997), 119.
69. Rowland Tappan Berthoff, *British Immigrants in Industrial America* (Cambridge: Harvard University Press, 1953), 5.
70. *Ibid.*
71. William E. Van Vugt, *Britain to America: Mid-Nineteenth Century Immigrants to the United States* (Urbana: University of Illinois Press, 1999), 9.
72. First Second and Third Reports from the Select Committee on Emigration from the United Kingdom with Minutes of Evidence, Appendix, and Index, *Irish University Press of British Parliamentary Papers* 5 (29 March 1827), 209.
73. Van Vugt, 11-2.
74. *Ibid.*, 125.
75. Berthoff, 133.
76. Richard Brookhiser, "The Way of the WASP," *Critical White Studies: Looking Behind the Mirror*, Richard Delgado and Jean Stefancic, eds. (Philadelphia: Temple University Press, 1997), 16-7.
77. Capt. John Smith, "The Proceedings of the English Colony in Virginia," 1612, *The Complete Works of Captain John Smith (1580-1631) in Three Volumes*, Vol. 1, Philip L. Barbour, ed. (Chapel Hill: University of North Carolina Press, 1986), 208-10.
78. John Winthrop, "Reasons to Be Considered for Justifying the Undertakers of the Intended Plantation in New England for Encouraging Such Whose Hearts God Shall Move to Join with Them in It," *The English in America 1578-1970*, Howard B. Furer, ed. (New York: Oceana Publications, 1972), 93.
79. Roedigger, 27.
80. *Ibid.*, 25.
81. *Ibid.*, 30.
82. James Iredell, March 1777, Letter Renouncing Allegiance to King George III, from the Rare Book, Manuscript and Special Collections Library, Duke University, 1.
83. *Ibid.*, 7.
84. *Ibid.*, 11.
85. *Ibid.*, 25.
86. *Ibid.*
87. Roediger, 45.
88. Wander, et al., 30.
89. Roedigger, 43.
90. Alexander Saxton, *The Rise and Fall of the White Republic: Class Politics and Mass Culture in Nineteenth-Century America* (London: Verso, 1990), 23-4.
91. Roediger, 55-6.
92. *Ibid.*, 56.
93. *Ibid.*, 59-60.
94. John M. Murrin, "A Protestant Era: Colonial Era to the Civil War," *Religion and American Politics: From the Colonial Era to the Present*, Mark A. Noll and Luke E. Harlow, eds. (New York: Oxford University Press, 2007), 24-6.
95. Harry S. Stout, "Rhetoric and Reality in the Early Republic: The Case of the Federalist Clergy," *Religion and American Politics: From the Colonial Era to the Present*, Mark A. Noll and Luke E. Harlow, eds. (New York: Oxford University Press, 2007), 66.
96. Stout, 72-3.
97. E. Digby Baltzell, *The Protestant Establishment: Aristocracy and Caste in America* (New York: Vintage, 1964), 9-10.
98. Louis B. Wright, *The First Gentlemen of Virginia: Intellectual Qualities of the Early Colonial Ruling Class* (Stanford: Stanford University Press, 1949), 44.
99. Peter Dobkin Hall, *The Organization of American Culture 1700-1900: Private Insti-*

tutions, *Elites, and the Origins of American Nationality* (New York: New York University Press, 1982), 22.

100. John Murrin, *Anglicizing an American Colony: The Transformation of Provincial Massachusetts* (dissertation, Ann Arbor,: University Microfilms, Inc., 1966), 24–5.

101. Hall, 58–9.

102. Baltzell, 110.

103. Joanne Jacobson, *Authority and Alliance in the Letters of Henry Adams* (Madison: University of Wisconsin Press, 1992), 50.

104. Anderson, 63.

105. Rev. J.H. Cone, "Anglo-Saxon Superiority," *The Maine Farmer* 68, no. 20 (15 March 1900), 2.

106. *Ibid.*, 488.

107. *Ibid.*

108. Bradford Perkins, *The Great Rapprochement: England and the United States 1895-1914* (London: Victor Gollanz), 51

109. Hazel McFerson, *The Racial Dimension of American Overseas Colonial Policy* (Westport, CT: Greenwood Press, 1997), 2.

110. George F. Pentecost, DD, "America in the Philippines," *The Arena* 103, no. 186 (May 1905), 490.

111. *Ibid.*, 487.

112. *Ibid.*, 488.

113. Elihu Root, "Address by the Secretary of War at the Marquette Club in Chicago, October 7, 1899, in Response to the Toast, 'The American Soldier," *The Military and Colonial Policies of the United States: Addresses and Reports by Elihu Root*, Robert Bacon and James Brown Scott, eds. (New York: AMS Press, 1970, reprinted from the Cambridge, Massachusetts, 1916, edition), 10.

114. *Ibid.*, 11.

115. Taft, 95–6.

116. Cruz, 86.

117. Abinales, 153.

Chapter II

1. Hans W. Gatzke, *Germany and the United States: "A Special Relationship?"* (Cambridge: Harvard University Press, 1980), 28

2. Albert Bernhardt Faust, *The German Element in the United States*, vol. 1 (Boston: Houghton Mifflin, 1909), 34.

3. *Ibid.*, 55.

4. *Ibid.*, 57.

5. Gatzke, 28.

6. Manfred Jonas, *The United States and Germany: A Diplomatic History* (Ithaca: Cornell University Press, 1984), 16–7.

7. Kathleen Neils Conzen, "Phantom Landscapes of Colonization: Germans in the Making of a Pluralist America," *The German-American Encounter: Conflict and Cooperation Between Two Cultures, 1800–2000*, Frank Trommler and Elliott Shore, eds. (New York: Berghahn Books, 2001), 11.

8. A Greg Roeber, "Through a Glass Darkly: Changing Ideas of American Freedom," *Transatlantic Images and Perceptions: Germany and America Since 1776*, David Barclay and Elizabeth Glaser-Schmidt, eds. (Washington, D.C.: Cambridge University Press, 1997), 20–1.

9. Conzen, 13.

10. Herman Wellenreuter, "Germans Make Cows and Women Work, " *Transatlantic Images and Perceptions: Germany and America Since 1776*, David Barclay and Elizabeth Glaser-Schmidt, eds. (Cambridge: Cambridge University Press, 1997), 47–8.

11. *Ibid.*, 50.

12. *Ibid.*, 52–6.

13. *Ibid.*, 57–9.

14. Hans-Jurgen Grabbe, "Weary of Germany—Weary of America: Perceptions of the United States in Nineteenth-Century Germany," *Transatlantic Images and Perceptions: Germany and America Since 1776*, David Barclay and Elizabeth Glaser-Schmidt, eds. (Cambridge: Cambridge University Press, 1997),71–2.

15. A.J.P. Taylor, *The Course of German History: A Survey of the Development of Germany Since 1815* (New York: Capricorn Books, 1962), 68–70.

16. R.R. Palmer, et al., *A History of the Modern World*, 10th ed. (New York: McGraw-Hill, 2007), 500–1.

17. John Gerow Gazley, *American Opinion of German Unification, 1848–1871* (New York: Longmans, Green, & Co., 1926), 17–9.

18. *Ibid.*, 20.

19. Jonas, 19.

20. Gazley, 23–6.

21. Carl Schurz to Theodore Petrasch, 18 September 1848, *Intimate Letters of Carl Schurz*, vol. 30, Joseph Schafer, ed. and trans. (Madison: State Historical Society of Wisconsin, 1928), 50.

22. Taylor, 77–87.

23. Jonas, 20.

24. *Ibid.*

25. James M. Bergquist, "The Forty-

Eighters: Catalysts of German-American Politics," *The German-American Encounter: Conflict and Cooperation Between Two Cultures, 1800-2000*, 23.

26. Carl Berthold, 23 February 1853, *News from the Land of Freedom: German Immigrants Write Home*, Walter D. Kaphoefner, Wofgang Helbich, Ulrike Sommer, eds. (Ithaca: Cornell University Press, 1991), 325.

27. Jonas, 20-1.
28. Bergquist, 26.
29. *Ibid.*, 27.
30. Hans L. Trefousse, *Carl Schurz: A Biography* (New York: Fordham University Press, 1998), 59-60.
31. Carl Schurz to Henry Meyer, 20 November 1856, *Intimate Letters of Carl Schurz*, vol. 30, Joseph Schafer, ed. and trans. (Madison: State Historical Society of Wisconsin, 1928), 173-4.
32. *Ibid.*, 174.
33. Bergquist, 27.
34. *Ibid.*, 28.
35. *Ibid.*
36. *Ibid.*, 29.
37. Walter D. Kamphoefner and Wolfgang Helbich, *Germans in the Civil War*, Susan Carter Vogel, tr. (Chapel Hill: University of North Carolina Press, 2006), 9.
38. *Ibid.*, 20.
39. Gazley, 124-5.
40. *Ibid.*, 127-8.
41. *Ibid.*, 170.
42. *Ibid.*, 183.
43. *Ibid.*, 194.
44. Carl Schurz to Margarethe Meyer Schurz, 24 July 1866, *Intimate Letters of Carl Schurz*, vol. 30, Joseph Schafer, ed. and trans. (Madison: State Historical Society of Wisconsin, 1928), 364.
45. Trefousse, 165.
46. Carl Schurz to Adolf Meyer 3 February 1868, *Intimate Letters of Carl Schurz*, vol. 30, Joseph Schafer, ed. and trans. (Madison: State Historical Society of Wisconsin, 1928), 421.
47. Gatzke, 36.
48. Jonas, 26.
49. Gazley, 289.
50. *Ibid.*, 290-2.
51. Jonas, 27-8.
52. *Ibid.*, 29.
53. Carl Schurz, "Address Delivered at the Peace Celebration in St. Louis," 1871, from the Western Historical Manuscript Collection, University of Missouri-St. Louis, 3.

54. *Ibid.*, 7.
55. Trefouse, 178.
56. Jonas, 32.
57. *Ibid.*, 30.
58. *Ibid.*, 31.
59. *Ibid.*
60. *Ibid.*, 32.
61. Daniel Fallon, "German Influences on American Education," *German-American Encounter: Conflict and Cooperation Between Two Cultures, 1800-2000*, Frank Trommler and Elliott Shore, eds. (New York: Berghahn Books, 2001), 77-8.
62. *Ibid.*, 79.
63. *Ibid.*, 79-80.
64. *Ibid.*, 80.
65. *Ibid.*, 82.
66. *Ibid.*
67. *Ibid.*, 83.
68. *Ibid.*, 84.
69. Daniel T. Rodgers, *Atlantic Crossings: Social Politics in a Progressive Age* (Cambridge: Harvard University Press, 1998), 82-3.
70. *Ibid.*, 222-3.
71. *Ibid.*, 84.
72. *Ibid.*, 235-6.
73. *Ibid.*, 236.
74. *Ibid.*, 242.
75. *Ibid.*, 246.
76. *Ibid.*, 223.
77. *Ibid.*, 247.
78. Anderson, 37-8.
79. Leroy G. Dorsey, *We Are All Americans, Pure and Simple: Theodore Roosevelt and the Myth of Americanism* (Tuscaloosa: University of Alabama Press, 2007), 119.
80. Albert Bernhardt Faust, *The German Element in the United States*, Vol. 2 (Boston: Houghton Mifflin, 1909), 465.
81. "Americans Prefer Germans," *The New York Times*, 9 August 1909, 1.
82. Imanuel Geiss, *German Foreign Policy, 1871-1914* (London: Routledge & Kegan Paul, 1976), 92.
83. Edward A. Freeman, *Outlines of History* (New York: Holt & Williams, 1872), 14-5.
84. *Ibid.*, 108.
85. J. W. Jackson, "The Racial Aspects of the Franco-Prussian War," *The Journal of the Anthropological Institute of Great Britain and Ireland* 1 (1872), 33-4.
86. *Ibid.*, 38-9.
87. *Ibid.*, 39.
88. *Ibid.*, 41.
89. *Ibid.*, 43.
90. James K. Hosmer, *A Short History of*

Anglo-Saxon Freedom (New York: Scribners and Sons, 1890), 3.

91. *Ibid.*, 16-7.
92. *Ibid.*, 20.
93. Josiah Strong, *The United States and the Future of the Anglo-Saxon Race* (London: Alfred Boot and Sons, 1889), 34.
94. Hosmer, 271.
95. *Ibid.*, 330-1.
96. John A. Kasson, "The Hohenzollern Kaiser," *The North American Review* 146, no. 377 (April 1888), 376.
97. Strong, 35.
98. Dorsey, 121.
99. Theodore Roosevelt, "Remarks to the Delegates of the German Societies Received at the White House, 19 November 1903," *The Works of Theodore Roosevelt: Presidential Addresses and State Papers,* Part 2 (New York: P.F. Collier & Son, 1901), 507.
100. Theodore Roosevelt, 15 June 1903, *The Works of Theodore Roosevelt,* 450.
101. Jonas, 67.
102. William Harbutt Dawson, *The German Empire 1867-1914* (Hamden, CT: Archon Books, 1966), 392-3.
103. Carl Schurz, "The United States and Germany," *The Independent,* 20 March 1902, 665.
104. *Ibid.*, 666-7.
105. Theodore Roosevelt to Hermann Speck von Sternberg, 27 November 1899, *Theodore Roosevelt: Letters and Speeches,* Louis Auchincloss, ed. (New York: The Library of America, 2004), 182.
106. Theodore Roosevelt to Whitelaw Reid, 11 September 1905, *The Letters of Theodore Roosevelt,* Elting Morsion, ed. (Cambridge: Harvard University Press, 1952), 18.
107. Theodore Roosevelt to Henry Cabot Lodge, 2 September 1905, *The Letters of Theodore Roosevelt,* Elting Morsion, ed. (Cambridge: Harvard University Press, 1952), 9.
108. Dorsey, 123.
109. *Ibid.*, 125.
110. Theodore Roosevelt, "True Americanism," *The Works of Theodore Roosevelt: American Ideals,* Vol. 2 (New York: P.F. Colliers, 1897), 42.
111. *Ibid.*, 46.
112. Paul M. Kennedy, *The Samoan Triangle: A Study of Anglo-German-American Relations* (Dublin: Irish University Press, 1974), 134.
113. *Ibid.*, 123.

114. *Ibid.*, 7
115. Lorrin A. Thurston, "The Growing Greatness of the Pacific," *The North American Review* 160, no. 461 (April 1895), 448.
116. *Ibid.*, 456.
117. *Ibid.*, 457-8.
118. George Melville, "Our Future on the Pacific: What We Have There to Hold and Win," *The North American Review* 166, no. 496 (March 1898), 293.
119. *Ibid.*, 294.
120. *Ibid.*, 291.
121. *Ibid.*, 287.
122. Kennedy, 3.
123. *Ibid.*, 13.
124. *Ibid.*, 25.
125. Theodore Roosevelt to Cecil Spring Rice, 14 April 1889, *Theodore Roosevelt: Letters and Speeches,* Louis Auchincloss, ed. (New York: The Library of America, 2004), 28.
126. Kennedy, 86.
127. *Ibid.*, 147.
128. *Ibid.*, 238-9.
129. Henry C. Ide, "Our Interest in Samoa," *The North American Review* 165, no. 489 (August 1897), 156.
130. *Ibid.*, 160-1.
131. *Ibid.*, 161.
132. *Ibid.*, 167.
133. *Ibid.*, 169-70.
134. Jonas, 55-6.
135. Holger H. Herwig, *The Politics of Frustration: The United States in German Naval Planning 1889-1941* (Boston: Little, Brown, 1976), 21.
136. *Ibid.*, 25-6.
137. Jonas, 57.
138. F.E. Chadwick, "Present-Day Phase of the Monroe Doctrine," *The Journal of Race Developmen* 4, no. 3 (January 1914), 310.
139. *Ibid.*, 311.
140. Jonas, 68.
141. Theodore Roosevelt to Alfred Thayer Mahan, 3 May 1897, *Theodore Roosevelt: Letters and Speeches,* Louis Auchincloss, ed. (New York: The Library of America, 2004), 95.
142. Theodore Roosevelt to Cecil Spring Rice, 13 August 1897, *Theodore Roosevelt: Letters and Speeches,* Louis Auchincloss, ed. (New York: The Library of America, 2004), 108-9.
143. *Ibid.*, 110.
144. Jonas, 69.
145. Theodore Roosevelt to Cecil Spring Rice, 3 July 1901, *Theodore Roosevelt: Letters and Speeches,* Louis Auchincloss, ed. (New York: The Library of America, 2004), 233.

146. Dawson, 393.
147. Jonas, 70-3.
148. Theodore Roosevelt to Cecil Spring Rice, 3 July 1901, *Theodore Roosevelt: Letters and Speeches*, Louis Auchincloss, ed. (New York: The Library of America, 2004), 233.
149. Theodore Roosevelt to Cecil Spring Rice, 13 May 1905, *Theodore Roosevelt: Letters and Speeches*, Louis Auchincloss, ed. (New York: The Library of America, 2004), 386.
150. *Ibid.*, 387.
151. Theodore Roosevelt to William Howard Taft, 20 April 1905, *The Letters of Theodore Roosevelt*, Elting Morison, ed. (Cambridge: Harvard University Press, 1952), 233.
152. *Ibid.*
153. Theodore Roosevelt to Whitelaw Reid, 28 April 1905, *The Letters of Theodore Roosevelt*, Elting Morison, ed. (Cambridge: Harvard University Press, 1952), 250.
154. Jonas 93-4.
155. *Ibid.*, 92.
156. *Ibid.*, 94.
157. J. Alden Nichols, *Germany After Bismarck: The Caprivi Era* (Cambridge: Harvard University Press, 1958), 55.
158. J. Ellis Barker, "The Future of Anglo-German Relations," *Eclectic Magazine of Foreign Literature*, June 1906, 533.
159. *Ibid.*, 534.
160. *Ibid.*
161. *Ibid.*, 538.
162. *Ibid.*, 543.
163. Sydney Brooks, "Great Britain, Germany, and the United States," *The Living Age*, 31 July 1909, 259.
164. *Ibid.*, 261.
165. *Ibid.*, 262.
166. *Ibid.*
167. *Ibid.*, 263-4.
168. *Ibid.*, 266.
169. W. G. Fitz-Gerald, "Does Germany Menace the World's Peace? the Truth About the Only 'Offensive' Navy," *The North American Review* 184, no. 613 (19 April 1907), 853.
170. *Ibid.*, 856.
171. *Ibid.*, 854-5.
172. *Ibid.*, 859-60.
173. "Germany and the Monroe Doctrine," *Outlook*, 4 November 1914, 521.
174. *Ibid.*, 523.
175. *Ibid.*, 524.
176. *Ibid.*

Chapter III

1. Hazel McFerson, *The Racial Dimension of American Overseas Colonial Policy* (Westport, CT: Greenwood Press, 1997), 80.
2. J. R. Hall, "Mid-Nineteeth-Century American Anglo-Saxonism: The Question of Language," *Anglo-Saxonism and the Construction of Social Identity*, Allen J. Frantzen and John D. Niles, eds. (Gainesville, Florida: University Press of Florida, 1997), 134.
3. MacFerson, 83-4.
4. Paul A. Kramer, "Empires, Exceptions, and Anglo-Saxons: Race and Rule Between the British and United States Empires, 1880-1910," *The Journal of American History* 88, no. 4 (March 2002), 1322-3.
5. Walter LaFeber, *The New Empire: An Interpretation of American Expansion, 1860-1898* (Ithaca: Cornell University Press, 1963, with 1998 preface), 3-4.
6. Paul Kennedy, *The Rise and Fall of the Great Powers* (New York: Random House, 1987), 242.
7. *Ibid.*, 243.
8. *Ibid.*, 243-4.
9. *Ibid.*, 245.
10. Robert L. Beisner, *From the Old Diplomacy to the New, 1865-1900* (Arlington Heights, IL: Harlan Davidson, 1986), 22-3.
11. Kennedy, 203.
12. *Ibid.*, 248.
13. John M. Taylor, *William Henry Seward: Lincoln's Right Hand Man* (New York: HarperCollins, 1991), 179-81.
14. Beisner, 10-2.
15. Glyndon G. Van Deusen, *William Henry Seward* (New York: Oxford University Press, 1967), 511-2.
16. Sidney Lens, *The Forging of the American Empire* (New York: Thomas E. Crowell, 1971), 157.
17. Ernest N. Paolino, *The Foundations of the American Empire: William Henry Seward and U.S. Foreign Policy* (Ithaca: Cornell University Press, 1973), 23.
18. *Ibid.*, 30.
19. LaFeber, 29.
20. *Ibid.*, 30-1.
21. *Ibid.*, 26.
22. William Henry Seward, "Democracy, the Chief Element of Government," 12 September 1860, *The Works of William Henry Seward*, Vol. 4, George Baker, ed. (New York: Houghton Mifflin, 1888), 319.
23. La Feber, 31.

24. William Henry Seward, "The Destiny of America," 14 September 1853, *The Works of William Henry Seward*, Vol. 4, George Baker, ed. (New York: Houghton Mifflin, 1888), 325.
25. Paolino, 147.
26. *Ibid.*, 210–2.
27. Beisner, 74.
28. Nell Irvin Painter, *Standing at Armageddon: The United States, 1877–1919* (New York: W.W. Norton, 1987), xxxiii–iv.
29. Beisner, 75.
30. Kristin L. Hoganson, *Fighting for American Manhood: How Gender Politics Provoked the Spanish-American and Philippine-American Wars* (New Haven: Yale University Press, 1998), 15–6.
31. Painter, 148.
32. Lens, 161.
33. Painter, 142.
34. Stuart Anderson, *Race and Rapprochement: Anglo-Saxonism and Anglo-American Relations, 1895–1904* (London: Associated University Presses, 1981), 73.
35. Lens, 166.
36. LaFeber, 58.
37. *Ibid.*, 59.
38. *Ibid.*, 60.
39. Robert Seager, II, *Alfred Thayer Mahan: The Man and His Letters* (Annapolis: Naval Institute Press: 1977), 2.
40. *Ibid.*, 37.
41. Alfred Thayer Mahan, "Hawaii and Our Future Sea Power," *The Interest of America in Sea Power, Present and Future* (Boston: Little, Brown, 1898), 35.
42. Alfred Thayer Mahan, *The Influence of Sea Power Upon History 1660–1783* (Boston: Little, Brown, 1890), 1.
43. Mahan, *The Influence of Sea Power Upon History 1660–1783*, 36–7.
44. Seager, 204.
45. Mahan, 34–5.
46. *Ibid.*, 35.
47. Richard D. Challener, *Admirals, Generals, and American Foreign Policy* (Princeton: Princeton University Press, 1973), 13.
48. *Ibid.*, 14.
49. Seager, 224.
50. Theodore Roosevelt, "Review of the Influence of Sea Power Upon History," *The Writings of Theodore Roosevelt*, William H. Harbaugh, ed. (Indianapolis: Bobs-Merrill, 1967), 41.
51. Alfred Thayer Mahan, "The United States Looking Outward," *The Atlantic Monthly*, August 1898, *The Interest of America in Sea Power, Present and Future* (Boston: Little, Brown, 1898), 6.
52. *Ibid.*, 7–8.
53. Foster Rhea Dulles, *America's Rise to World Power* (New York: Harper and Brothers, 1955), 32–3.
54. Seager, 225.
55. Challener, 26.
56. Alfred Thayer Mahan, "The Possibility of an Anglo-American Reunion," *The Interest of America in Sea Power, Present and Future* (Boston: Little, Brown, 1898), 108.
57. Seager, 348–9.
58. Mahan, "Hawaii and Our Future Sea Power," 34.
59. Challener, 26.
60. *Ibid.*, 27.
61. Mahan, "The Problem of Asia," *Harpers New Monthly Magazine*, March 1900, 543.
62. Mahan, "Hawaii and Our Future Sea Power," 33.
63. *Ibid.*, 36–7.
64. Alfred Thayer Mahan, "The Isthmus and Sea Power," *The Atlantic Monthly*, September 1893, reprinted in *The Interest of America in Sea Power, Present and Future* (Boston: Doubleday, 1918), 69.
65. *Ibid.*, 73.
66. Challener, 37.
67. *Ibid.*, 165–6.
68. *Ibid.*, 179–80.
69. Seager, 460.
70. Challener, 186–7.
71. Alfred Thayer Mahan, "The Problem of Asia," *Harpers New Monthly Magazine*, March 1900, 538.
72. *Ibid.*, 540.
73. Theodore Roosevelt to Alfred Thayer Mahan, 18 March 1901, *The Letters of Theodore Roosevelt*, Elting E. Morison, ed. (Cambridge: Harvard University Press, 1951), 19.
74. Seager, 465.
75. Mahan, 542.
76. Bruce Miroff, *Icons of Democracy: American Leaders as Heroes, Aristocrats, Dissenters, and Democrats* (Lawrence: University Press of Kansas, 1993), 160–1.
77. Rubin Francis Weston, "Racism and the Imperialist Campaign," *Race and U.S. Foreign Policy in the Ages of Territorial and Market Expansion, 1840 to 1900* (New York: Garland Publishing, 1998), 190.
78. Philip W. Kennedy, "Racial Overtones of Imperialism, 1900," *Race and U.S. Foreign Policy in the Ages of Territorial and Market Ex-

pansion, 1840 to 1900 (New York: Garland Publishing, 1998), 199.

79. Theodore Roosevelt to John Hay, 1 July 1899, *The Letters of Theodore Roosevelt*, Vol. 2, Elting E. Morison, ed. (Cambridge: Harvard University Press, 1951), 1024.

80. John Hay to Whitelaw Reid, 29 November 1898, *The Life and Letters of John Hay*, Vol. 2, William Roscoe Thayer, ed. (Boston: Houghton Mifflin, 1915), 198-9.

81. Theodore Roosevelt to John Hay, 1 July 1899, 1024-5.

82. *Ibid.*, 1025.

83. *Ibid.*

84. Seager, 520.

85. *Ibid.*, 520-1.

86. Theodore Roosevelt to William Wingate Sewall, 4 May 1898, *The Letters of Theodore Roosevelt*, Vol. 2, Elting E. Morison, ed. (Cambridge: Harvard University Press, 1951), 823.

87. Henry J. Hendrix, *Theodore Roosevelt's Naval Diplomacy: The U.S. Navy and the Birth of the American Century* (Annapolis: Naval Institute Press, 2009), 20-1.

88. Theodore Roosevelt to Paul Morton, 25 June 1904, *The Letters of Theodore Roosevelt*, Vol. 4, Elting E. Morison, ed. (Cambridge: Harvard University Press, 1951), 847.

89. *Ibid.*, 848.

90. Anderson, 148-9.

91. Theodore Roosevelt to Cecil Spring Rice, 11 August 1899, *The Letters of Theodore Roosevelt*, Vol. 2, Elting E. Morison, ed. (Cambridge: Harvard University Press, 1951), 1051-2.

92. *Ibid.*, 1053.

93. Hoganson, 29.

94. Hendrix, 104.

95. Theodore Roosevelt to Cecil Spring Rice, 13 June 1904, *The Letters of Theodore Roosevelt*, Vol. 4, Elting E. Morison, ed. (Cambridge: Harvard University Press, 1951), 830-2.

96. Theodore Roosevelt to John Hay, 26 July 1904, *The Letters of Theodore Roosevelt*, Vol. 4, Elting E. Morison, ed. (Cambridge: Harvard University Press, 1951), 865.

97. Hendrix, 105.

98. Theodore Roosevelt to Cecil Spring Rice, 16 June 1905, *The Letters of Theodore Roosevelt*, Vol. 4, Elting E. Morison, ed. (Cambridge: Harvard University Press, 1951), 1233.

99. Bradford Perkins, *The Great Rapprochement: England and the United States, 1895-1914* (London: Victor Gollanz, 1969), 52.

100. *Ibid.*

101. *Ibid.*, 6.

102. Kennedy, 226.

103. *Ibid.*, 210. In coal production, Germany produced 89 million tons in 1890 to 277 million tons in 1914 compared to Britain at 292 million tons.

104. *Ibid.*, 228. Britain produced 22.9 percent of world manufacturing and 23 percent of world trade. By 1913, it was only at 13.6 and 14 percent respectively. Between 1820 and 1840, annual productivity was 4 percent which shrank to 3 percent between 1840 and 1870 and decreased even further to 1.5 percent between 1875 and 1894.

105. "Two Foreign Policies," *The Economist*, 12 February 1898, 231.

106. Joseph Chamberlain, "Speech by Colonial Secretary Joseph Chamberlain at the Birmingham Town Hall Advocating Closer Ties with the United States, 13 May 1898," *Great Britain, Foreign Policy and Span of Empire 1689-1971*, Joel H. Wiener, ed. (New York: Chelsea, 1972), vol. 1, 509.

107. *Ibid.*, 509.

108. David H. Burton, *British-American Diplomacy 1895-1917 Early Years of the Special Relationship* (Malabar, FL: Krieger Publishing Company, 1999), 27.

109. *Ibid.*, 28.

110. *Ibid.*, 33.

111. John Hay to Henry White, 14 February, 1899, *the Life and Letters of John Hay*, Vol. 2, William Roscoe Thayer, ed. (Boston: Houghton Mifflin, 1915), 218.

112. Burton, 32.

113. Perkins, 52.

114. Charles Waldstein, "The English-Speaking Brotherhood," *The North American Review* 167, no. 501 (August 1898), 225.

115. *Ibid.*, 227.

116. *Ibid.*, 230.

117. *Ibid.*, 232.

118. *Ibid.*, 234.

119. *Ibid.*, 236.

120. Perkins, 158.

121. *Ibid.*, 161.

122. Philip Brown, "American Diplomacy in Central America," *The American Political Science Review* 6, no. 1 (February 1912), 154.

123. *Ibid.*, 155.

124. *Ibid.*, 156.

125. *Ibid.*, 160.

126. *Ibid.*

127. *Ibid.*, 161.

128. *Ibid.*, 163.

129. Hazel McFerson, *The Racial Dimension of American Overseas Colonial Policy* (Westport, CT: Greenwood Press, 1997), 2.

130. Theodore S. Woolsey, "The Government of Dependences," *The Foreign Policy of the United States: Political and Commercial*, Theodore S. Woolsey, E. W. Huffcut, A. Lawrence Lowell, et al., Annals of the American Academy of Political and Social Science, Vol. 13, Supplement 12 (May 1899), 3–4.

131. *Ibid.*, 10.

132. *Ibid.*, 11.

133. Theodore Roosevelt, Jr., *Colonial Policies of the United States* (New York: Doubleday, 1937), 145.

134. Theodore S. Woolsey, "The Government of Dependences," *The Foreign Policy of the United States: Political and Commercial*, 16–7.

135. Sidney Lens, *The Forging of an American Empire* (New York: Thomas Y. Cromwell Company, 1971), 186–7.

136. Elihu Root, "Address by the Secretary of War at the Marquette Club in Chicago, October 7, 1899, in Response to the Toast, 'The American Soldier,'" *The Military and Colonial Policies of the United States: Addresses and Reports by Elihu Root*, Robert Bacon and James Brown Scott, eds. (New York: AMS Press, 1970, reprinted from the Cambridge, Massachusetts, 1916, edition), 10.

137. *Ibid.*, 11.

138. Stuart Creighton Miller, "The American Soldier and the Conquest of the Philippines," *Reappraising an Empire: New Perspectives on Philippine-American History*, Peter W. Stanley, ed. (Cambridge: Harvard University Press 1984), 13–4.

139. Gates, 55–6.

140. *Ibid.*, 57–8.

141. James A. Le Roy, *The Americans in the Philippines: A History of the Conquest and First Years of Occupation with an Introductory Account of the Spanish Rule* (New York: AMS Press, reprint from Boston, 1914, edition), vol. 2, 287–8.

142. "Senator Beveridge on the Philippines," *The New York Times*, 10 January 1900, 5.

143. *Ibid.*

144. Leon Wolff, *Little Brown Brother: How the United States Purchased and Pacified the Philippine Islands at the Century's Turn* (New York: Doubleday & Company, 1961), 339.

145. Julian Go, "Introduction: Global Perspectives on the U.S. Colonial State in the Philippines," *The American Colonial State in the Philippines: Global Perspectives*, Julian Go and Anne L. Forster, eds. (Durham: Duke University Press, 2003), 4–5.

146. Untitled, *The Times of London*, 1 February 1899, 5.

147. Morrell Heald and Lawrence S. Kaplan, *Culture and Diplomacy: The American Experience* (Westport, CT: Greenwood Press, 1977), 143.

148. Theodore Roosevelt to William Howard Taft, 7 February 1900, *The Letters of Theodore Roosevelt*, Elting E. Morison (Cambridge: Harvard University Press 1951), 1175.

149. Bureau of Insular Affairs, *Reports of the Philippine Commission, the Civil Governor, and the Heads of the Executive Departments of the Civil Government of the Philippine Islands (1900–1903)* (Washington D.C.: War Department), 31.

150. Heald and Kaplan, 145–6.

151. Stanley Karnow, *In Our Image: America's Empire in the Philippines* (New York: Random House, 1989), 169–70.

152. Bureau of Insular Affairs, 9.

153. Dean C. Worcester, *The Philippines Past and Present* (New York: Macmillan, 1930), 273–5.

154. Romeo V. Cruz, *America's Colonial Desk and the Philippines, 1898–1934* (Quezon City: University of the Philippines Press, 1974), 24.

155. *Ibid.*, 26.

156. William Howard Taft, "Inaugural Address as Civil Governor of the Philippines," *The Collected Works of William Howard Taft*, David H. Burton, ed. (Athens: Ohio University Press, 2001), vol. 1, 79.

157. William Howard Taft, "The Duties of Citizenship Viewed from the Standpoint of Colonial Administration," *The Collected Works of William Howard Taft*, David H. Burton, ed. (Athens: Ohio University Press, 2001), vol. 1, 41.

158. McFerson, 109.

159. Bureau of Insular Affairs, 399.

160. *Ibid.*, 712.

161. David P. Barrows, "Education and Social Progress in the Philippines," *The Annals of the American Academy of Political and Social Science* 30, no. 1 (July 1907), 73.

162. Bureau of Insular Affairs, 412.

163. *Ibid.*

164. Norman G. Owen, "Introduction: Philippine Society and American Colonialism," *Compadre Colonialism: Studies on the*

Philippines Under American Rule, Norman G. Owen, ed. (Ann Arbor: University of Michigan, 1971), 1–3.
   165. Taft, 95–6.
   166. Cruz, 86.
   167. Patricio N. Abinales, "Progressive-Machine Conflict in Early Twentieth Century U.S. Politics and Colonial State Building in the Philippines," *The American Colonial State in the Philippines: Global Perspectives*, Julian Go and Anne L. Forster, eds. (Durham: Duke University Press, 2003), 153.
   168. Paul A. Kramer, "Empires, Exceptions, and Anglo-Saxons: Race and Rule Between the British and United States Empires, 1880–1910," *The Journal of American History* 88, no. 4 (March 2002), 1342.
   169. Thomas J. Noer, *Briton, Boer, and Yankee: The United States and South Africa 1870–1914* (Kent, OH: Kent State University Press, 1978), 6.
   170. Richard B. Mulanax, *The Boer War in American Politics and Diplomacy* (Lanham, MD: University Press of America, 1994), 9.
   171. *Ibid.*, 14.
   172. *Ibid.*, 15.
   173. Martin Kröger, "Imperial Germany and the Boer War," *The International Impact of the Boer War*, Keith Wilson, ed. (New York: Palgrave, 2001), 25–6.
   174. *Ibid.*, 28.
   175. Keith Wilson, "The Boer War in the Context of Britain's Imperial Problems," *The International Impact of the Boer War*, Keith Wilson, ed. (New York: Palgrave, 2001), 160.
   176. Noer, xi.
   177. Mulanax, 132.
   178. Theodore Roosevelt to Cecil Spring Rice, 2 December 1899, *The Letters of Theodore Roosevelt, the Letters of Theodore Roosevelt*, Elting E. Morison, ed. (Cambridge: Harvard University Press 1951), 1103–4.
   179. William N. Tilchin, "The United States and the Boer War," *The International Impact of the Boer War*, Keith Wilson, ed. (New York: Palgrave, 2001), 113.
   180. *Ibid.*, 114.
   181. *Ibid.*, 118.
   182. Noer, 73.
   183. Tilchin, "The United States and the Boer War," 109.
   184. Theodore Roosevelt to A. J. Sage, 9 March 1900, *The Letters of Theodore Roosevelt, the Letters of Theodore Roosevelt*, Elting E. Morison (Cambridge: Harvard University Press 1951), 1214–5.

   185. Paul A. Kramer, "Empires, Exceptions, and Anglo-Saxons: Race and Rule Between the British and United States Empires, 1880–1910," *The Journal of American History* 88, no. 4 (March 2002), 1341.
   186. F. V. Englenburg, "A Transvaal View of the South African Question," *The North American Review* 169, no. 515 (October 1899), 473–4.
   187. *Ibid.*, 475–6.
   188. *Ibid.*, 476–7.
   189. *Ibid.*, 478.
   190. *Ibid.*, 1339.
   191. Senator Augustus Bacon, "Independence for the Philippines," *Republic or Empire? the Philippine Question*, William Jennings Bryan, ed. (Chicago: W.B. Conkey, 1900), 545.
   192. Edward Stratemeyer, *Between Briton and Boer or Two Boys' Adventures in South Africa* (Boston: Lothrop, Lee & Shepard, 1900), 6–7.
   193. Kramer, 1344.
   194. Stratemeyer, 225–6.
   195. *Ibid.*, 292–3.
   196. *Ibid.*, 189.
   197. Kramer, 1344.

Chapter IV

   1. Arthur S. Link, *Wilson: The Struggle for Neutrality, 1914–15* (Princeton: Princeton University Press, 1960), 3.
   2. Woodrow Wilson, "Statement of the President, August 19, 1914, in the Early Days of the Great War," *President Wilson's Great Speeches and Other History Making Documents* (Chicago: Stanton and Van Vliet, 1917), 43–4.
   3. William Jennings Bryan to Woodrow Wilson, 28 August 1914, *Papers Relating to the Foreign Relations of the United States: The Lansing Papers, 1914–1920: Volume 1* (Washington, D.C.: United States Government Printing Office, 1939), 7.
   4. Link, 11.
   5. "Germany's Appeal to America," *The Independent*, 24 August 1914, 260.
   6. Theodore Roosevelt, *America and the Great War* (New York: Charles Scribner's, 1915), 16–7.
   7. *Ibid.*, 66–7.
   8. *Ibid.*, 72.
   9. Theodore Roosevelt to Edmond Robert Otto von Mach, *The Letters of Theodore Roosevelt*, Vol. 7, Elting E. Morison,

ed. (Cambridge: Harvard University Press, 1954), 832.

10. Roosevelt, 24.

11. Theodore Roosevelt to Arthur Hamilton Lee, 22 August 1914, *The Letters of Theodore Roosevelt*, Vol. 7, Elting E. Morison, ed. (Cambridge: Harvard University Press, 1954), 810.

12. Roosevelt, *America and the Great War*, 64–5.

13. Theodore Roosevelt to Arthur Hamilton Lee, 810.

14. Roosevelt, *America and the Great War*, 67–8.

15. Sydney Brooks, "The United States and the War," *The North American Review* 201, no. 711 (February 1915), 231.

16. *Ibid.*, 232.

17. *Ibid.*, 235.

18. *Ibid.*, 238.

19. *Ibid.*, 240.

20. Cecil Spring Rice to Dominick Spring Rice, 17 September 1915, *The Letters and Friendships of Sir Cecil Spring Rice*, Vol. 2, Stephen Gwinn, ed. (London: Constable, 1929, reprinted Freeport, New York: Books for Libraries Press, 1972), 285.

21. *Ibid.*, 286.

22. Cecil Spring Rice to Sir Valentine Chirol, 27 November 1914, *The Letters and Friendships of Sir Cecil Spring Rice: A Record*, Vol. II, Stephen Gwynn, ed. (London: Constable, 1929, reprinted Freeport, New York: Books for Libraries Press, 1972), 247.

23. *Ibid.*, 248.

24. Cecil Spring Rice to Lord Onslow, 23 September 1915, *The Letters and Friendships of Sir Cecil Spring Rice: A Record*, Vol. II, Stephen Gwynn, ed. (London: Constable, 1929, reprinted Freeport, New York: Books for Libraries Press, 1972), 306–7.

25. Robert W. Tucker, *Woodrow Wilson and the Great War: Reconsidering America's Neutrality 1914–1917* (Charlottesville: University of Virginia Press, 2007), 17.

26. Woodrow Wilson, "An Appeal to the Citizens of the Republic, Requesting Their Assistance in Maintaining a State of Neutrality During the Present European War," 18 August 1914, *President Wilson's Foreign Policy: Messages, Addresses, Papers*, James Brown Scott, ed. (New York: Oxford University Press, 1918), 67–8.

27. William C. Widenor, *Henry Cabot Lodge and the Search for an American Foreign Policy* (Berkeley: University of California Press, 1980), 188–9.

28. Henry Cabot Lodge to Theodore Roosevelt, 15 January 1915, *Selections from the Correspondence of Theodore Roosevelt and Henry Cabot Lodge* (New York: Charles Scribner's Sons, 1925), 451.

29. Charles Seymour, *American Diplomacy During the World War* (Hamden, CT: Archon Books, 1964), 130–1.

30. William Jennings Bryan to Woodrow Wilson, 1 December 1914, *Papers Relating to the Foreign Relations of the United States: The Lansing Papers 1914–1920* (Washington, D.C.: United States Government Printing Office, 1939), 10–1.

31. Daniel M. Smith, *The Great Departure: The United States and World War I, 1914–1920* (New York: John M. Wiley and Sons, 1965), 15.

32. Lawrence W. Levine, *Defender of the Faith: William Jennings Bryan: The Last Decade, 1915–1925* (New York: Oxford University Press, 1965), 6–7.

33. Daniel M. Smith, *Robert Lansing and American Neutrality* (Berkeley: University of California Press, 1958), 1.

34. *Ibid.*, 5.

35. Smith, *The Great Departure*, 18.

36. Robert Lansing, *War Memoirs of Robert Lansing* (Indianapolis: Bobbs-Merril, 1935), 75.

37. Robert Lansing, 19 November 1914, "Memorandum by the Counselor for the Department of State on Professor Hugo Münsterberg's Letter to President Wilson," *Papers Relating to the Foreign Relations of the United States: The Lansing Papers 1914–1920* (Washington, D.C.: United States Government Printing Office, 1939), 167.

38. *Ibid.*, 174.

39. Lansing, *War Memoirs*, 22–3.

40. William Jennings Bryan to Woodrow Wilson, 23 April 1915, *Papers Relating to the Foreign Relations of the United States: The Lansing Papers 1914–1920* (Washington, D.C.: United States Government Printing Office, 1939), 379.

41. Robert Lansing to William Jennings Bryan, 1 May 1915, *Papers Relating to the Foreign Relations of the United States: The Lansing Papers 1914–1920* (Washington, D.C.: United States Government Printing Office, 1939), 381.

42. Tucker, 109.

43. Lansing, *War Memoirs*, 19.

44. Robert Lansing to William Jennings Bryan, 5 May 1915, *Papers Relating to the Foreign Relations of the United States: The Lansing*

Notes—Chapter IV

Papers 1914-1920 (Washington, D.C.: United States Government Printing Office, 1939), 384.

45. William Jennings Bryan to Woodrow Wilson, 9 May 1915, *Papers Relating to the Foreign Relations of the United States: The Lansing Papers 1914-1920* (Washington, D.C.: United States Government Printing Office, 1939), 386.

46. *Ibid.*, 19-20.

47. Smith, *Robert Lansing and American Neutrality*, 18.

48. William Jennings Bryan to President Wilson, 10 August 1914, *Papers Relating to the Foreign Relations of the United States: The Lansing Papers, 1914-1920* (Washington, D.C.: United States Government Printing Office, 1939), 131-2.

49. Robert Lansing, 23 October 1914, "Summary of Information in Regard to Credits of Foreign Governments in This Country and the Relation to Trade," *Papers Relating to the Foreign Relations of the United States: The Lansing Papers, 1914-1920* (Washington, D.C.: United States Government Printing Office, 1939), 138-9.

50. Lansing, 128.

51. Ray H. Abrams, *Preachers Present Arms: The Role of the American Churches and Clergy in World Wars I and II, with Some Observations on the War in Vietnam* (Scottsdale, PA: Herald Press, 1933; revised 1969), 3.

52. *Ibid.*, 4.

53. *Ibid.*, 6-7.

54. *Ibid.*, 8.

55. *Ibid.*, 9-11.

56. Ross, 189.

57. Abrams, 22-3.

58. Ross, 189-90.

59. Charles Henry Parkhurst, "Kaiser Is Blamed: Dr. Parkhurst Would Blot Him Out as Public Menace," *The New York Times*, 23 August 1914, wp 6.

60. Abrams, 53-5.

61. Ross, 191.

62. Abrams, 101-3.

63. *Ibid.*, 116-7.

64. *Ibid.*, 119-20.

65. Peterson, 13.

66. Charles Roetter, *The Art of Psychological Warfare, 1914-1945* (New York: Stein and Day, 1974), 32-3.

67. *Ibid.*, 55-7.

68. Armin Rappaport, *The British Press and Wilsonian Neutrality* (Stanford: Stanford University Press, 1951), 11.

69. Peterson, 35.

70. *Ibid.*, 53.

71. *Committee on Alleged German Outrages* (London: His Majesty's Stationery Office, 1915), 87.

72. *Ibid.*, 55-6.

73. *Ibid.*, 113.

74. Peterson, 53-4.

75. *Ibid.*, 58.

76. James Morgan Read, *Atrocity Propaganda, 1914-1919* (New Haven: Yale University Press, 1941), 201.

77. "Lusitania Was Unarmed," *The New York Times*, 10 May 1915, p. 1.

78. "Press Calls Sinking of Lusitania Murder," *The New York Times*, 8 May 1915, p. 6.

79. Read, 17.

80. *Ibid.*, 18-9.

81. "The Law Still Stands," *The St. Louis Republic*, 10 May 1915, 6.

82. William Skaggs, *German Conspiracies in America* (London: T. Fisher, 1915), 11.

83. *Ibid.*, 14-6.

84. Brand Whitlock to General Moritz von Bissing 11 October 1915," *Papers Relating to the Foreign Relations of the United States: The Lansing Papers, 1914-1920* (Washington, D.C.: United States Government Printing Office, 1939), 131

85. Harold D. Lasswell, *Propaganda Technique in the World War* (New York: Garland Publishing, 1927; reprinted 1972), 34.

86. Brandon Whitlock to William Jennings Bryan, 30 October 1915, *Papers Relating to the Foreign Relations of the United States: The Lansing Papers, 1914-1920* (Washington, D.C.: United States Government Printing Office, 1939), 62.

87. Brand Whitlock to Walter Page, 13 October 1915," *Papers Relating to the Foreign Relations of the United States: The Lansing Papers, 1914-1920* (Washington, D.C.: United States Government Printing Office, 1939), 61.

88. James M. Beck, "The Case of Edith Cavell: A Reply to Dr. Albert Zimmermann, Germany's Under Secretary for Foreign Affairs," *The New York Times*, 31 October 1915, p. sm 1.

89. *Ibid.*, 2.

90. Roetter, 11-2.

91. Rappaport, 133-4.

92. "Washington Exposes Plot," *The New York Times*, 1 March 1917, p. 1.

93. Peterson, 315.

94. George Bruntz, *Allied Propaganda and the Collapse of the German Empire* (Stanford: Stanford University Press, 1938; reprinted New York: Arno Press, 1972), 31-2.

95. George Creel, *Complete Report of the Chairman of the Committee on Public Information, 1917, 1918, 1919* (Washington, D.C.: Government Printing Office, 1920; reprinted New York: Da Capo Press, 1972), 1.

96. George Creel, *How We Advertised America* (New York: Harper, 1920; reprinted New York: Arno Press, 1972), 4-5.

97. Creel, *Complete Report of the Chairman of the Committee on Public Information*, 8.

98. Creel, *How We Advertised America*, 4.

99. Creel, *Complete Report of the Chairman of the Committee on Public Information*, 24.

100. Ross, 268.

101. Higham, 208.

102. Widenor, 38.

103. Tucker, 25.

104. Kathleen Burk, *Britain, America, and the Sinews of War, 1914-1918* (Boston: Allen & Unwin, Inc., 1985), 4.

105. *Ibid.*, 14.

106. *Ibid.*, 15.

107. *Ibid.*, 16.

108. *Ibid.*, 18.

109. Sir Cecil Spring Rice to Sir Edward Grey, 20 May 1915, *The Letters and Friendships of Sir Cecil Spring Rice*, Stephen Gwinn, ed. (London: Constable, 1929, reprinted Freeport, New York: Books for Libraries Press, 1972), Vol. 2, 270-1.

110. Burk, 20-1.

111. Cecil Spring Rice to Sir Edward Grey, 25 August 1914, *The Letters and Friendships of Sir Cecil Spring Rice*, Vol. 2, Stephen Gwinn, ed. (London: Constable, 1929, reprinted Freeport, New York: Books for Libraries Press, 1972), 218.

112. *Ibid.*

113. *Ibid.*, 224.

114. Theodore Roosevelt to Cecil Spring Rice, 5 February 1915, *The Letters of Theodore Roosevelt*, Vol. 8, Elting E. Morison, ed. (Cambridge: Harvard University Press, 1954), 888-9.

115. Theodore Roosevelt to John St. Loe Strachey, 22 February 1915, *The Letters of Theodore Roosevelt*, Vol. 8, Elting E. Morison, ed. (Cambridge: Harvard University Press, 1954), 897.

116. *Ibid.*, 898.

117. Stuart Wallace, *War and the Image of Germany: British Academics 1914-1918* (Edinburgh: John Donald Publishers, 1988), 6.

118. *Ibid.*, 60-1.

119. *Ibid.*, 63-4.

120. Alexander Deconde, *Ethnicity, Race, and American Foreign Policy: A History* (Boston: Northeastern University Press, 1992), 55.

121. Stephen J. Gross, "The Perils of Prussianism: Main Street America, Local Autonomy, and the Great War," *Agricultural History* 78, no. 1 (Winter 2004), 79.

122. Woodrow Wilson, "Address to the Daughters of the American Revolution," 11 October 1915, *President Wilson's Great Speeches and Other History Making Documents* (Chicago: Stanton and Van Vliet, 1917), 73.

123. Deconde, 82.

124. John Higham, *Strangers in the Land: Patterns of American Nativism* (New Brunswick: Rutgers University Press, 1955), 197.

125. Sir Cecil Spring Rice to Sir Valentine Chirol, 13 November 1914, *The Letters and Friendships of Sir Cecil Spring Rice*, Stephen Gwinn, ed. (London: Constable, 1929, reprinted Freeport, New York: Books for Libraries Press, 1972), Vol. 2, 244.

126. Deconde, 84.

127. Widenor, 217.

128. John Horne and Alam Kramer, *German Atrocities, 1914: A History of Denial* (New Haven: Yale University Press, 2001), 278-9.

129. M.F. Egan, "Kultur and Our Need of It," *Studies: An Irish Quarterly Review* 4, no. 14 (June 1915), 211-2.

130. Paul L. Atwood, *War and Empire: The American Way of Life* (New York: Pluto Press, 2010), 111.

131. Higham, 201.

132. *Ibid.*, 209.

133. Woodrow Wilson, Address to Congress, 7 December 1915, *President Wilson's Great Speeches and Other History Making Documents* (Chicago: Stanton and Van Vliet, 1917), 94.

134. *Ibid.*, 95.

135. Widenor, 70-1.

136. *Ibid.*, 167.

137. Henry Cabot Lodge to Theodore Roosevelt, 22 February 1915, *Selections from the Correspondence of Theodore Roosevelt and Henry Cabot Lodge* (New York: Charles Scribner's Sons, 1925), 457.

138. Widenor, 198.

139. Theodore Roosevelt to Henry Cabot Lodge, 8 December 1914, *Selections from the Correspondence of Theodore Roosevelt and Henry Cabot Lodge* (New York: Charles Scribner's Sons, 1925), 450.

140. Theodore Roosevelt to James Bryce, 30 November 1915, *The Letters of Theodore Roosevelt*, Vol. 7, Elting E. Morison, ed. (Cambridge: Harvard University Press, 1954), 994.

141. Brian Lloyd, *Left Out: Pragmatism, Exceptionalism, and the Poverty of American Marxism, 1890-1922* (Baltimore: Johns Hopkins Unversity Press, 1997), 274.
142. *Ibid.*, 289.
143. Stewart Halsey Ross, *Propaganda for War: How the United States Was Conditioned to Fight the Great War of 1914-1918* (Jefferson, NC: McFarland, 1996), 146.
144. *Ibid.*, 147.
145. Frederic Louis Huidekoper, "Is America Prepared for War?" *The North American Review* 182, no. 591 (February 1906), 162.
146. Arnold White, "Germany's Aim in Foreign Politics," *The North American Review* 180, no. 581 (April 1905), 560.
147. *Ibid.*, 561.
148. Carlton Hayes, "The War of the Nations," *Political Science Quarterly* 29, no. 4 (December 1914), 689.
149. *Ibid.*, 693.
150. *Ibid.*
151. *Ibid.*, 694.
152. *Ibid.*, 704.
153. *Ibid.*, 701-2.
154. *Ibid.*, 700.
155. *Ibid.*, 706.
156. *Ibid.*, 707.
157. Archibald R. Colquhoun, "Why the British Empire Is at War," *The North American Review* 200, no. 708 (November 1914), 680.
158. *Ibid.*, 688.
159. *Ibid.*, 690.
160. *Ibid.*, 691.
161. *Ibid.*, 692.
162. Victor S. Yarros, "The German and Anglo-American View of the State," *International Journal of Ethics* 28, no. 1 (October 1917), 46.
163. *Ibid.*, 45.
164. *Ibid.*, 48.
165. *Ibid.*, 47.
166. *Ibid.*, 48-9.
167. *Ibid.*, 49-50.
168. *Ibid.*, 51.
169. Ross, 172.
170. *Ibid.*, 173.
171. Theodore Roosevle to Arthur Hamilton Lee, 2 September 1915, *The Letters of Theodore Roosevelt*, Elting E. Morison, ed. (Cambridge: Harvard University Press, 1954),Vol. 8, 967.
172. Roosevelt, 23-4.
173. *Ibid.*, 50-1.
174. *Ibid.*, 276-7.
175. Henry Cabot Lodge to Theodore Roosevelt, 20 January 1915, *Selections from the Correspondence of Theodore Roosevelt of Henry Cabot Lodge 1884-1918, Vol. II* (New York: Charles Scribner's Sons, 1925), 452-3.
176. Ross, 146.
177. H.C. Peterson, *Propaganda for War: The Campaign Against American Neutrality, 1914-1917* (Norman: University of Oklahoma Press, 1939), 12-3.
178. *Ibid.*, 167-7.
179. Ross Gregory, *Walter Hines Page: Ambassador to the Court of St. James's* (Lexington: University of Kentucky Press, 1971), 62.
180. Walter H. Page to Woodrow Wilson, 15 October 1914, *The Life and Letters of Walter H. Page*, Burton J. Hendrick, ed. (Garden City, New York: Doubleday, Page & Co., 1923), 371-2.
181. *Ibid.*
182. Ray Stannard Baker, *Woodrow Wilson: Life and Letters: Facing War, 1915-1917* (New York: Doubleday, Doran, & Company, 1937), 447-8.
183. Tucker, 189.
184. Cecil Spring Rice to Arthur Balfour, 23 February 1917, *The Letters and Friendships of Sir Cecil Spring Rice*, Vol. 2, Stephen Gwinn, ed. (London: Constable, 1929, reprinted Freeport, New York: Books for Libraries Press, 1972), 381.
185. Cecil Spring Rice to Arthur Balfour, 23 March 1917, *the Letters and Friendships of Sir Cecil Spring Rice*, Vol. 2, Stephen Gwinn, ed. (London: Constable, 1929, reprinted Freeport, New York: Books for Libraries Press, 1972), 387-8.
186. Woodrow Wilson, "Why We Went to War," 2 April 1917, *President Wilson's Great Speeches and Other History Making Documents* (Chicago: Stanton and Van Vliet, 1917), 12.
187. *Ibid.*, 13.
188. *Ibid.*, 17.
189. *Ibid.*, 17-8.
190. *Ibid.*, 18-9.
191. *Ibid.*, 20.
192. Gwynn, 389.
193. Higham, 218.
194. George Louis Beer, *The English-Speaking Peoples: Their Future Relations and Joint International Obligations* (New York: Macmillan, 1917), 127.
195. *Ibid.*, 129.
196. *Ibid.*, 170-1.
197. *Ibid.*, 100.
198. *Ibid.*, 172.
199. *Ibid.*, 177.

Bibliography

Government Documents

Bureau of Insular Affairs. *Reports of the Philippine Commission, the Civil Governor, and the Heads of the Executive Departments of the Civil Government of the Philippine Islands 1900-1903.* Washington, D.C.: War Department.

Committee on Alleged German Outrages. London: His Majesty's Stationery Office, 1915.

Complete Report of the Chairman of the Committee on Public Information, 1917, 1918, 1919. Washington, D.C.: Government Printing Office, 1920; reprinted New York: Da Capo Press, 1972.

First, Second and Third Reports from the Select Committee on Emigration from the United Kingdom with Minutes of Evidence, Appendix and Index. *Irish University Press of British Parliamentary Papers* 5, 29 March 1827.

Iredell, James March. 1777, Letter Renouncing Allegiance to King George III. Rare Book, Manuscript and Special Collections Library, Duke University.

Papers Relating to the Foreign Relations of the United States: The Lansing Papers, 1914-1920: Volume 1. Washington, D.C.: United States Government Printing Office, 1939.

Root, Elihu. *The Military and Colonial Policies of the United States: Addresses and Reports by Elihu Root.* Robert Bacon and James Brown Scott, eds. New York: AMS Press, 1970, reprinted from the Cambridge, Massachusetts, 1916, edition.

Correspondences and Papers

Hay, John. *The Life and Letters of John Hay, Vol. 2.* William Roscoe Thayer, ed. Boston: Houghton Mifflin, 1915.

Lansing, Robert. *War Memoirs of Robert Lansing.* Indianapolis: Bobbs-Merrill, 1935.

News from the Land of Freedom: German Immigrants Write Home. Walter D. Kaphoefner, Wofgang Helbich, and Ulrike Sommer, eds. Ithaca: Cornell University Press, 1991.

Page, Walter H. *The Life and Letters of Walter H. Page.* Burton J. Hendrick, ed. Garden City, New York: Doubleday, Page & Co., 1923.

Roosevelt, Theodore. *Letters and Speeches.* Louis Auchincloss, ed. New York: The Library of America, 2004.

_____. *the Letters of Theodore Roosevelt.* Elting Morsion, ed. Cambridge: Harvard University Press, 1952.

_____. "Review of the Influence of Sea Power Upon History." *The Writings of Theodore Roosevelt.* William H. Harbaugh, ed. Indianapolis: Bobs-Merrill, 1967.

_____. *The Works of Theodore Roosevelt: Presidential Addresses and State Papers*, Part 2. New York: P.F. Collier & Son, 1901.

_____. *The Works of Theodore Roosevelt: American Ideals*, Vol. 2. New York: P.F. Collier & Son, 1897.

Schurz, Carl. *Intimate Letters of Carl Schurz.* Joseph Schafer, ed. and trans. Madison: State Historical Society of Wisconsin, 1928.

Selections from the Correspondence of Theodore Roosevelt and Henry Cabot Lodge. New York: Charles Scribner's Sons, 1925.

Seward, William Henry. *The Works of William Henry Seward*, Vol. 4. George Baker, ed. New York: Houghton Mifflin, 1888.

Smith, Capt. John. *The Complete Works of Captain John Smith (1580-1631) in Three Volumes*, Vol. 1. Philip L. Barbour, ed. Chapel Hill: University of North Carolina Press, 1986.

Spring Rice, Cecil. *The Letters and Friendships of Sir Cecil Spring Rice*, Vol. 2. Stephen

Gwinn, ed. London: Constable, 1929, reprinted Freeport, New York: Books for Libraries Press, 1972.

Taft, William. *The Collected Works of William Howard Taft*. David H. Burton, ed. Athens: Ohio University Press, 2001.

Wilson, Woodrow. *President Wilson's Foreign Policy: Messages, Addresses, Papers*, James Brown Scott, ed. New York: Oxford University Press, 1918.

_____. *President Wilson's Great Speeches and Other History Making Documents*. Chicago: Stanton and Van Vliet, 1917.

Printed Primary Sources

"Americans Prefer Germans." *The New York Times*, 9 August 1909, 1.

The Anglo-Saxon Chronicle. M.J. Swanton, tr. New York: Routledge, 1996.

"The Anglo-Saxon Race." *Christian Observer*, 6 July 1850.

"Are Americans Anglo-Saxon?" *The Spectator*, 30 April 1898.

Bacon, Senator Augustus. "Independence for the Philippines." *Republic or Empire? The Philippine Question*. William Jennings Bryan, ed. Chicago: W.B. Conkey, 1900.

Barker, J. Ellis. "The Future of Anglo-German Relations." *Eclectic Magazine of Foreign Literature*, June 1906, 533.

Barrows, David P. "Education and Social Progress in the Philippines." *The Annals of the American Academy of Political and Social Science* 30, no. 1 (July 1907).

Beck, James M. "The Case of Edith Cavell: A Reply to Dr. Albert Zimmermann, Germany's Under Secretary for Foreign Affairs." *The New York Times*, 31 October 1915.

Bede. *The Ecclesiastical History of the English People*. Judith McClure and Roger Collins, tr. Oxford: Oxford University Press, 1999.

Beer, George Louis, *The English-Speaking Peoples: Their Future Relations and Joint International Obligations*. New York: Macmillan, 1917.

Besant, Sir Walter. "The Future of the Anglo-Saxon Race." *North American Review* 376 (August 1896), 129.

Brooks, Sydney. "The United States and the War." *The North American Review* 201, no. 711 (February 1915).

Brown, Philip. "American Diplomacy in Central America." *The American Political Science Review* 6, no. 1 (February 1912), 154.

Chadwick, F.E. "Present-Day Phase of the Monroe Doctrine" *The Journal of Race Development* 4, no. 3 (January 1914), 310.

Chamberlain, Joseph. "Speech by Colonial Secretary Joseph Chamberlain at the Birmingham Town Hall Advocating Closer Ties with the United States, 13 May 1898." *Great Britain, Foreign Policy and Span of Empire 1689–1971*, Vol. 1. Joel H. Wiener, ed. New York: Chelsea, 1972, 509.

Colquhoun, Archibald R. "Why the British Empire Is at War." *The North American Review* 200, no. 708 (November 1914).

Cone, Rev. J.H. "Anglo-Saxon Superiority." *The Maine Farmer* 68, no. 20 (15 March 1900).

Cornwall, M.D., and E. Edward. "Are the Americans an Anglo-Saxon People?" *The New York Times*, 14 January 1900.

Creel, George. *How We Advertised America*. New York: Harper, 1920; reprinted New York: Arno Press, 1972.

Egan, M.F. "Kultur and Our Need of It." *Studies: An Irish Quarterly Review* 4, no. 14 (June 1915).

Englenburg, F. V. "A Transvaal View of the South African Question." *The North American Review* 169, no. 515 (October 1899).

Faust, Albert Bernhardt. *The German Element in the United States*, Vol. 1. Boston: Houghton Mifflin, 1909.

Fitz-Gerald, W. G. "Does Germany Menace the World's Peace? The Truth About the Only 'Offensive' Navy." *The North American Review* 184, No. 613 (19 April 1907), 853.

Freeman, Edward A. *Outlines of History*. New York: Holt & Williams, 1872.

Geoffrey of Monmouth. *The History of the Kings of Britain*. Lewis Thorpe, tr. Middlesex, England: Penguin, 1966.

"Germany and the Monroe Doctrine." *Outlook*, 4 November 1914.

"Germany's Appeal to America." *The Independent*, 24 August 1914.

Gildas. *The Ruin of Britain and Other Works*. Michael Winterbottom, tr. London: Phillimore & Co., 1978.

Hawkins, Dexter A. *The Anglo-Saxon Race: Its History Character and Destiny*. New York: Nelson & Philips, 1875.

Hayes, Carlton. "The War of the Nations." *Political Science Quarterly* 29, no. 4 (December 1914).

Hosmer, James. *A Short History of Anglo-Saxon Freedom: The Polity of the English-Speaking Race*. Boston: Berwick & Smith Printers, 1890.

Huidekoper, Frederic Louis. "Is America Prepared for War?" *The North American Review* 182, no. 591 (February 1906).

Ide, Henry C. "Our Interest in Samoa." *The North American Review* 165, no. 489 (August 1897).

Jackson, J. W. "The Racial Aspects of the Franco-Prussian War." *The Journal of the Anthropological Institute of Great Britain and Ireland* 1 (1872).

Kasson, John A. "The Hohenzollern Kaiser." *The North American Review* 146, no. 377 (April 1888).

"The Law Still Stands." *The St. Louis Republic*, 10 May 1915.

"Lusitania Was Unarmed." *The New York Times*, 10 May 1915.

Mahan, Alfred Thayer. "Hawaii and Our Future Sea Power." *The Interest of America in Sea Power, Present and Future*, Boston: Little, Brown, 1898.

_____. *The Influence of Sea Power Upon History 1660-1783*. Boston: Little, Brown, 1890.

_____. "The Isthmus and Sea Power." *The Atlantic Monthly*, September 1893, reprinted in *The Interest of America in Sea Power, Present and Future*. Boston: Doubleday, 1918.

_____. "The Possibility of an Anglo-American Reunion." *The Interest of America in Sea Power, Present and Future*. Boston: Little, Brown, 1898.

_____. "The Problem of Asia." *Harpers New Monthly Magazine*, March 1900.

_____. "The United States Looking Outward." *The Atlantic Monthly*, August 1898, *The Interest of America in Sea Power, Present and Future*. Boston: Little, Brown, 1898.

Melville, George. "Our Future on the Pacific: What We Have There to Hold and Win." *The North American Review* 166, no. 496 (March 1898).

Morey, William C. "The Sources of American Federalism." *Annals of the Academy of American Political Science* 6 (September 1895).

Parkhurst, Charles Henry. "Kaiser Is Blamed: Dr. Parkhurst Would Blot Him Out as Public Menace." *The New York Times*, 23 August 1914.

Payson, Reverend George S. "Anglo-Saxon Supremacy." *Outlook*, 14 March 1896.

Pentecost, DD, George F. "America in the Philippines." *The Arena* 103, no. 186 (May 1905).

"Press Calls Sinking of Lusitania Murder." *The New York Times*, 8 May 1915.

Roosevelt, Theodore, *America and the Great War*. New York: Charles Scribner's, 1915, 16–7.

Roosevelt, Theodore, Jr. *Colonial Policies of the United States*. New York: Doubleday, 1937.

Schurz, Carl. "The United States and Germany." *The Independent*, 20 March 1902.

"Senator Beveridge on the Philippines." *The New York Times*, 10 January 1900.

Shattuck, Charles. "The True Meaning of the Term 'Liberty' in Those Clauses in the Federal and State Constitutions Which Protect "Life, Liberty, and Property." *Harvard Law Review* 4, no. 8 (15 March 1891).

Skaggs, William, *German Conspiracies in America,* London: T. Fisher, 1915.

Stratemeyer, Edward. *Between Briton and Boer or Two Boys' Adventures in South Africa*. Boston: Lothrop, Lee & Shepard, 1900.

Straton, John Roach. "Will Education Solve the Negro Problem?" *The North American Review* 170, no. 523 (June 1900).

Strong, Josiah. *The United States and the Future of the Anglo-Saxon Race*. London: Alfred Boot and Sons, 1889.

Thurston, Lorrin A. "The Growing Greatness of the Pacific." *The North American Review* 160, no. 461 (April 1895).

Trent, W. P. "A New South View of Reconstruction." *The Sewanee Review* 9, no. 1 (January 1901).

"Two Foreign Policies." *The Economist*, 12 February 1898.

Untitled. *The Times of London*, 1 February 1899.

Waldstein, Charles. "The English-Speaking Brotherhood." *The Living Age* 167 (August 1898).

"Washington Exposes Plot." *The New York Times*, 1 March 1917.

White, Arnold. "Germany's Aim in Foreign Politics." *The North American Review* 180, no. 581 (April 1905).

Woolsey, Theodore S. "The Government of Dependencies." *The Foreign Policy of the United States: Political and Commercial*. Theodore S. Woolsey, E. W. Huffcut, A. Lawrence Lowell, et al., eds., Annals of the American Academy of Political and Social Science, Vol. 13, Supplement 12, May 1899.

Yarros, Victor S. "The German and Anglo-American View of the State." *International Journal of Ethics* 28, no. 1 (October 1917).

Secondary Sources

Abrams, Ray H. *Preachers Present Arms: The Role of the American Churches and Clergy in World Wars I and II, with Some Observations on the War in Vietnam.* Scottsdale, PA: Herald Press, 1933; revised 1969.

Anderson, Benedict. *Imagined Communities: Reflections on the Origin and Spread of Nationalism.* London: Verso, 1983.

Anderson, Stuart. *Race and Rapprochement: Anglo-Saxonism and Anglo-American Relations, 1895–1904.* London: Associated University Presses, 1981.

Atwood, Paul L. *War and Empire: The American Way of Life.* New York: Pluto Press, 2010.

Baker, Ray Stannard. *Woodrow Wilson: Life and Letters: Facing War, 1915–1917.* New York: Doubleday, Doran, & Company, 1937.

Baltzell, E. Digby. *The Protestant Establishment: Aristocracy and Caste in America.* New York: Vintage, 1964.

Barclay, David, and Elizabeth Glaser-Schmidt, eds. *Transatlantic Images and Perceptions: Germany and America Since 1776.* Cambridge: Cambridge University Press, 1997.

Beisner, Robert L. *From the Old Diplomacy to the New, 1865–1900.* Arlington Heights, IL: Harlan Davidson, 1986.

Beowulf. Seamus Heaney, tr. New York: W. W. Norton, 2000.

Brooks, Nicholas. *Anglo-Saxon Myths: State and Church 400–1066.* London: Hambledon Press, 2000.

Brown, George Hardin. *Bede the Venerable.* Boston: Twayne, 1987.

Bruntz, George. *Allied Propaganda and the Collapse of the German Empire.* Stanford: Stanford University Press, 1938; reprinted New York: Arno Press, 1972.

Burk, Kathleen. *Britain, America, and the Sinews of War, 1914–1918.* Boston: Allen & Unwin, 1985.

Burton, David H. *British-American Diplomacy, 1895–1917: Early Years of the Special Relationship.* Malabar, FL: Krieger Publishing Company, 1999.

Challener, Richard D. *Admirals, Generals, and American Foreign Policy.* Princeton: Princeton University Press, 1973.

Crossley-Holland, Levom. *The Anglo-Saxon World.* Woodbridge, Suffolk: Boydell, 1982.

Cruz, Romeo V. *America's Colonial Desk and the Philippines, 1898–1934.* Quezon City: University of the Philippines Press, 1974.

Dawson, William Harbutt. *The German Empire 1867–1914.* Hamden, CT: Archon Books, 1966.

Deconde, Alexander. *Ethnicity, Race, and American Foreign Policy: A History.* Boston: Northeastern University Press, 1992.

Delgado, Richard, and Jean Stefancic, eds. *Critical White Studies: Looking Behind the Mirror.* Philadelphia: Temple University Press, 1997.

De Wolfe, Barbara, ed. *Discoveries of America: Personal Accounts of British Emigrants to North America During the Revolutionary Era.* Cambridge: Cambridge University Press, 1997.

Dorsey, Leroy G. *We Are All Americans, Pure and Simple: Theodore Roosevelt and the Myth of Americanism.* Tuscaloosa: University of Alabama Press, 2007.

Dulles, Foster Rhea. *America's Rise to World Power.* New York: Harper and Brothers, 1955.

Finke, Laurie A., and Martin B. Schichtman. *King Arthur and the Myth of History.* Gainesville: University of Florida Press, 2004.

Frantzen, Allen J., and John D. Niles, eds. *Anglo-Saxonism and the Construction of Social Identity.* Gainesville: University of Florida Press, 1997.

Furer, Howard B., ed. *The English in America 1578–1970.* New York: Oceana Publications, 1972.

Gatzke, Hans W. *Germany and the United States: "A Special Relationship?"* Cambridge: Harvard University Press, 1980.

Gazley, John Gerow. *American Opinion of German Unification, 1848–1871.* New York: Longmans, Green, & Co., 1926.

Geiss, Imanuel. *German Foreign Policy, 1871–1914.* London: Routledge & Kegan Paul, 1976.

Go, Julian, and Anne L. Forster, eds. *The American Colonial State in the Philippines: Global Perspectives.* Durham: Duke University Press, 2003.

Gregory, Ross. *Walter Hines Page: Ambassador to the Court of St. James's.* Lexington: University of Kentucky Press, 1971.

Gross, Stephen J. "The Perils of Prussianism: Main Street America, Local Autonomy, and the Great War." *Agricultural History* 78, no. 1 (Winter 2004).

Hall, Peter Dobkin. *"The Organization of American Culture 1700–1900: Private Institutions, Elites, and the Origins of American*

Nationality. New York: New York University Press, 1982.

Heald, Morrell, and Lawrence S. Kaplan. *Culture and Diplomacy: The American Experience*. Westport, CT: Greenwood Press, 1977.

Hendrix, Henry J. *Theodore Roosevelt's Naval Diplomacy: The US Navy and the Birth of the American Century*. Annapolis: Naval Institute Press, 2009.

Henson, Don. the *Origins of the Anglo-Saxons*. Hockwold-Cum-Wilton, Norfolk: Anglo-Saxon Books, 2006.

Herwig, Holger H. the *Politics of Frustration: The United States in German Naval Planning, 1889–1941*. Boston: Little, Brown, 1976.

Higham, John. *Strangers in the Land, Patterns of American Nativism, 1860–1925*. New Brunswick: Rutgers University Press, 1955.

Hoganson, Kristin L. *Fighting for American Manhood: How Gender Politics Provoked the Spanish-American and Philippine-American Wars*. New Haven: Yale University Press, 1998.

Hollister, C. Warren. the *Making of England, 55 BC-1399*, 3d Ed. Lexington, MA: D.C. Heath, 1976.

Holmes, Graeme M. *Britain and America: A Comparative Economic History, 1850–1939*. London: David & Charles Publishers Limited, 1976.

Horne, John, and Alam Kramer. *German Atrocities, 1914: A History of Denial*. New Haven: Yale University Press, 2001.

Jacobson, Joanne. *Authority and Alliance in the Letters of Henry Adams*. Madison: University of Wisconsin Press, 1992.

Jonas, Manfred. the *United States and Germany: A Diplomatic History*. Ithaca: Cornell University Press, 1984.

Kamphoefner, Walter D., and Wolfgang Helbich. *Germans in the Civil War*. Susan Carter Vogel, Tr. Chapel Hill: University of North Carolina, 2006.

Karnow, Stanley. in *Our Image: America's Empire in the Philippines*. New York: Random House, 1989.

Kaufmann, Eric P. the *Rise and Fall of Anglo-America*. Cambridge: Harvard University Press, 2004.

Kennedy, Paul M. the *Rise and Fall of the Great Powers*, New York: Random House, 1987.

_____. the *Samoan Triangle: A Study of Anglo-German-American Relations*. Dublin: Irish University Press, 1974.

Kramer, Paul A. "Empires, Exceptions, and Anglo-Saxons: Race and Rule Between the British and United States Empires, 1880–1910." *The Journal of American History* 88, no. 4 (March 2002).

Krenn, Michael, ed. *Race and US Foreign Policy in the Ages of Territorial and Market Expansion, 1840 to 1900*. New York: Garland Publishing, 1998.

LaFeber, Walter. *The New Empire: An Interpretation of American Expansion, 1860–1898*. Ithaca Cornell University Press, 1963, with 1998 preface.

Lasswell, Harold D. *Propaganda Technique in the World War*. New York: Garland Publishing, 1927; reprinted 1972.

Lens, Sidney. *The Forging of the American Empire*. New York: Thomas E. Crowell, Co., 1971, 157.

Le Roy, James A. *The Americans in the Philippines: A History of the Conquest and First Years of Occupation with an Introductory Account of the Spanish Rule*. New York: AMS Press, reprint from Boston, 1914, edition.

Levine, Lawrence W. *Defender of the Faith: William Jennings Bryan: The Last Decade, 1915–1925*. New York: Oxford University Press, 1965.

Link, Arthur S. *Wilson: The Struggle for Neutrality, 1914–15*. Princeton: Princeton University Press, 1960.

Lloyd, Brian. *Left Out: Pragmatism, Exceptionalism, and the Poverty of American Marxism, 1890–1922*. Baltimore: Johns Hopkins University Press, 1997.

MacDougal, Hugh A. *Racial Myth in English History: Trojans, Teutons, and Anglo-Saxons*. Hanover: University Press of New England, 1982.

McFerson, Hazel. *The Racial Dimension of American Overseas Colonial Policy*. Westport, CT: Greenwood Press, 1997.

Miroff, Bruce. *Icons of Democracy: American Leaders as Heroes, Aristocrats, Dissenters, and Democrats*. Lawrence: University Press of Kansas, 1993.

Mulanax, Richard B. *The Boer War in American Politics and Diplomacy*. Lanham, MD: University Press of America, 1994.

Murrin, John. *Anglicizing an American Colony: The Transformation of Provincial Massachusetts*. Dissertation, Ann Arbor: University Microfilms, 1966.

Nichols, J. Alden. *Germany After Bismarck: The Caprivi Era*. Cambridge: Harvard University Press, 1958.

Noer, Thomas J. *Briton, Boer, and Yankee: The United States and South Africa 1870–1914*. Kent, OH: Kent State University Press, 1978.

Noll, Mark A., and Luke E. Harlow, eds. *Religion and American Politics: From the Colonial Era to the Present*. New York: Oxford University Press, 2007.

Owen, Norman G., ed. *Compadre Colonialism: Studies on the Philippines Under American Rule*. Ann Arbor: University of Michigan Press, 1971.

Painter, Nell Irvin. *Standing at Armageddon: The United States, 1877–1919*. New York: W.W. Norton, 1987.

Palmer, R.R., et al. *A History of the Modern World*, 10th ed. New York: McGraw-Hill, 2007.

Paolino, Ernest N. *The Foundations of the American Empire: William Henry Seward and U.S. Foreign Policy*. Ithaca: Cornell University Press, 1973.

Perkins, Bradford. *The Great Rapprochement: England and the United States 1895–1914*. London: Victor Gollanz, 1969.

Peterson, H.C. *Propaganda for War: The Campaign Against American Neutrality, 1914–1917*. Norman: University of Oklahoma Press, 1939.

Rappaport, Armin. *The British Press and Wilsonian Neutrality*. Stanford: Stanford University Press, 1951.

Read, James Morgan. *Atrocity Propaganda, 1914–1919*. New Haven: Yale University Press, 1941.

Rodgers, Daniel T. *Atlantic Crossings: Social Politics in a Progressive Age*. Cambridge: Harvard University Press, 1998.

Roediger, David R. *The Wages of Whiteness: Race and the Making of the American Working Class*. London: Verso, 1991.

Roetter, Charles. *The Art of Psychological Warfare, 1914–1945*. New York: Stein and Day, 1974.

Ross, Stewart Halsey. *Propaganda for War: How the United States Was Conditioned to Fight the Great War of 1914–1918*. Jefferson, NC: McFarland, 1996.

Rothenberg, Paula S., ed. *White Privilege: Essential Readings on the Other Side of Racism*. New York: Worth Publishers, 2005.

Rouse, Robert, and Cory Rushton. *The Medieval Quest for Arthur*. Stroud, Gloucestershire: Tempus Publishing, 2005.

Saxton, Alexander. *The Rise and Fall of the White Republic: Class Politics and Mass Culture in Nineteenth-Century America*. London: Verso, 1990.

Seager, Robert, II. *Alfred Thayer Mahan: The Man and His Letters*. Annapolis: Naval Institute Press: 1977.

Seymour, Charles. *American Diplomacy During the World War*. Hamden, CT: Archon Books, 1964.

Slotkin, Richard. *Gunfighter Nation: The Myth of the Frontier in Twentieth Century America*. New York: Athenaeum, 1992.

Smith, Daniel M. *The Great Departure: The United States and World War I, 1914–1920*. New York: John M. Wiley and Sons, 1965, 15.

_____. *Robert Lansing and American Neutrality*. Berkeley: University of California Press, 1958.

Stanley, Peter W., ed. *Reappraising an Empire: New Perspectives on Philippine-American History*. Cambridge: Harvard University Press, 1984.

Tappan Berthoff, Rowland. *British Immigrants in Industrial America*. Cambridge: Harvard University Press, 1953.

Taylor, A.J.P. *The Course of German History: A Survey of the Development of Germany Since 1815*. New York: Capricorn Books, 1962.

Taylor, John M. *William Henry Seward: Lincoln's Right Hand Man*. New York: HarperCollins, 1991.

Thistlethwaite, Frank. *The Anglo-American Connection in the Early Nineteenth Century*. New York: Russel & Russel, 1959.

Trefousse, Hans L. *Carl Schurz: A Biography*. New York: Fordham University Press, 1998.

Trommler, Frank and Elliott Shore, eds. *The German-American Encounter: Conflict and Cooperation Between Two Cultures, 1800–2000*. New York: Berghahn Books, 2001.

Tucker, Robert W. *Woodrow Wilson and the Great War: Reconsidering America's Neutrality 1914–1917*. Charlottesville: University of Virginia Press, 2007.

Van Alstein, Richard. *Genesis of American Nationalism*. Waltham, MA: Blaidswell Publishing Company, 1970.

Van Deusen, Glyndon G. *William Henry Seward*. New York: Oxford University Press, 1967.

Van Vugt, William E. *Britain to America: Mid-Nineteenth Century Immigrants to the United States*. Urbana: University of Illinois Press, 1999.

Wallace, Stuart. *War and the Image of Ger-

many: British Academics 1914–1918*. Edinburgh: John Donald Publishers, 1988.
Watson, Ritchie Devon, Jr. *Normans and Saxons: Southern Race Mythology and the Intellectual History of the American Civil War*. Baton Rouge: Louisiana State University Press, 2008.
Weston, Rubin Francis. *Racism in U.S. Imperialism: The Influence of Racial Assumptions on American Foreign Policy, 1893–1946*. Columbia: University of South Carolina Press, 1972.
Widenor, William C. *Henry Cabot Lodge and the Search for an American Foreign Policy*. Berkeley: University of California Press, 1980.
Wilson, Keith, ed. *The International Impact of the Boer War*. New York: Palgrave, 2001.
Wolff, Leon. *Little Brown Brother: How the United States Purchased and Pacified the Philippine Islands at the Century's Turn*. New York: Doubleday & Company, 1961.
Worcester, Dean C. *The Philippines Past and Present*. New York: Macmillan, 1930.
Wright, Louis B. *The First Gentlemen of Virginia: Intellectual Qualities of the Early Colonial Ruling Class*. Stanford: Stanford University Press, 1949.

Index

Adams, Henry 112
Adams, Herbert Baxter 17
Aguinaldo, Emilio 35, 36
Alaska 79, 80, 97
Alaska Boundary Dispute 113
Alaska Boundary Tribunal 130
American Association for Labor Legislation (AALL) 52
American Revolution (War of Independence) 3, 16, 20, 25, 31, 34, 37, 39, 76, 77, 79, 86, 99, 110, 112, 115, 117, 132, 135, 141, 149, 150, 168
Anglo-Saxon 20, 23, 34, 64, 157
The Anglo-Saxon Chronicle 11
Anglo-Saxonism 1, 7, 15, 17, 27, 35, 37, 75, 77, 83, 101, 109, 115, 118, 119, 129, 133, 148, 152, 157, 160, 164, 165, 169, 170, 171, 173–175, 177, 178
Anglo-Saxonists 16, 23, 27, 34, 113, 166
Australia 2, 15, 25, 61, 63, 91, 102, 113, 124, 126, 157, 168
Austria 43, 47, 64, 112, 120, 121, 123, 130, 132, 134

Bacon, A.O. 112
Baja California 62
Bale, John 13
Balfour, Arthur James 164
Baltzell, E. Digby 33
Barnard, Henry 50
Beck, James M. 142
Bede 2, 9–11
Beer, George Louis 166–168
Beethoven, Ludwig van 55
Belgium 5, *122*, 123, *124*, 126, *127*, *131*, 136, 137, 139, 141, 142, 146–148, 150, 153, 154, 157, 158, *159*, 162, 163, 165, 168, 169, 175
Bergess, John W. 17
Berlin 47, 50, 51, 68, 156
Besant, Sir Walter 25, 26
Bethman-Hollweg, Chancellor 121
Bismarck, Otto von 38, 46–49, 52, 53, 56, 62, 68, 96, 98, 111, 155, 156, 158
Bismarck Archipelago 62

Bissing, Moritz von 141
Blaine, James G. 64
Boer War 35, 63, 69, 109–119
British Empire 2, 4, 7, 34, 37, 73, 91, 109, 110, 116, 119, 131, 138, 144, 147, 157, 158, 166, 168
Brooks, John Graham 53
Brooks, Sydney 70, 71, 125
Brown, Phillip 100–101
Bryan, William Jennings 118, 121, 129, 130, 132–136, 142, 144, 153, 163, 168
Bryce, Lord James 139
Bryce Report 139, 140, 143, 175

California 17, 61, 76, 100, 126
California (battleship) 92
Canada 2, 15, 25, 61, 91, 102, 124, 126, 157, 168
Carnegie, Andrew 112, 136, 153
Cavell, Edith 142
Central Powers 118, 125, 128, 129, 132, 133, 135, 154, 174, 175
Chamberlain, Joseph 54, 97
China 61, 80, 81, 89, 90, 93, 94, 96, *154*
Civil War, American 3, 15, 20–22, 28, 34, 46–48, 51, 58, 60, 75, 77, 78, 80–83, 85, 135, 147, 173
Clayton-Bulwer Treaty 97, 98
Colquhoun, Archibald 157, 158
Committee of Public Information (CPI) 143
Cornwall, Edward 27
Costa Rica 100
Creel, George 143
Cuba 87–89, 91, 92, 100, 123, 136

Darwin, Charles 3, 23, 24, 27, 34, 82
Democratic Party 44, 46
Denmark 43, 65
Dewey, George 65
Dicey, Edward 98
Diderichs, Otto von 65
Dominican Republic 133
Donelson, Andrew J. 42
Drake, Sir Francis 88
Dreadnought 92

201

Index

East Indies 102, 155
Ecuador 89
El Salvador 100
Elizabeth I 88
Ellis, Barker 68, 69
Engelenburg, F.V. 114
England 7, 9, 10, 12–14, 15, 16–21, 25–31, 56, 57, 60, 63, 66, 67, 73, 86, 88, 90, 116, 126, 127, 135, 146, 147, 150, 164, 166, 172, 174
Entente Cordiale 96
Entente powers 5, 118, 135, 136, 142, 153, 154, 162, 163, 166, 168, 174

Faust, Albert Bernhardt 54
Fiji 61, 63
First World War 1–7, 38, 53, 67, 68, 72–74, 80, 118–169, 171–176
Fiske, John 17
Fitzgerald, W.G. 71, 72
Florida 92
Ford, Henry 153
France 1, 5, 34, 35, 39, 47, 48, 49, 55, 61–65, 67, 68, 78, 81, 84, 96, 121, *124*, 132, 134, 136, 137, 141, 147, 150, 151, 153, 154, 156, 163, 164, 169
Frankfurt Assembly 42, 43, 49
Franz Ferdinand 120–122
Freeman 54, 55

Geoffrey of Monmouth 2, 11–13, 98
German Confederation 42
German immigration 4, 39–43, 174
German unification 46–53
Germantown, Pennsylvania 39
Germany 1, 4–5, 19, 25, 27, 34, 35, 36–39, 41–74, 77, 78, 81, 86, 87, 92, 96, 98, 100, 111, 112, 119–176
Gibraltar 88
Gildas 7–12
Glorious Revolution of 1689 14
Goethe, Johann von 55
Grant, Madison 166, 176
Great Britain 1–7, 15, 24–27, 28–37, 38, 42, 49, 51, 54–57, 60–71, 75–77, 78, 82, 83, 86, 87–99, 102, 110–117, 118, 119, 121, 128, 129, 132–135, 137, 142, 144, 147, 148, 151–153, 157, 158–160, 163, 164, 168–170, 171, 174, 176, 177
Greece 55
Grey, Sir Edward 120, 125, 146, 147, 176
Guatemala 89, 100, 101

Habsburg Dynasty 43
Haiti 133
Hastings, Battle of 21
Hawaii 79, 85, 87, 89, 98
Hawkins, Dexter 20
Hay, John 66
Haydn, Franz Josef 55
Hayes, Carlton 155–157
Hay-Pauncefote Treaty 98

Hegel, Georg 55
Henry, Prince of Prussia 65
Henry VIII 13
Hohenzollern Dynasty 57, 69, 119, 155, 160, 174
Holland 84
Holy Alliance 42
Honduras 100, 101
Hosmer, James K. 17, 56, 57
Humboldt, Alexander 55

Ide, Henry 63
immigration, British 28, 29
immigration, U.S. 6, 27, 32, 78, 79, 80, 87, 94, 169, 176, 177
India 88, 94, 96, 102–104, 114
The Influence of Sea Power Upon History 84, 85
Insular Affairs, Bureau of (BIA) 107
Insular Cases of May 1901 105
Iredell, James 31, 32
Italy 55, 130, 164

Jackson, J.W. 55
Jameson, Leander Starr 110
Jameson Raid 110
Japan 59–65, 73, 75, 79, 81, 89, 90, 93–95, 111, 128, 143
Jefferson, Thomas 15, 31, 32, 50, 51

Kasson, John 83
Kidd, Benjamin 24
Kruger, Paul 110
Ku Klux Klan 176
Kultur 119, 150, 151
Kulturkampf 49

Lansing, Robert 129–135, 144
Lee, Arthur Hamilton 123, 162
Linnaeus, Carol 55
Lodge, Henry Cabot 59, 82, 128, 144, 150, 152, 153, 163, 168
London 28
Ludwig, Maria (Molly Pitcher) 39
Lusitania 5, 126, 132, 133, *134*, 140–142, 150, 169, 175
Luther, Martin 55
Luxembourg 162, 163

Magna Carta 18, 54, 99
Mahan, Alfred Thayer 63, 66, 71, 82–90, 92, 117
Manifest Destiny 3, 16, 76, 77, 80, 173
Manila 102–104, 106, 109
McAdoo, William 83
McKinley, William 97, 104–106
Melville, George 61, 62
Mexican War 100
Mexico 16, 48, 77, 101, 123, 133, 142, 143, 166
Moltke, Helmut von 55

Monroe Doctrine 48, 49, 59, 66, 67, 70–72, 79, 99–109, 169
Morey, William 19, 20
Morgan, J.P. 146
Moroccan Crisis 67, 68
Mozart, Wolfgang Amadeus 55
Munsterberg, Hugo 132, 155

Napoleon III 48
Naturalization Act of 1790 76
Navy, U.S. 60, 82–87
Netherlands 61, 102, 113, 155, 163
Nevada 92
New England 34, 41, 50, 56, 172
New Guinea 62, 63, 86
New York (Battleship) 92
New York (State) 39, 45, 62
New York City 28, 47, 62, 126, 130, 134, 136, 140, 173
New Zealand 2, 16, 25, 61, 91, 102, 124, 157, 168
Nicaragua 89, 100, 101
Norman Conquest 12, 13, 15, 16, 18–22, 172, 173
Northwest Ordinance of 1787 76

Orange Free State 110, 114
Oregon Country 17
Ottoman Empire 112
Oxford pamphlets 148

Page, Walter Hines 163, 164
Panama 89, 100
Parker, Foxhall 43
Payson, George 27
Peabody, Elizabeth 50
Pennsylvania 92
Pensionado 36
Philippine Civil Service 36
Philippines 6, 35, 36, 60, 63–65, 72, 89, 91, 92, 101–109, 117, 123, 174
Polk, James K. 42
Prussia 39–42, 46–51, 55, 57, 69, 71, 154

Raleigh, Sir Walter 88
Rapprochement, Anglo-American 4, 6, 16, 28, 35, 54, 64, 65, 86, 87, 95, 97–99, 109, 112, 113, 115, 117, 118, 131, 144, 146, 151, 164, 171, 174
Reformation, English 13
Republican Party 44–46
Revolution of 1848 41–44
Rizal, Jose 109
Roman Empire 8, 12
Roosevelt, Theodore 35, 53, 58, 82, 85, 87, 90, 100, 101, 103, 112, 113, 121, **127**, 128, 146–148, 162, 168
Root, Elihu 36, 37, 48, 87, 103, 104, 107
Russia 34, 35, 38, 78, 80, 90, 93–96, 98, 111, 121, **126**, 134, 150, 156, 166, 176

Samoa 60–64, 70, 83, 86, 111, 174
Samoa Crisis 60, 63, 111
Schiller, Johann von 55
Schleswig-Holstein 43
Schurman Commission 106
Schurz, Carl 43, 45, 47–50, 58, 59, 112
Scott, Sir Walter 99
Second Empire 48
Seed, George 98
Serbia 120, 121
Seward, William Henry 78–81
Shakespeare, William 99
Shattuck, Charles 17, 18
Skaggs, William 141
Social Darwinism 17, 27, 61, 69, 75, 83, 87, 116, 118, 148, 156, 158, 173, 174
Social Democratic Party 49, 156
South Africa 2, 3, 16, 33, 63, 91, 109–115, 124, 157, 168
Spain 4, 28, 35, 36, 47, 60, 61, 63, 64, 66, 84, 86–88, 91, 98, 102, 105, 107, 109, 113, 136
Spanish-American War 4, 35, 46, 76, 100, 111
Spanish Armada 2, 13
Spring Rice, Cecil 62, 66, 67, 94, 95, 125, 126, 146, 150, 164, 166
State Department 49, 80, 97, 129, 130, 135, 144, 145
Sternberg, Speck von 59, 66
Steuben, Baron Frederick von 39
Strachey, John St. Loe 147
Stratemeyer, Edward 115, 116
Straton, John Roach 22, 23
Strong, Josiah 56, 57
Sussex Pledge 164

Taft, William Howard 106, 107, 130, 163
Taft Commission 107–109
Temple, Sir William 13
Teutonic theory 4, 38, 54–58, 69, 74, 111, 121–123, 151, 166, 169, 174, 175
Texas 17
Thirty Years' War 39
Thurston, Lorrin 61
Transvaal 110, 113
Treaty of Guadalupe Hidalgo 77
Treitschke, Heinrich von 147, 156
Trent, W.P. 21
Trump, Donald 6, 7, 176, 177
Turner, Frederick Jackson 17

United States 1–6, 15–27, 28–37, 38–53, 54–74, 75–77, 78–90, 91–101, 102–109, 110–117, 118–143, 144–170, 171–178
Utah 92

Van der Berghe, Pierre L. 33
Veblen, Thorsten 153
Venezuela 66, 67, 70
Vienna, Congress of 41

Waldstein, Charles 25
Washington, George 15, 153, 168, 172
Western Front 1
White Anglo-Saxon Protestant (WASP) 4, 5, 30, 32–34, 58, 75, 82, 130, 148–150, 173–175
Whitlock, Brand 141, 142
Wilhelm II 5, 38, 54, 58–60, 62, 64, 65, 67–69, 71, 111, 122, 123, *134*, 136, *140*, 156, 165, 168
Wilson, Woodrow 1, 68, 118–121, 124, 126, 127, *127*, 128130, 132–135, 137, 143, 144, *145*, 147, 149, 150, 152, 153, 162–166, *167*, 168, 170, 174, 175, 177
Winthrop, John 15
Woolsey, Theodore 102, 103
Wright 52
Wyoming 92

Yarros, Victor 158, 160

Zenger, John Peter 39
Zimmerman Telegram 166

www.ingramcontent.com/pod-product-compliance
Lightning Source LLC
Chambersburg PA
CBHW032057300426
44116CB00007B/784